monsoonbooks

BEYOND THE VENEER

Born in New York City, Ioannis Gatsiounis was a journalist for American media until 2000 when he relocated to Southeast Asia. Beginning in Jakarta, he reported on post-Suharto Indonesia for major publications in America. On a visit to neighboring Malaysia, he discovered a land that was underreported and teetering between First and Third Worlds. His unflinching and trenchant commentaries, penned in a climate of fear and intimidation, have secured his reputation as a leading expert on Malaysia. He resides in Kuala Lumpur, Malaysia.

BEYOND THE VENEER

IOANNIS GATSIOUNIS

monsoon

monsoonbooks

Published in 2008
by Monsoon Books Pte Ltd
52 Telok Blangah Road
#03-05 Telok Blangah House
Singapore 098829
www.monsoonbooks.com.sg

ISBN: 978-981-08-0657-6

Copyright © Ioannis Gatsiounis, 2008
The moral right of the author has been asserted.

Cover photograph copyright © Getty Images

All rights reserved. No part of this publication may be reproduced, stored in a retrieval system, or transmitted, in any form or by any means without the prior written permission of the publisher, nor be otherwise circulated in any form of binding or cover other than that in which it is published and without a similar condition being imposed on the subsequent purchaser.

This publication represents the opinions and views of the author based on his personal experience, knowledge and research, and does not reflect the views of the publisher. The publisher makes no representation or warranties with respect to the content of this book, and specifically disclaims any implied warranties or merchantability or fitness for any particular purpose, and shall in no events be liable for any loss of profit or any other commercial damage, including but not limited to special, incidental, consequential or other damages.

National Library Board Singapore Cataloguing in Publication Data

Gatsiounis, Ioannis.
Beyond the veneer : Malaysia's struggle for dignity and direction / Ioannis Gatsiounis. – Singapore : Monsoon Books, 2008.
p. cm.
Includes index.
ISBN-13 : 978-981-08-0657-6 (pbk.)
1. Malaysia – Politics and government. 2. Human rights – Malaysia. 3. Malaysia – Race relations – Political aspects. 4. Islam and state – Malaysia. I. Title.
JQ1062.A58
320.9595 -- dc22   OCN228721439

Printed in Singapore
12 11 10 09 08   1 2 3 4 5 6 7 8 9

Contents

INTRODUCTION	9
BEFORE AND AFTER THE 2008 ELECTION	
Pre-election Hopes for Malaysian Opposition	15
A New Democratic Era in Malaysia	19
The Malaysian Race Card	24
HUMAN RIGHTS	
Indonesia vs Malaysia: The Media and Democracy	31
Activism in Malaysia Lives and Dies by the Sword	35
For Malaysians, a Day for Speaking Out	39
Malaysia Moving Backward on Human Rights	41
Abdullah Revives Malaysian Authoritarianism	48
Malaysia's Mid-life Crisis	54
Opposition Steals a March in Malaysia	58
ACCOUNTABILITY	
Abdullah's Honeymoon is Over in Malaysia	67
Malaysia Aims to NIP Corruption in the Bud	70
Anti-graft War Backfires in Malaysia	73
Malaysia's Blind Path to Progress	79
Hail, Hail Malaysia's Pak Lah	86
REVIEWS AND PROFILES	
Holding Malaysian Politicos to their Words	95
Malaysia Under Mahathir's Shadow	99
Addressing Muslim Rage	106
Faith: Part of the Problem	110
Malaysia's Leader-in-Waiting	117
Malaysian PM's Competing Instincts Collide	126
RACE AND RELIGION	
The Racial Divide Widens in Malaysia	135
In Malaysia, "Too Sensitive" for Debate	139
Malaysia Takes the Rock out of Music	143

No place for Terror in Malaysia	149
The Search for a Malaysian Race	154
Mahathir's Mixed Legacy on Race	161
Malaysia Makes its Case on Conversion	167
Islam Hadhari in Malaysia	172
Malaysia's Islamists Soften the Line	186
The Year of the Rat	190

GEOPOLITICS
Malaysia's Axis Mysteriously Shifting	201

GRAND PLANS
Branding Itself Globally	211
Malaysia's Distant 2020 Vision	216
Malaysia Changes Gear	223
Malaysia's MSC: Super Corridor or Dead End?	226
A Megaproject Bears Witness to Malaysia's Faith in Economic Planning	230

THE WORLD BEYOND
Western Media Fade, New Media Rise in Asia	239
China and the Media	243
Greece Neglecting Needs of Muslim Immigrants	248
Promoting US Values in Muslim Lands	252
Hollywood Still Seduces the World	256

EPILOGUE	263
INDEX	267

Introduction

This collection of articles covers issues and events that led to Malaysia's "political tsunami" in March 2008, when the ruling coalition's suffered its worst election showing since independence.

The articles pick up in 2003, which was where, at the time, I thought they would end. To my eye Malaysia appeared placid and untroubled, good for an article or two but lacking in the tensions and dynamism to sustain a news narrative.

But the longer I stuck around the more it felt like Malaysia was trying to run the rat race of globalization on one good leg. This was the leg it showed to the cameras, in the form of the Petronas Towers and superhighways, in what it touted as racial harmony and progressive Islam. But looking at social, political and civilizational factors one soon discovered that Malaysia had much in common with undeveloped countries it appeared to be unlike. Corruption was rampant. The public had lost faith in key institutions like the police and judiciary. The rich–poor divide was the highest in the region. Politics were communal, ensuring that diversity was a weakness and not a strength. Restrictions on speech and conscience were undermining public reasoning and by turn development. Malaysia was dressed for success but there was something fishy about the fabric. And the fabric was about to become a lot harder to overlook.

In late 2003 Abdullah Badawi was named Malaysia's first new prime minister in 22 years. He inherited some of the issues that triggered the "political tsunami," though he and his party would often do little to help matters, and in some cases would recklessly aggravate them. A nation that at the beginning of the decade had seemed to be speeding toward developed status would soon find itself fractured and adrift.

This collection follows that dissolution and response to it. It is, ultimately, a tale of self-realization: everyday Malaysians waking up to what their blind allegiance to an entrenched leadership had unleashed; and deciding to become more active stakeholders in their nation's development. The election results have led Malaysians to contemplate a future without race-based politics. Though resisting the temptation to revert will not be easy (see page 24).

The collection is also concerned with how Malaysia fits into the global context. Malaysia offers some valuable lessons regarding the challenges of nation building in the 21st century, particularly to those countries pursuing an authoritarian-capitalist path to development, as Malaysia has. Malaysia vividly captures the trendy development model's strengths, particularly rapid economic development, and its flaws, including the tendency to dehumanize and compromise the integrity of key institutions. The election results represent no less than a yearning for more than what the authoritarian-capitalist model can provide, and a shift we're likely to see in the path a adopted by countries in the decades to come: a form of development that is as socio-centric as it is economic-centric.

Credit for this book must go partially to my editors, for sharing my conviction that Malaysia is an underreported story and granting me the space to share it. I am indebted to readers for their constructive feedback and encouragement in a country where forthright analysis is not celebrated. Official obscurantism has shaped notions of right and wrong. Unflattering realities are expected to be kept unsaid. But then it has been my aim to take the socio-political pulse of Malaysia and it would be a disservice to readers and the nation to pretend all is healthy.

On a personal level, the heart has grown quite fond of Malaysia. Traveling elsewhere I soon come to miss the country's myriad quirks, and the optimism and generosity in abundance here. So many Malaysians have opened their hearts and shared their insights with me along the journey that there is not the space to thank them by name here. All of you have the power to help make Malaysia the great nation it has shown glimpses of becoming, and I look forward to celebrating that day with you.

Kuala Lumpur
June 2008

BEFORE AND AFTER THE 2008 ELECTION

Pre-election Hopes for Malaysian Opposition

There is a cautious optimism running through the opposition as Malaysia gears up for a March 8 vote that many are calling the most crucial general election in the country's 50-year history.

Cautious because the long-ruling government controls the media and school curriculum, oversees a broken electorate system tilted to its advantage, and doesn't look kindly on freedom of expression; optimistic because Prime Minister Abdullah Badawi's four-year-old government has been plagued by a series of scandals and allegations of corruption.

At the same time, there is growing anxiety about the nation's global competitiveness, race relations are tense, and the Internet is exposing Malaysians to the depth and breadth of official disregard.

This election arguably represents the best chance the opposition has to weaken the ruling coalition's Barisan Nasional (BN) stranglehold on power in at least a decade. The opposition's modest aim is to win one-third of parliament's 222 seats, which it hasn't done since 1969 and if achieved would put a check on the ruling government's power to amend the constitution.

"We will do well, no question about it," de facto opposition leader Anwar Ibrahim told *Asia Times Online*. "We will deny the BN government a two-thirds majority. Now the problem is, when you are talking about the so-called elections, you are talking about a fraudulent process. You are talking about phantom voters, you are talking about [gerrymandering]."

That is the voice of a man leading the battle cry with one arm shielding his face. Indeed just four years ago Anwar watched the elections from prison, waiting out a politically motivated conviction for corruption and sexual misconduct, as Abdullah co-opted the opposition's bread-and-butter issues of good governance and accountability to hand the opposition its worst defeat in history. The BN won 91% of parliamentary seats, although only 64% of the popular vote.

Fast forward to the present and Abdullah's scandal-plagued administration has forfeited the right to stake a claim to those issues. Anwar is a free man and his stump speeches are attracting large crowds around the country—even though his corruption conviction bars him from running for public office until April. It is hardly a coincidence that the March 8 elections are slated for a month before Anwar is eligible to run.

Discontent over inequality, electoral fraud, inflation and a corrupt judiciary have spilled onto the streets in recent months—rare in a country where public meetings of more than five people are illegal without a permit. Two-thirds of Indians and Chinese, who combined make up 35% of the population, said they disapprove of the way the Malay-dominated government is addressing inequality and ethnicity, according to a recent poll by the independent Merdeka Center.

Nonetheless, the opposition will face a tough challenge converting popular discontent into actual votes. Despite carping about the government, many Malaysians have proven loath to vote for change. And yet Abdullah's government has in taken their allegiance for granted.

Whichever way the electorate leans, this election will likely have a dramatic and lasting impact. If the BN wins handily, the public will have sent the message that injustice, authoritarianism, and a political culture of mediocrity is still acceptable. It could also relegate the opposition to political irrelevance and ease the pressure on the BN-led government to change its ways.

That's a prospect Anwar considered in his sparse office along a leafy street in the Kuala Lumpur suburb of Petaling Jaya, before saying, "I don't share that view. I think that we are moving on. People know that; we see the crowds." Anwar is the fulcrum of the disparate opposition parties, which include the Islamist party known as PAS, the Chinese-based Democratic Action Party (DAP) and his own multi-religious and multi-racial People's Justice Party (PKR). Anwar is arguably their biggest asset, a religious man espousing justice, equality and progressive economic policies.

But walking that tightrope in Malaysia's race-based political landscape has alienated voters as well. Many Muslim Malays question whether the former Islamic youth leader is still on their side, or if he's bending over backwards to appease what many of them narrowly consider infidels. Some non-Muslims fear Anwar is too Islamic and that if in power he would give Islam a greater role in the socio-political domain. Meanwhile some Malaysians, irrespective of race, question the sincerity of his reform agenda. Anwar was once a fast-rising star in the United Malays National Organization (UMNO), which heads the BN, rising to finance minister and deputy prime minister before being sacked in 1998 by then premier Mahathir Mohamad and later imprisoned. As the BBC's Stephen Sackur asked Anwar after his release in 2005, "If you're telling me that over all of that time you were making protests about corruption, how come you kept getting promoted?"

Still, Anwar is an inspiration to many. He is a cosmopolitan populist who grasps both the needs and desires of common folk and the unsympathetic realities of globalization. More than any other Malaysian politician, he has laid bare official malaise, and despite being out of government since 1998 he has remained the current government's biggest fear.

Anwar's unique attributes, however, will not make much of a difference come March 8 unless the opposition runs a smarter campaign than it did in 2004. Toward that end the loose coalition of parties is fielding one candidate per constituency so as not to self-cannibalize opposition votes. PAS, for instance, will run in mostly Malay constituencies, DAP in Chinese ones.

DAP says that given power it will give 6,000 ringgit (US$1,877) a year to poor households and see to it that government contracts are awarded more fairly. (Abdullah has not disturbed the shopworn government tradition of awarding projects without tender.) PKR meanwhile has introduced an assistance plan that would be based on need to replace the 37-year-old affirmative action program that mostly benefits the majority Malays over minority groups.

Anwar says Malays will not lose out under his party's plan because a minority of well-off Malays have profited from the current structure at the expense of the poor Malays. Converting that message into votes won't be easy, however. Many Malaysians readily acknowledge that Malaysia is endemically corrupt but often in the next breath ask, "Where isn't their corruption?" They are often unaware of how the severe limits on freedoms of conscience and expression—in the name of promoting peace and stability—are impairing development and competitiveness.

The opposition may get a lift from the Internet, which the government has been at a loss to regulate and is increasingly being leveraged by everyday Malaysians to raise political awareness and highlight areas of poor governance. That being said, Malaysians by-and-large have a low threshold for hard truth. The bulk of the population with access to uncensored media on the Internet still turns primarily to the state-run media for their "news"—although a couple of online news sites have garnered larger readerships than certain mainstream outlets. The government papers these days are predictably frontloaded with headlines suggesting Malaysia's economy is booming amid growing national nervousness about its underlying health and medium-term prospects. The spin is used to feed suspicions about the untested opposition's economic credentials and Abdullah himself milked the formula last week when he urged Malaysians not to take the "risk" and "experiment" in voting for the opposition.

The BN is in particular bringing news of its Midas touch to Kelantan, the only state currently controlled by the political opposition. A win there, the BN feels, would offset the expected loss of parliamentary seats elsewhere. Many predict the BN will in the end secure a two-thirds majority, but the opposition, at least in the run-up to the polls, has reason to be hopeful.

First published March 5, 2008 (*Asia Times*)

* * *

A New Democratic Era in Malaysia

The Malaysian government's authoritarian instincts were finally checked by democracy at Saturday's highly anticipated general elections, where the long-ruling Barisan Nasional (BN) government suffered one of its worst poll results in its 50-year history of uninterrupted rule.

The BN won a mere 51% of the popular vote, down significantly from the 64% it notched at the 2004 polls, securing only a simple majority rather than the two-thirds of parliamentary seats it had sought. When the dust settled, opposition parties, which rode a wave of popular discontent about government corruption and neglect, won 82 of 222 parliamentary seats, 37% compared with the 9% previously held, and wrested control of four states—Perak, Kedah, Penang and Selangor—while bolstering their hold on the northeastern state of Kelantan.

The new parliamentary equation will effectively curb the BN's ability to amend the constitution, including over issues related to citizens' rights and the role of religion. The opposition's strong performance came despite allegations of BN vote-rigging, stiff restrictions on political expression and assembly, and a pro-government bias in the state-influenced print and broadcast media. At around 2 am on Sunday, Prime Minister Abdullah Badawi and his deputy Najib Razak appeared dazed before a blitz of camera flashes, with Abdullah meekly announcing, "We've lost, we've lost."

The main opposition parties, including the multi-racial People's Justice Party (PKR), the Democratic Action Party (DAP), and the Pan-Malaysian Islamic Party (PAS) all exceeded expectations at the polls. Malaysian voters had until now tolerated corruption and authoritarianism among its leaders in exchange for relative social and economic stability.

Over the weekend, voters sent the message that they want a more sophisticated approach to nation-building. "The people have expressed in no uncertain terms that they want accountability, transparency, and the rule of law," said Anwar Ibrahim, de facto leader of the opposition People's Justice Party (PKR).

A swing away from the BN was widely expected among Indian and Chinese voters, who have felt increasingly marginalized by a long-standing affirmative action program known as the New Economic Policy (NEP), which benefits the majority Muslim Malays over minority Chinese and Indians, and the more assertive role Islam has been given during Abdullah's term.

The Chinese-majority state of Penang fell to the opposition Democratic Action Party (DAP) after 36 years of BN rule and several BN Indian leaders, including long-time cabinet member Samy Vellu, lost their seats. Less anticipated, however, was the large defection of Muslim Malay voters to the opposition camp. The United Malays National Organization (UMNO), which leads the BN coalition, has long fashioned itself as the protector of ethnic Malay interests.

It had until now maintained political support by instilling fears, reiterated in the run-up to Saturday's polls, that a vote for the opposition would divide and weaken the nation. However, many Malays proved undaunted, joining hands with Indians and Chinese to punish Abdullah's administration for failing to tackle corruption, crime and inflation.

BN was routed in the Malay-majority states of Kedah and Kelantan, while in many areas Malay support for UMNO was not much more than 55%, according to Ibrahim Suffian, program director of the Merdeka Center for Opinion Research. That significant numbers of Malays, Chinese and Indians voted for the opposition, despite UMNO's fear mongering, will lessen the likelihood that discord will play out along racial lines.

It is not clear whether and how UMNO will respond to the democratic setback. The party has been known to react unkindly when its stranglehold on power has been threatened. In 1999, for instance, when PAS won the rural eastern state of Terengganu, then prime minister Mahathir Mohamad later deprived the state of development funds. He also restricted publication and distribution of the party's newspaper *Harakah*. After enacting its revenge, UMNO won the state back in 2004.

Voter rejection of the BN this time is more encompassing, not only cutting across racial lines but along rural and urban ones. The results also signal to Malaysians—long trained to think otherwise—that they possess the ability to check official abuses.

Abdullah in the hot seat

After the resounding setback, UMNO's first order of business may be to pressure Abdullah to resign—perhaps opening the door for his deputy Najib to take over the party's leadership. A spokesman for Abdullah said he has no plans to step down, and on Sunday senior UMNO leaders met at the premier's official residence to show their support for him. He was swiftly sworn in as premier on Monday morning through UMNO's and the BN's simple majority.

Yet even Abdullah's resignation will not likely restore legitimacy to UMNO and the BN. The ruling coalition's Indian and Chinese component parties are now widely seen as UMNO tokens, with their leaders cushioning their positions at the expense of their constituencies. UMNO, meanwhile, has in many voters' eyes become synonymous with mediocrity, feudalism, racism and patronage. The party's young rising stars were expected to adopt a more progressive approach, but to many they have become indistinguishable from the old guard, which in turn has eroded public confidence in UMNO's ability to reform itself. Mahathir, for one, has accused Abdullah's son-in-law and UMNO deputy youth chief Khairy Jamaluddin of being emblematic of this trend and said that he "played a big role" in the BN's losses over the weekend.

It's perhaps telling of the mood in Malaysia that Information Minister Zainuddin Maidin (dubbed the "misinformation" minister by the opposition) lost his parliamentary seat in Kedah, while blogger Jeff Ooi won the Jelutong parliamentary seat with DAP. The government had leveraged the traditional media it tightly controls to report that Malaysia is an economic miracle, respected by the world and breezing toward developed country status under visionary BN rule. Web portals and blogs like Ooi's, however, have exposed Malaysians to the country's less flattering realities and awakened them to the fact that becoming a developed country will require replacing the political culture of mediocrity and impunity.

Saturday's results may pave the way for that shift. Both the opposition and the BN will feel the pressure to perform: the opposition has been given a precious opportunity and the BN can no longer take the public's allegiance for granted.

Incoming chief minister of Penang and DAP secretary general Lim Guan Eng's sober victory address to reporters on Sunday morning suggested that he is not underestimating the hard work ahead.

Opposition icon Anwar, meanwhile, said he plans to start assisting the opposition to form governments in the states it now controls. A politically motivated corruption charge prevents him from running until next month, though it is expected that another member of the party will step aside so he can contest in a by-election.

New winds of democracy are expected to blow through Parliament as well, where the BN's dominance had in the past all but turned the legislative branch into a rubberstamp of the executive. Dissenting voices will now be harder to ignore in Parliament, which under a previously unassailable BN majority lacked a culture of debate and accountability.

As opposition leaders hailed Saturday's results, the streets of the capital Kuala Lumpur have been eerily quiet—as perhaps they should be out of respect for the country's still fragile social balance and during what amounts to a traumatic moment for some in a society that is not accustomed to genuine democratic change. If the BN and citizenry handle the transition gracefully, Malaysia will have taken an all-important step in its political development.

First published March 11, 2008 (*Asia Times*)

* * *

BEYOND THE VENEER

The Malaysian Race Card

Anwar Ibrahim's big victory in Malaysia's elections looked on the surface like a triumph for both democracy and multiculturalism—a major accomplishment in this profoundly divided state. The Pan-Malaysian Islamic Party and the Chinese-based Democratic Action Party (DAP) contributed to the opposition gains, but it was Anwar's multiethnic People's Justice Party that bagged the largest share of the popular vote and parliamentary seats. Yet events immediately following the vote—when rabble-rousing politicians once again started playing the race card—show just how dangerous the splits remain.

Race has always played a peculiar role here, in this country of 25 million cobbled together by the British from disparate kingdoms. Ethnic Malays today make up 55 percent of the population. Ethnic Chinese represent an additional 25 percent, and Indians 8 percent. The Chinese minority has long been perceived as dominating Malaysia's business community, causing widespread resentment among poorer Malays and sparking vicious riots in the 1960s. Since then, successive governments have justified restrictions on civil rights by pointing to this bloody history, and to their credit they have managed to avoid major violence for 40 years. But sweeping affirmative-action programs benefiting ethnic Malays, put in place in 1971, have kept tensions bubbling just under the surface.

Anwar's People's Justice Party vowed to replace this race-based assistance program with one that would help the needy regardless of ethnicity. And since its formation in 2003 his party has been growing in strength, thanks to support from Malays, Chinese and Indians alike, all frustrated by the lackluster economic performance of the ruling National Front (BN) coalition and its leader, Prime Minister

Abdullah Badawi. But by the middle of last week the opposition had succumbed to tribal instincts, with the various parties squabbling among themselves over jobs in state governments and threatening boycotts if they didn't get the seats they thought they deserved.

At the same time, members of the National Front's lead party, the United Malays National Organization (UMNO), have continued to play the race card. Indeed, politicians affiliated with this party seem to feel it is their duty to do so. UMNO has portrayed itself as the champion and protector of the ethnic Malays, and some members have promoted *ketuanan* Melayu (Malay supremacy). Worryingly, some of UMNO's younger politicians, once hailed as progressives, are now doing the same thing. UMNO youth chief Hishammuddin Hussein, for instance, has made a habit of brandishing the *keris*, the Malay dagger, at the party's annual assembly—a gesture widely understood as a veiled threat to any race that dares challenge Malay supremacy. His deputy, and Badawi's son-in-law, Khairy Jamaluddin, recently warned that any split among the Malays—that is, any defection from UMNO—would be exploited by the Chinese.

Ironically, the same camps that play the race card are often just as quick to warn Malaysians of the consequences of acting on those feelings. And for the most part, that message has sunk in. Most Malaysians now recognize just how important the nation's peace and stability are; indeed, they're the bedrock on which Malaysia's rapid economic development has depended. Yet as the dust of the elections settles, there are few signs the rhetoric over race is going to diminish. In the wealthy and mostly Chinese state of Penang, the Chinese DAP won power after 36 years of rule by the Malay-dominated BN. Incoming Chief Minister Lim Guan Eng quickly vowed to end the crude affirmative-action policy, which, he said, "only breeds cronyism, corruption and inefficiency." In response, the prime minister warned the state not to marginalize Malays and said that "the state government must not try to create an atmosphere which can cause racial tensions."

By many accounts race relations are now more tense than at any time since 1969. Ninety percent of Chinese students attend Chinese-language schools, while the majority of Malays attend public schools. Islam has taken a greater prominence in the social and political domains, breeding resentment among Indians and Chinese. Chinese and Indians, meanwhile, have become more vocal in opposing discriminatory policies, but they have given little indication that if they were granted greater equality they would rise above their own clannish tendencies. The enmity could erupt into violence. And if it does, it may, ironically, be triggered by the same affirmative-action policies that have done so much to prevent violence over the years.

The tragedy is that most Malaysians seem tired of the fractious politics of the past. Many Malaysians of all races have grown exasperated with Badawi's failure to tackle corruption, crime and inflation. And they recognize that race-based politics is impairing social and economic progress. But unless the opposition parties can rise above the nation's ethnic cleavages by learning to put national rather than ethnic interests at the forefront, ordinary Malaysians are unlikely to.

First published March 15, 2008 (*Newsweek*)

HUMAN RIGHTS

Indonesia vs Malaysia: The Media and Democracy

Neighbors Malaysia and Indonesia are often depicted in opposing lights. Indonesia is the turbulent big brother with deep scars from a brutal dictatorship and a crisis of Islamic militancy on its hands. Malaysia is the rapidly developing "model Islamic democracy," a beacon of hope in the region—a reputation reinforced by the ruling coalition Barisan Nasional's (BN) rout of the Muslim fundamentalist-led opposition in parliamentary general elections last month.

Ironically, though, Indonesia, which just completed what was only its second general election since independence in 1945, has already embraced a more democratic tradition than Malaysia, which purports to have held "free and fair" elections since the 1950s. And the decision of Indonesian president B J Habibie, to free up the media after Suharto's fall in 1998 has played a significant role.

In Indonesia on Monday, 24 parties contested for parliamentary seats. They may not all have gotten equal media coverage, but there are few if any allegations that a state-organized conspiracy impaired their showing. In Malaysia's elections last month, on the other hand, just two coalitions were represented, and only one received what might be called "fair" coverage.

For those in the BN, the state-controlled media's performance was nothing short of stellar. They not only gave the "moderates" an unfair advantage in the weeks leading up to the election (the leading opposition party's paper cannot publish more than twice a month and distribution is restricted), but in effect, quelled public concern over numerous allegations that the Election Commission and the BN conspired to commit election fraud.

Wong Chun Wai, deputy chief group editor of Malaysia's largest pro-government English-language daily, *The Star*, bristled at this analysis. He said his paper ran the opposition's advertisements. "The Malaysian media [are] as democratic as [they] can be. There's no need to change [them]." He pointed out that the opposition Chinese-led Democratic Action Party actually gained seats in the March 21 election, and as for other opposition parties that scored poorly, this was because of their stated aims, not because of media coverage.

But others say the power of the media to influence voters, especially during election time, should not be underestimated.

By many accounts the Malaysian media's campaign coverage was slicker and more ambitious than in past elections. At the least, it was unabashed and relentless. One front-page headline called Malaysia's economy "booming," a description some economists would hardly endorse. Non-disparaging coverage of the opposition was often relegated to the lower corners of inside pages. A frequently run television spot featured Malaysians extolling how tolerant, vibrant and blissful life is in Malaysia. The ad listed no sponsor. But with the BN ruling since the 1950s, the message was implicit enough.

Five months ago there was a twinge of hope that the media situation here in Malaysia might change. That's when Abdullah Badawi was appointed prime minister by his predecessor, the long-ruling strongarm Mahathir Mohamad. Abdullah was seen as the tolerant gentleman determined to stamp out corruption. But optimism waned when Abdullah sacked an editor of an English-language daily for publishing an article that criticized government foreign policy. And it has eroded further, say experts, with the election rout.

With the media's strong showing, "What incentives do [the government] have to open the doors?" asked Eric Paulsen, coordinator of the Voice of People of Malaysia.

One can think of plenty: to develop a knowledge-based economy; to check power and stamp out corruption; to spur public debate on important issues. But getting the government to sign on is a different matter. BN's performance last month was its best since 1955. Why tamper with success?

A number of analysts say mass public mobilization is perhaps the only thing that will pressure the Malaysian government to change. In Indonesia, public protest led to the dictator Suharto's resignation and consequently the repeal of media restrictions. And although the government has since occasionally threatened to curb those freedoms, myriad activists in Indonesia have made clear that the freedoms won't be lifted without a fight.

By contrast, Malaysians historically have shown little affinity for social activism. And times are good for many. The economy is stable; the standard of living here is higher than in Indonesia; Malaysia lacks the sense of desperation that can galvanize action. As well, the government has strict laws preventing public demonstration; the Internal Security Act, which reserves the right to jail offenders without trial, has scared away many would-be activists.

"Barring no meltdown, nothing will change," said Ibrahim Suffian of the Merdeka Center for Opinion Research.

The closest thing to a "meltdown" in Malaysia in recent times came in the late 1990s, when Mahathir jailed his charismatic deputy Anwar Ibrahim on allegations of sodomy and corruption. Public distrust of the government and media, coinciding with the Internet boom, witnessed a proliferation of reformation websites, and thousands taking to the streets.

"Now one or two [reformation] sites—from over a hundred—are left," said Suffian.

During the scandal, the hardline opposition Parti Islam SeMalaysia (PAS) won control of a second state. And while many voters turned to the opposition because they felt betrayed by Mahathir and the BN, the media in no small way helped people and parties mobilize.

Since that election a few credible independent websites have surfaced. (Mahathir promised not to interfere with web-based content.) But generally Malaysians are content taking in the state-controlled press. From food stalls to dentist offices, Malaysians can be found soaking up the state newspapers, even when complimentary copies of international papers are available.

A Merdeka Center poll found that most Malaysians don't believe what they read in the state-controlled press. But then one has to wonder what they're reading "serious" newspapers for if not for "useful" information—to be mindlessly entertained?

Sometimes the public's indifference has led to outright defense of the situation. One hears often enough from Malaysians that they are not mature enough yet for open media, echoing a line left over from the colonial days and milked often by the ruling coalition ever since.

But lawyer Sivarasa Rasiah, a vice president of the opposition People's Justice Party (PKR), does not blame the public. "It's quite normal not to seek information," Rasiah said. "The onus is on us, and we have failed to get to them."

Rasiah said that for the opposition to stand any chance in future elections (Malaysia's next parliamentary election isn't likely to be called until 2009), they will have to rethink how to reach the public. "It's the main obstacle we face," he said. "It's the only way we can break down the [ruling coalition's] blockade."

Opposition leaders say they will tap into the Internet but know it won't be enough. One leader said without irony, "We might have to do what they did in Eastern Europe in the communist era: quietly roam in long coats and sell on street corners."

Indeed, many observers are too pleased with the election results to reflect on its meaning—or simply find the ends justify the means. One editorial writer noted that with this election, "Malaysia demonstrated that the 'green wave'—the tide of political Islam that seems to be engulfing the Muslim world—can be stopped democratically."

M G Pillai, writing on his independent website, sees it differently: "With this general election we have descended firmly into the Third World we had spent years to get out of."

But as long as the state-controlled media are calling the shots, Malaysians will continue to get a more flattering view of themselves. The morning after Indonesia's elections, Malaysia's *Star* newspaper ran a front-page headline that read: "Shortages and confusion over voting card hamper Indonesian elections." That news was hard to find outside Malaysia.

First published April 9th, 2004 (*Asia Times*)

* * *

Activism in Malaysia Lives and Dies by the Sword

This article was written during the nadir of Malaysia's reformation movement. It should offer a sense of just how swiftly the situation has evolved since then; and why: Abdullah noted minimal public pressure to carry out his reform mandate and chose the safe route of protecting vested interests within the party. In the process, though, he confused the lack of pressure with a lack of desire for reform and unwittingly revived the reformation movement.

A few short years ago Anwar Ibrahim was Southeast Asia's most famous prisoner. Put away on what many here still believe were falsified counts of corruption and sodomy, the progressive Muslim and charismatic former deputy under premier Mahathir Mohamad became a symbol of injustice in Malaysia, exposing the dark reality of a nation deceptively billing itself as a model Islamic democracy.

Thousands took to the streets to protest Anwar's jailing, riots broke out, hundreds of reformation websites were launched. At parliamentary polls, voters voiced their disgust by turning away from strongarm leader Mahathir, who orchestrated the witch-hunt, and his long-ruling National Front (Barisan Nasional or BN).

Now only a handful of reformation websites remain. And last week, as Anwar began his final appeal against his nine-year prison sentence for sodomy, only about 200 supporters showed up outside the courthouse—this on the heels of a parliamentary election romp by the ruling National Front coalition.

Five years after his arrest, Anwar is arguably as neglected as he is famous.

The concern, say some, is that this has left the call reform in the hands of a small band of activist organizations, and they lack an inspiring figurehead to galvanize mass support.

Prime Minister Abdullah Badawi has promised reforms including greater transparency and accountability, but without greater public pressure the reforms are likely to materialize slowly, if at all. Abdullah's standing within his United Malays National Organization (UMNO), the dominant party in the BN, is tenuous, and an aggressive reform drive may stir the hornets' nest. By contrast, if history is any indication, appeasing the public can wait.

"History shows that [the government] can take the Malaysian people for a ride," said Joseph Paul of Amnesty International in Malaysia. "They've been told promises before, they haven't been delivered, and the issues have been dropped." He added: "As long as the public doesn't speak out, there will continue to be the sense that you can put their concerns on the back burner."

Malaysians say they are concerned about a range of issues, including official corruption, the breakdown of civil society, limits on expression and the country's overall competitiveness. But few actually pressure the government to address these issues.

"And yet look at where Malaysia is with economic development compared with neighboring countries," Abdul Razak Baginda of the Malaysian Strategic Research Center said. By not standing up to the government, "Malaysians have to some extent been very practical."

Others say success here is too often quantified solely on economic terms and that this has resulted in an inflated sense of achievement, at the expense of grasping and nurturing social aspects of the development equation.

Azizuddin Ahmad, secretary general of the Muslim Youth Movement of Malaysia (ABIM), founded by Anwar Ibrahim, said many Malaysians are concerned with social issues, they just don't feel at liberty to express them.

"The law doesn't protect people's rights to speak out," Ahmad said. Almost 100 people are being detained indefinitely under the Internal Security Act (ISA) for "jeopardizing national security." The media are state-controlled. The Police Act is so vague as to give the Malaysian police virtually unlimited powers of enforcement. One must obtain a permit to demonstrate.

Or as Mahathir once warned, perverting the maxim "Those who live by the sword shall die by the sword": "Those who rise by street demonstrations will fall through street demonstrations."

And yet, Ahmad said, at the end of the day, official intimidation doesn't legitimize remaining silent. Generally, Ahmad said, "People who are sincere and passionate and serious about [an issue] don't have fear." He cited neighboring Indonesia, where street demonstrations ended Suharto's iron-fisted rule and are now commonly used to speak out against everything from rising chicken prices to corruption. Some argue that Malaysians are less inclined to demonstrate than

Indonesians because their standard of living is higher. But more developed countries like South Korea and Taiwan have vibrant civil societies. Even in oppressed societies like Iran "ordinary people are proving themselves irrepressible," remarked Nicholas Kristoff in Saturday's *New York Times*.

Malaysia's parliamentary elections in March raised numerous and well-documented allegations of fraud, but no mass response followed.

This may be due in part to Malaysians' perception of leadership. According to Paul of Amnesty International, the trouble in Malaysia is, "Leaders are seen as there to be served, not to serve."

And Paul said Malaysians have grown more apolitical. Despite a climate of fear in the 1960s, "Back then there were lots of students involved in activism—people were caught up in the universal struggle for human rights and they openly discussed [it]."

Now, said Masjaliza Hamzah of the women's-rights group Sisters in Islam, there's a general sense that only troublemakers and nimrods protest government policy. Mahathir was a main perpetrator of this view, equating street demonstrations with mob rule and voting for the opposition as an attempt to "overthrow the government."

"Actually, these idiots are nothing if not for what we have given them ... until when are they going to be idiots?" he said in 2001.

Abdullah also hasn't taken much more kindly to free expression. Last month he declared his support for the ISA. He recently had a newspaper editor fired from an UMNO mouthpiece for straying from the government line. Responding to allegations that ISA prisoners are beaten, deprived of sleep and forced to commit sexual acts by authorities, Abdullah said at a press conference on Tuesday: "I have never heard of such atrocities." He urged those with proof to could come talk to him. The same day, his Information Minister Abdul Kadir Sheikh Fadzir said "Don't make things difficult for the government. We want the media to be free. If they can discipline themselves, there's no problem."

Meanwhile, the Abdullah administration insists it is dedicated to reform. Fair play, though, the government is making clear, is not part of the deal. For that to happen, the public may well have to enlist more of its own.

First published May 21, 2004 (Asia Times)

* * *

For Malaysians, a Day for Speaking Out

Malaysian leaders and the state-run media are known to use Independence Day here to tell Malaysians that they live in a free, prosperous and harmonious society. And many Malaysians play along with the idea as it sure is comforting to hear. But skepticism may be challenging obedience as the national virtue, if the exchange of ideas taking place via the country's handful of independent news outlets on Malaysia's 48th Independence (*Merdeka*) Day last week is any indication. At the least Malaysians appear to be getting more exasperated with their country's shortcomings, at the same time becoming more pointed in their criticism of them.

Malaysians find themselves with no shortage of targets at which to take aim. Prime Minister Abdullah Badawi's anti-graft drive is inching along at a snail's pace; he has fried a few big fish but has not dissuaded the culture that feeds the practice. Several of Malaysia's most renowned university professors have resigned or been dismissed in controversy. Meanwhile, multinationals continue to bypass Malaysia for developing countries with ostensibly better talent pools and cheaper labor costs. National carmaker Proton has hit the red, its future uncertain, having seen its domestic market share drop to 44% in 2004 from 60% in 2000.

Then there's the nagging issue of race. While the Indians and Chinese, Malaysia's two largest minority groups, have grudgingly accepted the long-standing affirmative action program designed to make the majority Muslim Malays more competitive, they have always held out hope that the plan would eventually be scrapped. Those hopes were dashed in July, when the ruling United Malays National Organization's (UMNO) youth wing leader called for a revival of the plan at the party's assembly, then brandished a traditional Malay dagger while his supporters chanted, "Long live Malays."

A letter writer attributed the sour mood this *Merdeka* Day to a "failure to thrive. The things that are wrong with Malaysia could be destroying the very few things that are right with it."

Over the years the government has managed to obscure many of Malaysia's more pressing problems—including racial tensions, an inclination toward mediocrity, creeping Islamic fundamentalism and a moribund education system—by adroitly drawing attention away from them. Indeed on the surface Malaysia has begun to resemble a developed country, with "smart" cities, sky trains and a world-class highway system. Key statistics are impressive. Poverty has shrunk to about 10% from 49% in 1970. Household income is second highest in Southeast Asia. Unemployment is about 4%. A tightly controlled mainstream media delivers the message. The government bought further time when Badawi took over the premiership from the authoritarian Mahathir Mohamad promising key reforms.

But two years at the helm, Badawi hasn't delivered much. His party has proven complacent and hostile to notions of change. The impressive numbers, the inexorable construction, the talk of reform is doing less to mask the disconnect, while Internet news sites and blogs have become an outlet for lamenting the fact.

One is left to wonder, if the government can't instill gratitude during that nation's independence day, what can it expect the rest of the year?

First published September 2005 (*Asia Times*)

* * *

Malaysia Moving Backward on Human Rights

The Malaysian government has long held that promoting human rights over national security would undermine the country's economic development. As a multi-ethnic country with a history of racial and religious antagonisms, relaxing restrictions on individual freedoms would invite destabilization and undermine progress, officials have long claimed.

That philosophy was deeply entrenched during Mahathir Mohamad's 22-year rule as prime minister, when the country leaped from being a backwater to an industrialized powerhouse despite an abysmal rights record. Hopes ran high that Mahathir's successor, current Prime Minister Abdullah Badawi, would reverse that trend and allow for more political and social openness. Nearly three years into his term, however, those once-high hopes have waned as Abdullah has chosen to leave in place many of the strictures that characterized Mahathir's rule.

Compared with Asia's more dynamic democracies, social progress has badly lagged economic development in Malaysia. Government officials are still grappling with how to cultivate a dynamic, progressive citizenry without relinquishing control. At the same time, class disparity is widening, corruption runs rampant and many argue that the courts and police long ago lost their moral legitimacy as impartial arbiters. After years of affirmative-action programs, race relations between the majority Muslim Malays and minority Chinese and Indians are still on edge.

Abdullah has acknowledged these concerns while paying lip service to the crucial connection between human rights and nation-building.

"Abdullah has allowed for greater public dialogue regarding promotion of human rights," said lawyer Param Cumaraswamy, a founding member of Malaysia's Human Rights Committee. "The climate has been more open and we're seeing more discussions between the government and civil-society groups."

At the same time, there are doubts Abdullah has the political will to put his more liberal rhetoric into action.

"Badawi is hiding behind the impression he gives that he's a good man with a soft approach," said human-rights lawyer P Uthayakumar. Of the hundreds of letters Uthayakumar says he has written to Abdullah about specific instances of human-rights abuses, he said: "Almost none have received a response."

Behind Abdullah's nice-guy image there have been a string of developments that raise serious doubts about his commitment to protect and promote human rights and more democracy. Chief among those concerns are media freedoms, police conduct, religious persecution and his administration's continued reliance on draconian legislation to curb dissent, say rights advocates.

The 1984 Printing Presses and Publications Act, which through annual re-licensing requirements keeps media owners on guard against offending the government, is still firmly in place. Moreover, Abdullah has frequently reprimanded the local media when it falls out of step with the government's news agenda. On June 26, a Mandarin-language call-in radio program, The Mic Is On, With Love, Without

Obstacles, was ordered by the government to change its format after airing a segment critical of a controversial order affecting Chinese-language schools.

Nor has Abdullah's government been above overt censorship. Mahathir's recent criticism of Abdullah's policies, in which he has referred to his successor's reform agenda as a "big bluff," has notably been blacked out of the mainstream media. Mahathir has instead vented his criticisms over the Internet-based media he once sought to silence.. (Through a legal loophole, Internet media in Malaysia are not constrained by the renewable-licensing requirements the print and broadcast media face.)

"We've seen some opening up and at the same time a strong willingness to black out issues to suit [Abdullah's] political agenda," said Sonia Randhawa, executive director at the Kuala Lumpur-based Center for Independent Journalism. "He may not have the dominant personality of Mahathir, but he has quietly cultivated close links with the media to informally pressure them to pursue the agenda of the government."

One example: a bloody police crackdown on a peaceful demonstration against Abdullah's decision to raise fuel prices sharply in May was not carried by any mainstream media.

Where Abdullah has pursued substantive reforms, he has often met firm resistance. For instance, his plans to set up an Independent Police Complaints and Misconduct Commission (IPCMC) to address the police force's long record of corruption, inefficiency and abuse was widely lauded by rights advocates. It would be "the single biggest advancement in human rights in this country," contended Uthayakumar. However, the official police website promised retaliation and threatened to allow crime to escalate if the proposed new watchdog body was established.

Some observers suggest that the most worrying trend is creeping Islamization through the judiciary. A number of recent court decisions have set the *sharia* (Islamic law) courts against the civil courts and have challenged the supremacy of Malaysia's secular constitution, which guarantees equality and freedom of worship.

One recent decision involved a woman who was born Muslim but had renounced Islam in 1998 to convert to Christianity. However, *sharia* courts refused to recognize her apostasy. Another controversial decision involved a Hindu-born soldier who was buried as a Muslim after *sharia* courts decided that he had converted to Islam. The courts refused to hear testimony from his widow, who insisted her spouse was not a Muslim.

Malaysia's parliament last year passed a new Islamic Family Law that aims to provide legal protections for Muslim men to engage in polygamy and divorce. The bill led social activist Marina Mahathir to say, "Only in Malaysia are Muslim women regressing. In every other Muslim country in the world, women have been gaining rights, not losing them." Abdullah has since agreed to review the bill.

Abdullah's defenders say he should not be held accountable for the rising tide of conservative Islam and its associated abuses, which they contend were on the ascent before he assumed power. Moreover, Abdullah, a religious scholar, has championed what he calls Islam Hadhari, or Civilizational Islam, a moderate brand of the religion that stresses technological and economic competitiveness, moderation, tolerance and social justice.

Critics point out that Islam Hadhari has been used to entrench Islam into Malaysia's multi-ethnic fabric. For instance, Islam Hadhari played prominently in the recently promulgated Ninth Malaysia Plan, a five-year socio-economic policy template.

"This is the first time the nation's economic and social plan has used religion to shape the national agenda," said Lim Teck Ghee, director for the Center for Public Policy Studies at the Asian Strategy and Leadership Institute in Kuala Lumpur.

Ethnic favoritism threatens Malaysia's delicate social balance.

Non-Muslim members of parliament recently withdrew a formal letter addressed to Abdullah requesting better protection of religious minorities' rights after the request sparked a backlash in Abdullah's United Malays National Organization (UMNO). They were reacting partially to a state-approved demolition campaign of a number of Hindu temples that officials have claimed lack proper registration documents.

"I said that they should withdraw the memorandum and they agreed," Abdullah was quoted as saying. "So it is over."

A close ally of Abdullah, Minister in the Prime Minister's Department Mohamed Nazri, called on non-Muslims not to interfere in discussions about Islam and threatened to use the Sedition Act against those who insulted Islam.

Some argue that recent abuses are rooted in Abdullah's non-confrontational, self-effacing style, which marks a stark contrast to former prime minister Mahathir's forceful leadership. That has opened the way for competing interest groups to more openly speak their mind and pursue policies that favor the majority Malays over minority Chinese and Indians.

"It's partly due to the opening up of the system," said Joseph Roy, director of Amnesty International's Malaysian chapter. "But Badawi has to be stronger, clearer where he stands, otherwise people will take advantage and there will be more human-rights abuses on a systematic level and few fundamental changes on the ground."

Ivy Josiah, executive director of Women's Aid Organization, said, "Badawi needs to set the bar on human rights standards."

To illustrate her point, Josiah mentioned a recent forum held in the northern state of Penang organized to discuss overlapping jurisdictions between civil and *sharia* courts. Five hundred Muslim protesters under an "Anti-Inter-Faith Commission Body" banner demanded that the event be canceled. Rather than taking a clear stand and providing protection to the seminar goers, according to

Josiah, Abdullah said merely that it was a sensitive issue and he refused to intervene. According to witnesses, the event was canceled at the request of police, who feared that the demonstrators would barge into the premises.

Many of Abdullah's more progressive policies have been slowly implemented. For instance, his much-vaunted National Integrity Plan (NIP), which aimed at reducing inefficiency and corruption in government by imbuing Malaysians with a greater sense of right and wrong, has been poorly executed; most Malaysians remain unfamiliar with the plan's key principles and only in April did UMNO's powerful youth wing agree to draw up an action plan to implement it, two years after it was first promulgated.

"If Mahathir were Abdullah with Abdullah's agenda, things would move," said K S Nathan of the Institute of Southeast Asian Studies in Singapore. "A strategy would be in place, backed by strong convictions. Mahathir was the first to say the buck stops here; Badawi is passing the buck around."

Though different in style, the two Malaysian leaders share similar political instincts—if not tactics. Like Abdullah, Mahathir promised liberal reforms during his first three years in office, including allowing more freedom of expression. Soon after assuming the premiership, Mahathir released a batch of prisoners who were then being held under the Internal Security Act (ISA), which allows for indefinite detention without trial.

Yet both Mahathir and Abdullah have relied heavily on the ISA and other draconian laws in the name of national security to crack down on political opposition. Both leaders have also displayed a tendency to justify their own abuses by harping on other, usually Western, countries' policy discrepancies. Mahathir famously lashed out at the United States' Jewish population, which he often claimed sought to undermine Muslim nations. An HRW report noted that "The government has recently expanded its use of the Internal Security

Act to include individuals accused of counterfeiting and forging documents." Brad Adams, HRW's Asia director, said: "Abdullah has urged the US to close Guantanamo, yet his own government is holding detainees indefinitely without trial."

To be sure, human-rights considerations in a multi-ethnic country such as Malaysia are seldom black and white. Some contest that there are reasons for rights proponents to feel encouraged by developments under Abdullah, says Elina Noor with the Institute of Strategic and International Studies (ISIS) in Kuala Lumpur. Top ministers in Abdullah's cabinet, she points out, rejected a plan by authorities in Malacca state to set up a moral police force to spy on people and deter behavior considered indecent under Islamic law.

An Islamic body tried to set up a similar force in Kuala Lumpur that was disallowed when Abdullah told his cabinet that no group has the right to spy on people. "The government is actually doing a lot to moderate these issues," Noor said. However, she also conceded that many Malaysians are understandably worried about "how sporadic the efforts are."

Three years into Abdullah's term, many Malaysians are unsure where his government really comes down on promoting rights. Political historians believe that, similar to Mahathir, Abdullah will show his true colors some time during the three-year mark of his five-year term.

But with little passed in the way of legal reforms to deter human-rights abuses, he "is left with everything in his palm to be used should he feel insecure or threatened, when he feels the need to fight back," said Elizabeth Wong, secretary general of the National Human Rights Society in Malaysia. "And politicians in possession of the trump card rarely fail to use it when they feel the need."

First published July 20, 2006 (*Asia Times*)

Abdullah Revives Malaysian Authoritarianism

Prime Minister Abdullah Badawi took to the premiership four years ago, postured as a humble, well-meaning repairman. His words cut past Malaysia's shiny facade to fix the ethnic, social and economic fissures that after years of official neglect had worn away at the multiracial country's foundations.

He spoke of good governance, of weeding out corruption, of closing one of the region's largest rich-poor divides. He introduced Islam Hadhari, a "balanced" approach to the faith that lightly hinted all was not right with Malaysia's deeply political and increasingly conservative brand of Islam. And he delivered his message with a soft voice and sensitive gaze that seemed in retrospect sincere about defusing deep-seated political and racial resentments.

In the time since, Malaysia has spiraled toward political instability, culminating in three major street demonstrations over the last five weeks. The latest demonstration occurred last Tuesday outside of Parliament and involved a coalition of non-governmental organizations (NGOs) objecting to a proposed constitutional amendment to extend the term of the election commission's chairman. Last month an estimated 20,000 people turned up downtown here calling for electoral reforms. All the rallies were deemed illegal, as the government refused to issue permits, and have resulted in violent crackdowns and dozens of arrests.

The embattled leader accuses the protestors of threatening national stability and on Monday said he would not hesitate to authorize use of the draconian Internal Security Act (ISA), which allows for indefinite detention without trial, adding, "I'll do it without feeling guilty, without feeling sad." On Thursday, he made good on his word, signing detention orders for five leaders of the Hindu Rights Action Force (Hindraf), which recently held a 10,000-strong rally in downtown Kuala Lumpur to protest the perceived marginalization of Malaysia's Indian community.

A long-standing affirmative action program subsidizes the majority Malays, though Indians are economically the worst off among Malaysia's three main ethnic groups: the Malays, Chinese and mostly Tamil Indians. The Malay-led government has labeled Hindraf "terrorists" via official statements and over the state-controlled media.

Abdullah's strong-arm tactics, however, do not address the root cause of the socio-political crisis, nor will they easily resolve the boiling situation. Sources of resentment and division include the country's affirmative action program, which favors the majority ethnic Malays over minority groups, and a brand of Islam which is slowly but surely encroaching into the public and political sphere. Abdullah's ruling party, the United Malays National Organization (UMNO), has made a habit during its five-decade rule of squelching dissent and brazenly proceeding as it sees fit.

But this go-round of protests—the first major demonstrations in 10 years—is a potentially explosive culmination of long neglected grievances. The 1998 *reformasi* demonstrations, in contrast, targeted official corruption. The judicial crisis of 1988, which caused a split within UMNO and effectively ended the judiciary's independence, did not lead to judicial reform. The race riots of 1969, which violently pitted ethnic Malays against Chinese, gave rise to the still in-effect affirmative action program then known as the New Economic Policy (NEP), which intended to help the Malays reach economic parity with the Chinese. It has been abused by well-to-do Malays and still has yet to reach its stated aims.

The first serious call for review of the current crisis began last year. And staunch resistance to changing the status quo within UMNO persists. When a video tape surfaced in September showing a prominent lawyer allegedly brokering judicial appointments with a chief justice, Abdullah's de facto law minister and other senior officials defended the integrity of the judiciary while impugning the whistleblowers.

The government's habit of reacting to crises by digging in its heels—rather than redressing them through legal prosecutions and reforms—has contributed to what was already an uneven brand of development. Economically, in broad terms, Malaysia has performed well. Poverty is expected to fall below 3 % by 2010; unemployment is low; Malaysia now imports, rather than exports, labor.

But socially and institutionally, it has not kept pace. Innovative and critical thinking is famously in short supply, while race and religion dominate the political landscape and are now seriously threatening national stability. The judiciary and media and other key institutions are widely seen to lack credibility, while the government dismisses international concerns over its abuses as an "internal affair."

It wasn't supposed to be like this. By the time Abdullah took over for his authoritarian predecessor Mahathir Mohamad, it was already apparent that Malaysia's lopsided growth was unsustainable. Abdullah's repairman rhetoric was for many Malaysians apt, uplifting, and unifying—a much-needed political reality check. He has since failed to deliver on most of those pledges.

Some of Abdullah's defenders have explained this away as a matter of a well-meaning leader up against an entrenched government system. But this explanation doesn't absolve him for the numerous scandals linked to his administration. His deputy internal security minister, former director general of the anti-corruption agency, and the inspector general of police have all faced allegations of corruption.

The attorney general has declared them all clean, raising questions about Abdullah's and his administration's political will to push for more rule by law. Some scandals have even allegedly involved Abdullah's own family members. In 2005, an independent inquiry into then Iraqi leader Saddam Hussein's oil-for-food scandal cleared Abdullah of involvement, but implicated two of his relatives for paying bribes to Iraqi officials.

His ambitious son-in-law Khairy Jamaluddin is now busy establishing a foothold in both business and politics—counter to Abdullah's initial promises to break the perceived corrupt nexus of government and big business seen under his predecessor. In particular, Khairy was involved in a controversial merger between the privately held and relatively unknown ECM Libra Capital and a major government-linked company, Avenue Capital.

Complaints of foul play have even come from within the ruling party: Then Information Minister Abdul Kadir Sheikh Fadzir claimed the 2004 general election, which swept Abdullah to power with an overwhelming majority, was the most corrupt he had witnessed in his decades-long career. To be sure, Abdullah has inherited a race-based political system that many say is outdated and increasingly inimical to the country's future. But despite the once-grand rhetoric he has not checked the tendency of leaders in his camp to play the race card for political gain.

By many accounts race relations have worsened under his watch and UMNO's senior politicians have not helped matters. The party's annual assembly last year was among the most racially charged in the party's 50 years in power. This year's was quieter, but on the whole the party is showing few signs of parting with its discriminatory strategy to maintain power. After the Hindraf rally, the state of Malacca's chief minister was quoted saying, "The Malays have never taken to the streets, so do not force us to do so as we will draw our *parang* [machete] to defend [Malay supremacy] in this country."

For his part, Abdullah justified Thursday's use of the ISA against political opponents on the grounds that it was necessary for "national stability," but thought better of applying it against senior UMNO members who publicly threatened to use violence against Malaysia's minority communities.

A deeper problem, however, is the unwillingness of all the races to think pro-actively about what their respective communities can do to bridge the racial divide. The finger is reflexively pointed at the "other," while the government maintains that the solution is not to talk about differences.

Some here are puzzled by how dramatically Abdullah's agenda has veered from its stated course. But that is to negate his political past; his staunch support for UMNO's brand of oppression harks back to his days as a cabinet minister under Mahathir.

After the opposition rode a wave of public outrage over official abuse to score significant electoral gains in 1999, four opposition leaders and a newspaperman were charged with offenses against the state. Mahathir was on vacation at the time, leaving then deputy Abdullah to deny that it was a case of "political revenge" and saying the often perceived pliant courts were "the best place for them to prove their innocence."

During the *reformasi* period, Abdullah also warned street demonstrators of "very tough" action. He famously accused Al Gore of supporting "terrorism" and inciting riots when the then-US vice president gave a speech here applauding Malaysian demonstrators for championing democracy and justice.

"He sounds like the [previous] PM [Mahathir], he is crude in his attacks on the opposition," said Nasir Hashim, president of Malaysia's Socialist Party at the time, in an analysis that many Malaysians will find apropos of the present, adding that Abdullah's "insecurity" over his inter-party support led him to sound and behave like other UMNO leaders. Indeed, if Abdullah were to have fulfilled his initial pledges, the 68-year-old leader would have had to first change himself, to put the national interest above his party's, to cultivate the moral authority to stand up to the entrenched and often corrupt interests in his own midst. The fact that Abdullah hasn't garnered support and built up connections in the traditional UMNO way, including through developing strong business ties, may also help to explain why he has recently taken his hard authoritarian turn against the political opposition.

On Friday, a day after signing the ISA detention orders, Abdullah met with 13 NGOs to discuss issues affecting the Indian community. This seemed duplicitous to many, after weeks of street demonstrations and Abdullah insisting the protests were not an acceptable way for Malaysians to voice their complaints and grievances, unwittingly suggesting that it was street demonstrations that finally got his ear.

His administration's use of the ISA, overtly targeting what the government has referred to as Indian "terrorists," simultaneously sent a message to the ground swell of dissatisfaction with Abdullah's leadership, which increasingly cuts across ethnic lines. Still, many are predicting the ruling coalition Abdullah leads to handily win the general elections, widely expected to be called in the first quarter next year.

Indeed, without systemic electoral reforms, the cards are once again stacked in the UMNO-led coalition's favor. It controls the political machinery: the media, the national purse strings, the election commission, even the school curriculum, where university students and academics are required to take a pledge promising to "always be loyal" to the government. A resounding electoral victory will reinforce the status quo, but is unlikely to rescue Malaysia from its growing political impasse.

First published December 18, 2007 (*Asia Times*)

Malaysia's Mid-life Crisis

In preparation for Malaysia's golden anniversary next month, banners have been hung on the streets around the Petronas Towers in downtown Kuala Lumpur showing Malay, Indian and Chinese children blissfully bicycling and running through a village at dusk. The sign reads: "One legacy. One destiny."

But behind the message of unity, the United Malays National Organization (UMNO), the conservative race-based party that has run Malaysia since independence, is ushering in the country's 50-year anniversary by ratcheting up its trademark fear-based communal rule. Last week Deputy Prime Minister Najib Razak controversially referred to Malaysia, which includes 40% non-Muslims, as an Islamic state. "Islam is the official religion and we are an Islamic state," Najib said.

The incendiary statement may have been an election ploy; on Wednesday Najib ordered component parties of the National Front (Barisan Nasional, or BN) that UMNO heads to prepare for an election by early next year. More likely it was the result of a desperate politician resorting to desperate political measures. Najib's aspirations to become prime minister are well known and have been cast into doubt by an ongoing murder trial in which the main suspects—including prominent political analyst Abdul Razak Baginda and two elite police officers—have been closely linked to Najib.

Opposition leaders and the murder victim's cousin say there is a photo linking Najib with the Mongolian model found blown up with C4 explosives in a patch of jungle outside Kuala Lumpur. Najib has declined to answer questions about the woman and he may be spared having to testify. Nonetheless, the ongoing case has hurt UMNO's political standing, and the party appears to be appealing to its well-worn tactic of playing the race and religion card to divert attention.

In the larger scheme of things, Najib's comments might have been meaningless. UMNO has long relied on communal rhetoric to sustain its five-decade grip on power. But the comments also come at a time when the nominally secular country is undergoing what some view as a pronounced Islamization; when several court decisions have denied individuals the right to be recognized by the religion of their choosing; when race relations are on the skids; and when official provocation is on the rise—in a word, as the country finds itself in the throes of a mid-life crisis.

In response to Najib's remark, the Malaysian Chinese Association (MCA), a component party of the BN, issued statements assuring its constituency that Malaysia is a secular state. UMNO Youth chief and Education Minister Hishammuddin Hussein, famous for speeches in which he brandishes Malay daggers and warns Malaysia's minority Chinese and Indian communities not to question Malay "supremacy," hit back by telling the MCA (sans dagger this time) not to issue "any more statements that Malaysia is a secular state."

Internet opposition

A few years ago, when the state-run print and broadcast media monopolized public opinion, Najib's and Hishammuddin's comments would have been spared public probity. But with the recent proliferation of blogs and independent news websites, the ruling elite are increasingly being exposed to outside criticism.

Take, for instance, Minister in the Prime Minister's Office Nazri Abdul Aziz, who during a recent parliamentary session repeatedly shouted "*bodoh*" (stupid) across the floor at a fellow parliamentarian. The nine-minute clip was posted on YouTube, and Malaysian bloggers had a field day asking in effect, "Who is running our country?"

On Monday, UMNO information chief Muhammad Muhammad

Taib filed a police report against Raja Petra Kamarudin, the editor of popular Web portal *Malaysia-today.net*, for allegedly degrading Islam and stirring communal tensions. The website has built a name for itself by aggressively reporting on alleged abuses of power at the highest levels, including within Prime Minister Abdullah Badawi's inner circle.

UMNO probably didn't foresee what happened next. By Monday afternoon, with news of the police report out, the site's pages loaded slowly as its server hit 97% capacity, according to Raja Petra. By Tuesday, Raja Petra had posted a warning to UMNO as clear as that which the party was trying to send to him and bloggers. In an article titled "See you in hell, Muhamad son of Muhamad," Raja Petra reminded readers of the former state-level chief executive's attempt to bring 2.4 million ringgit (US$693,000) into Australia in 1997.

Raja Petra's style of recalcitrance is one of UMNO's biggest fears: dissenters who refuse to go quietly, dissenters who could inspire others to speak out just as fearlessly over the Internet. His is arguably not a common response in feudal Malaysia. And UMNO, through remarks like Najib's and the crackdown on bloggers, are putting Malaysians' tolerance to an important new test.

On Tuesday the government said it would formulate laws that would potentially allow for detention without trial to punish "offending" bloggers. On July 13, Nathaniel Tan, a webmaster for the opposition People's Justice Party (PKR), was detained for five days by police after he was said to have "classified" documents alleging that Deputy Internal Security Minister Johari Baharom had taken bribes to free known gangsters from prison.

Not only did the circumstances surrounding Tan's detention draw attention to Johari, it also put the spotlight back on Najib. Some bloggers speculated that Tan's arrest was meant to distract the independent online media from the Mongolian-murder trial.

A few months ago, around the time that Malaysia's arch-conservative Information Minister Zainuddin Maidin announced that the government had to control bloggers and classify them as "professionals" or "non-professionals," several prominent websites, including *Malaysia Today*, added blog roundups to their homepages (with one of the blogs therein proposing to extend the "professional or non-professional" label to politicians).

But bloggers are not the only Malaysians concerned about UMNO's mounting crackdown on dissent. Former UMNO chief and longtime prime minister Mahathir Mohamad and his onetime deputy and current opposition figurehead Anwar Ibrahim have both in recent weeks concluded that UMNO has "rotted." Meanwhile, a band of academics has begun campaigning against Akujanji, a pledge of loyalty to the government that every college student must sign and over the years has been used to suppress free expression.

Last week, meanwhile, the Internal Security Ministry ordered all the major media not to publish on the question of whether Malaysia is an Islamic state. Only the prime minister and deputy prime minister are authorized to comment on it, said the ministry. But on Wednesday a diverse group of Malaysians held a forum to discuss the matter, in short emphasizing that while the constitution declares Islam as Malaysian's official religion, the secular-based constitution, not *sharia* law, was intended as the country's legal framework.

Despite this dissent, many political analysts predict an UMNO-BN landslide at the next general elections, which will occur when the prime minister decides to call them. That, they say, is because most Malaysians have been indoctrinated by the government to fear political change and still vote on ethnic lines. In an ironic twist, Mahathir, who ruled with an iron fist for 22 years, recently suggested that Malaysians tend to vote blindly and said, "The country deserves the government it gets."

The real victim in all this is the Malay community, whom UMNO claims it is serving and protecting. By politicizing religion, UMNO has tarnished Malaysia's international and domestic reputation as a bastion of moderate Islam. Meanwhile, UMNO's unwavering support for an affirmative-action program favoring ethnic Malays over minority Chinese and Indians has bred animosity among non-Muslims and led them to scapegoat Malays for the country's shortcomings, while ignoring their significant contributions to nation-building. Moreover it has too often become an excuse among non-Muslims not to reflect on their own respective community's roles in the country's vicious socio-political spiral and to take pro-active steps to reverse the trend.

The racial divide has and continues to play into UMNO's hands. The government elite and a growing band of concerned Malaysians have set the stage for country's 50th anniversary. Malaysians of all ethnicities must now decide where they will stand, if it's best to leave nation-building primarily in government hands, or if now is the time to become more active stakeholders in the country's future.

First published July 28, 2007 (*Asia Times*)

* * *

Opposition Steals a March in Malaysia

This pivotal day and its aftermath left many Malaysians to ponder whether the government's authoritarian streak or street demonstrations were inimical to the national interest. After all, the rally concerned a fundamental democratic right, voting.

The week after the rally, Deputy Prime Minister Najib Razak said that the demonstrators had disrupted business in the Jamek Mosque area. I witnessed quite the contrary. Many of the shops along the choked streets remained open, and it was not until police stormed through, barking and cracking their batons against walls, that store fronts were shut. The same week on the front page of a state paper, Mr N. Siva Subramaniam, commissioner for the government Human Rights Commission, was quoted as saying there were no incidents of police violence at the rally. In the hope he would not repeat the claim, I rang him up and offered to send him video footage I had captured of unprovoked police stomping a demonstrator. On the wall behind that scene was a portrait of Malaysia's first prime minister in a shot taken during independence, shouting, "Freedom! Freedom! Freedom!"

Bad weather and government intimidation failed to prevent an estimated 40,000 people from gathering in the Malaysian capital to demand electoral reforms, marking the country's largest public protest in nearly 10 years and a stiff new opposition challenge to Prime Minister Abdullah Badawi's scandal-plagued administration.

On Friday, Abdullah said the government would not tolerate street demonstrations, while his son-in-law, Khairy Jamaluddin, called the activists "monkeys" and said if the protesters sought to challenge the ruling coalition that has ruled the country since independence to do so at the polls—ignoring, or merely failing to comprehend, the premise of the rally.

Police checkpoints were stationed at all major arteries into the city and as far as the northern state of Kedah to prevent ralliers from attending, those involved in the demonstrations said. On Saturday, thousands of police were on hand, blocking off roads and cordoning protesters in various locations, to keep them from gathering en masse. Outside the Jamek Mosque train terminal police fired tear gas at largely quiescent demonstrators. According to government news reports, 245 people were arrested and later released.

The ralliers, many wearing yellow t-shirts, planned to march from the Jamek Mosque area to the king's palace to deliver a memorandum containing their electoral reform demands, including a cleanup of the voter rolls and free and fair access to the state-controlled media. Elections have in the past been plagued by allegations of phantom voting, vote-buying and manipulative gerrymandering. The election commission has failed to address these issues, said rally organizers BERSIH (Clean), a coalition of 26 non-governmental organizations as well as non-ruling political parties.

An incident witnessed by this correspondent at about 4pm on Tun Perak Road on Saturday was a window into the ill health of Malaysian democracy. As riot police stood watch behind shields, ralliers began to move parallel to them down the sidewalk. Those in the front urged the others to pull forward, but there was a pronounced apprehension about the crowd—a stutter in the step, as if the notion of free expression was only vaguely familiar. Some twirled Malaysian flags. Others waved to police in a gesture of goodwill. Then suddenly police blitzed from the side, sending protesters scurrying. Some of those caught were dragged to the ground and kicked and punched by several officers before being hauled away. Minutes later, police rushed the shop-lined alleys behind the Jamek Mosque area, barking and banging their clubs against drawn shop fronts, as shopkeepers and customers sought cover behind lattice gates. Plainclothesmen demanded those with cameras to shut them off or risk arrest. Back on Tuanku Abdul Rahman Road, police fired water cannons from atop police trucks crawling toward retreating protesters. An estimated 30,000 protestors managed to reach the king's palace and deliver the memorandum, according to the rally's organizers. Fitri Shukri, 31, a consultant who traveled from the northern state of Penang to attend the rally, said overall he was encouraged by the day: "This is a start. We know it takes time. But sitting at home won't help and Malaysians are beginning to realize it."

Abdullah came to power in late 2003, promising greater transparency and to fight the country's endemic graft. However, the general perception is that he has failed to deliver and there is a growing sense as he becomes entrenched in power that he no longer intends to. He has retained a number of high-ranking officials widely suspected of corruption. The anti-corruption agency remains under the purview of the ruling government. Critics also charge Abdullah with neglecting to address judicial corruption and electoral fraud and other cases of official abuse and neglect.

Malaysia's race-based political landscape means agendas often play out along ethnic lines. Saturday's protest witnessed the participation of a large number of members from the opposition, the ethnic Malay-dominated, Islamic PAS party, which apart from running on a clean governance platform would like to turn Malaysia into an Islamic state. But a much broader swath of Malaysian society was represented: activists, ordinary citizens, young, old, Indian, Malay, Chinese. Police expressed alarm at the large number of children present, state media reported.

"It was a citizens' event involving an issue that is quite universal," said activist Tian Chua. The last time Malaysians took to the street on such a scale was during the *reformasi* movement in 1998 after the nation's then deputy prime minister Anwar Ibrahim was sacked after challenging former prime minister Mahathir Mohamad's hold on power and later received a black eye from a beating in jail by police chief Rahim Noor.

Public participation in the political process waned sharply after *reformasi*, however. Indeed, a much overlooked consequence of the period is that the government has used that tumultuous turn of events to repel many Malaysians from being active stakeholders of the national development process. The ruling elite now often brands those vocalizing dissatisfaction with official policy short-sighted troublemakers intent on destabilizing the nation, and many

Malaysians today echo that government line.

The government's rhetoric of fear and intimidation was employed once again during Saturday's protest. For instance, Abdullah was quoted as saying, "They are challenging the patience of the people who want the country to be peaceful and stable." Anonymously sent text messages warned people to stay away from Freedom Square, where an "illegal anti-government" rally would be held. It was illegal in the sense that gatherings of more than five people require a police permit and organizers were unable to obtain one on the grounds that it would block traffic and disturb business.

That the demonstration still managed to attract so many people (though supporters estimated as many as 40,000, police estimates put the number at 4,000) is testament to the level of dissatisfaction over Abdullah's governance, said Tian. Although the ralliers themselves were peaceful, and state security officials violent, it did not stop the state-run *New Straits Times* newspaper from running a story on Sunday entitled, "Illegal gathering causes traffic chaos in city." The story was buried on page four, reserving the front page for a photo of a girl who had had a heart transplant chomping on chicken from a skewer.

This despite that fact that international eyes were trained on Malaysia over the weekend, as much if not more over the government's handling of the rally than the calls of the demonstrators. The government's violent response to basic democratic rights has led some advocates and analysts to draw comparisons with the repressive military regime in Myanmar, which likewise aggressively extinguished street protests in August and September.

The New York-based rights group Human Rights Watch said in a statement, "If Malaysia wants to count itself a democracy, it can begin by upholding constitutional guarantees of free speech and assembly. The way the system works now, only the ruling coalition can get its messages out."

General elections are expected to be held by early next year and as it stands the voices for reform will probably only be heard in protests to those polls, which they argue will be systematically stacked in Abdullah's favor.

First published November 13, 2007 (*Asia Times*)

ACCOUNTABILITY

Abdullah's Honeymoon is Over in Malaysia

In the wake of last month's general assembly for the United Malays National Organization (UMNO), empathy for Prime Minister Abdullah Badawi is supplanting the restlessness eddying around his vaunted anti-graft war.

Few expected allegedly corrupt officials to nab top posts, or a party veteran to lambaste the affair as "the worst case of money politics in history." Nor did they expect a visibly nonplussed Abdullah to ask anyone with information on the allegations to please step forward—sounding, in the process, more like the helpless father of a kidnapped child than the transformational leader he set out to be when he succeeded former premier Mahathir Mohamad one year ago.

But flash back to the months leading up to the assembly. It was then, as Abdullah's war on graft seemed to be losing focus and determination, that calendars were marked in anticipation of the UMNO assembly. According to the logic, if Abdullah could just win his party's presidency, he would have the job security to pursue his battle in earnest. Win it he did, with overwhelming support.

This raises the question, do the assembly's "shock results," as one daily newspaper here put it, justify "extending Abdullah's honeymoon"?

Waging a reform war will always find resistance, especially among a party steeped in religion and race like UMNO and a citizenry weaned on feudalism and communalism. No time to pursue one will be ideal. And yet now may be as propitious a time as Abdullah will get.

"Abdullah has overwhelming support within the populace," said Dr Chandra Muzaffar, president of the International Movement for a Just World. "And now it's time to prove he's capable of wielding a big stick."

It's a matter of tone-setting, Muzaffar added, which may well determine whether history will remember Abdullah as a transitional or transformational leader.

Abdullah's defenders say he has set the tone, that he has marked his first year with substantive first steps. They note that he has appointed quality people to government-linked companies; set up a royal police commission to oversee an institution long plagued by allegations of lethargy, corruption and racism; launched a National Integrity Plan (NIP) that outlines how the whole of Malaysia can help fight graft.

Others say these measures still leave doubt about Abdullah's sincerity and vision as a reformer. To set up institutions and frameworks is one thing, to see them through is another. The NIP, for instance, according to an official with its overseeing body, the National Integrity Institute, is an extension of Mahathir's Vision 2020. In that plan, to make Malaysia a fully developed country by the year 2020, Mahathir called for a "highly moral and spiritual society with the highest ethical standards." Some observers say corruption and ethics worsened during Mahathir's 22-year reign.

Efforts on the ground level seem to be lacking and call into question Abdullah's determination. In the capital Kuala Lumpur, pirated CDs are sold openly. Gambling centers and brothels still do business down the block from police stations. Customs officials and police officers are reportedly as receptive to bribes as they've always been.

Abdullah's defenders say these things take time to clean up. But as Singapore's former prime minister Lee Kuan Yew, who oversaw the nation-state's leap from the Third World to First through strict and efficient governance, points out in his memoirs, "It was not that difficult to clean up these organized rackets." Lee's memoirs are a reminder of the possible. "It is easy to start off with high moral standards, strong convictions and determination to beat down corruption," Lee writes. "But it is difficult to live up to these good intentions unless the leaders are strong and determined enough to deal with all transgressors, and without exception."

Abdullah's detractors say he has shied away from confronting allegedly corrupt big fish within UMNO. Months back, this move was thought to be a wise gambit, a kind of wooing before the hunting. But increasingly it's being read as an opportunistic case of retreat.

"Abdullah is not eager to implement change," said Tian Chua, vice president of the People's Justice Party (PKR). "His fight so far has been one of dignity: to defend his dignity and prevent being humiliated. So he's been careful not to upset the status quo too much while remaining popular enough to be liked by the people."

As Abdullah himself was quoted as saying in 2000, after becoming the premier-in-waiting, "For the time being, I have done well just keeping my certain posture."

Abdullah's gentle approach appeals to ordinary Malaysians. But it may be undermining his leadership within UMNO. Mahathir ruled UMNO with an iron fist. And while Abdullah is known to be "soft but firm," so far as premier he has shown himself to be more soft than firm, and some in the party may be capitalizing—that's one way of reading the assembly's "shock results."

The outcome of that election, attributed to circumstances beyond Abdullah's control, may have bought him a little more time to wage his proclaimed war, but before long Malaysians will expect him to deliver. Depending where Abdullah's real heart lies will determine whether that's a day he'll relish.

First published October 20, 2004 (*Asia Times*)

Malaysia Aims to NIP Corruption in the Bud

The NIP was to leverage all sectors of society. But four years after it was introduced I venture to guess that most Malaysians would be stumped if you asked them what "NIP" stands for let alone its basic aims. One is left to wonder whether Abdullah was serious about seeing the NIP through in the first place.

Prime Minister Abdullah Badawi recently unveiled a National Integrity Plan (NIP) to inculcate Malaysians with a better sense of right and wrong. It seeks to reduce corruption and inefficiency and foster greater religious understanding in a nation that is 55 percent Malay Muslim, with sizeable Indian, Chinese and indigenous minorities.

The plan is backed by a 152-page blueprint that calls on all sectors of society to play a role and recommends family value-based park outings, "My House Is My Heaven" seminars and putting profiles of the country's leaders on a website.

But the NIP says little if anything about greater government transparency, expanded media freedoms, or the establishment of an independent judiciary and the Malaysian Anti-Corruption Agency, which now reports directly to the prime minister's office. These steps, say critics, are vital to curb corruption and build a more civil society.

"You can't just create a plan and tell people to do it step-by-step," said Eric Paulsen, coordinator of the non-governmental organization (NGO) Voice of the People of Malaysia. "Certain fundamentals have to be addressed first," he said.

Samsudin Osman, the chairman of NIP's overseeing body, the

newly formed Integrity Institute of Malaysia, told *Asia Times Online* that the Anti-Corruption Agency (ACA) and media are free to act as they wish. "No one dictates to them how they should proceed," Osman said.

But rights groups tell a different story—of journalists being harassed and fired for straying from the government line, of ACA cases being closed by the prime minister's office despite evidence against ministers, of a public afraid to speak out for fear of reprisal (activists have been jailed without trial).

Lim Kit Siang, leader of the opposition Democratic Action Party, said, "A plan is better than no plan." But, he added, "All these unresolved issues raise questions of political will."

In other areas the Abdullah Administration is working to put those questions to rest. Last week Abdullah's administration announced that the police, immigration and customs departments will soon undergo a transfer of civil servants in order to curb corruption, abuse of power and misappropriation. Abdullah has promised more overhauls and further scrutiny of how business and government practices are conducted.

A majority of Malaysians, including opposition supporters, welcome Abdullah's early calls for change; under his predecessor Mahathir Mohamad corruption turned rampant. Key institutions like the judiciary lost credibility. Dissent was squelched.

Abdullah's early moves are an acknowledgement of the mess he's been handed, and of how far the country remains from its stated goal of becoming a fully developed country by 2020. Economic growth has not been matched by the political, cultural, spiritual, educational, and creative growth called for in the NIP. In that sense, the NIP appears to be a timely step in the right direction.

And yet several recent decisions by Abdullah and deals involving his family members are raising questions about Abdullah's own integrity. In March, *Malaysian Business* reported that Abdullah's only son became one of the 10 richest Malays in the country when shares of the oil and gas firm he owns, Scomi, soared more than 1,000 percent upon going public last year. Then last week, news broke that Abdullah's son-in-law Khairy Jamaluddin is set to become a senior executive at the state-controlled investment company, Khazanah Nasional, an allegation the 28-year-old has neither confirmed nor denied.

Abdullah has also retained several questionable characters from the old regime in his cabinet. He had promised that all cabinet members will have to report their assets—but only to him, it turns out.

The March parliamentary elections were marred by accusations of voter fraud. Abdullah said he was leaving it to the Election Commission to investigate. Opposition leaders say the commission serves the ruling coalition and won't investigate properly.

"Sometimes the sloganeering of the past seems to be the order of the day," said Abdul Razak Baginda, executive director of the Malaysian Strategic Research Center. "And if the [NIP] is to work, which I think it can, we have to be more honest with ourselves."

That will happen only if the government elite renovate their thinking and strive not only to make those they govern more accountable but themselves as well. After all, a fish rots from the head down, a point the NIP's 152-pages of good intentions never makes, nor can it change.

First published May 13, 2004 (*Asia Times*)

* * *

Anti-graft War Backfires in Malaysia

It has become evident to many Malaysians that Prime Minister Abdullah Badawi's war on graft never really got started.

But few would have predicted that three years on, Abdullah and his family would become the target of a mounting chorus of accusations, linked to the same allegations of corruption, nepotism, and abuse of power that the once-reform-minded premier has so publicly campaigned against.

Much attention has focused on the meteoric rise of Abdullah's only son, Kamaluddin, and his son-in-law, Khairy Jamaluddin—both for the most part political and business unknowns before Abdullah assumed the premiership in 2004. While their role cannot be overlooked in what increasingly has the markings of a family business empire in the making, Abdullah's approach to managing the country has done little to break the endemic patronage that has long hobbled Malaysia's political and economic progress. Indeed, his style of governance may in fact be encouraging it.

A turning point in Abdullah's premiership arguably came last October in the run-up to the general assembly for the ruling party he heads, the United Malays National Organization (UMNO). At the time, Abdullah's promise to battle corruption "without fear or favor" was meeting resistance among the conservative party's old guard. Then, on the eve of the assembly, in an apparently unprecedented move by a Malaysian prime minister, Abdullah reportedly distributed RM3 million (more than US$856,000) to each division chief for "development" purposes.

Opposition members said the gesture smacked of vote-buying.

Abdullah for his part denied any foul play. At the very least, the gesture signaled to the party's old guard that Abdullah is as committed as his predecessor—former premier Mahathir Mohamad—to oiling UMNO's patronage machine. And even where the UMNO elite have not benefited directly from Abdullah's style of governance, they have been able to take stock in what appears to be a man being swallowed by the system he had earlier promised to change.

Most recently, Abdullah was accused of procuring a new $50 million jet for his personal use. The plane, he explained, was being leased from a government company for use by top officials, including the king. Either way, Abdullah's administration has shown a special fondness for the country's royal sultanates. His government directly awarded a RM400 million palace project to two little-known companies, Kumpulan Seni Reka and Maya Maju.

In response to the contract, opposition leader Lim Kit Siang asked in Parliament: "Who are [the companies]? Are they a crony company? Why wasn't there an open tender? Why wasn't there a contract? Why do we need this new palace?" Those questions are still being debated, but the opposition is making much hay of the allegations for its own political benefit.

Meanwhile, Abdullah's own family members have during his term likewise, fairly or unfairly, found themselves at the center of controversy. His son Kamaluddin's business activities, including his position as leading shareholder of Scomi Group, a local oil-and-gas company, have come under particularly sharp scrutiny. Scomi's share price skyrocketed 588% four months after listing on the local bourse in May 2003.

While the growth of Malaysia's energy industry has since certainly played a role in pumping up the company's shares, Kamaluddin's family clout is also thought to have inflated investor confidence. Mahathir, now a vocal Abdullah critic, estimates that Scomi has secured RM1 billion worth of government contracts during

Abdullah's tenure. Industry analysts, meanwhile, are perplexed as to how Kamaluddin, 38, could suddenly be worth an estimated $90 million.

More controversially, a Scomi subsidiary, Scomi Precision Engineering, was fingered in 2004 by US and European intelligence officials for supplying dual-use centrifuges to Libya, which allegedly could have been used in the country's covert nuclear-weapons program. The company was hastily cleared of any wrongdoing by both the Foreign Ministry and police, even as the United States was applying pressure for full disclosure about Scomi's business dealings.

Defending family honor

Meanwhile, Abdullah has stoutly defended his son's independence as a businessman, saying that Kamaluddin "has never abused his ties with me ... He has never asked help from the government or anything that required a bailout for him." Abdullah has likewise defended his son-in-law Khairy's recent advances in politics and business, which have drawn opposition scrutiny.

Khairy, deputy chief of UMNO's youth wing, has been described in some political circles as "Malaysia's most powerful 31 year old." Several of Khairy's closest confidantes are also known to be close to Abdullah, including businessman and newspaperman Kalimullah Hassan, whom the premier appointed editor-in-chief of the UMNO-controlled *New Straits Times* newspaper.

Both Khairy and Hassan have been linked to controversial financial dealings between ECM Libra and Avenue Capital. On December 27, 2005, ECM chairman Hassan along with two other company co-founders announced that they would each sell 1% of their shareholdings in the company to Khairy in a deal that was transacted at 71 sen per share, for a total of RM9.2 million. Khairy is on record saying that the deal was financed through the company, but many viewed his invitation to join ECM as a way to earn the company valuable political connections.

Soon thereafter, ECM acquired government-linked financial company Avenue Capital Resources and reportedly was not required to raise any outside capital to make the multimillion-dollar acquisition. Critics, including most prominently former premier Mahathir, say the deal lacked transparency. ECM has persistently denied any foul play.

Khairy has also been loosely linked to Khazanah Holdings, the state-run investment arm that Abdullah chairs and which manages an estimated RM25 billion worth of government funds. Two years ago, Khairy was widely tipped to become Khazanah's chief operating officer, but amid a public outcry the appointment didn't go through.

However, Ganendran Sarvananthan, 29, said to be Khairy's close friend during his time in school in England, was in February 2006 appointed to the surprisingly senior position of Khazanah's executive director of investments.

It is of course entirely possible that there is no political connection to any of Abdullah's family's growing businesses, as the embattled premier has consistently argued. But with opposition criticism mounting, if Abdullah were true to his word about an "unconditional" anti-corruption drive, the authorities should have probed at least some of the allegations. To date, no such probes have been launched.

Rather, top appointments in the government's fight against graft could be viewed as hindering that process. Former Anti-Corruption Agency (ACA) officer Mohamad Ramli Manan recently filed a police report alleging that the ACA's current director general, Zulkipli Mat Noor, was involved in various crimes—from living beyond his means to sexual misconduct—when he was a top cop with the Royal Malaysian Police.

Ramli said the ACA had begun to investigate Zulkipli's conduct beginning in 1997, but since he filed his original complaint to the attorney general's office last July, there have been no signs that the relevant authorities plan to move on the case. The Parliamentary Select Committee on Integrity last week decided to call both Zulkipli and whistle-blower Ramli in for closed-door hearings.

As currently constituted, the ACA is not an independent outfit, but rather reports to the Prime Minister's Office. The agency's corruption-related arrests have risen from 339 in 2003, to 497 in 2004, and 485 in 2005, but critics contend that the ACA has merely netted minnows and not any big fish. Indeed, some of the agency's once-prime suspects have later landed in the Prime Minister's Office as top-level appointees.

Transparency and accountability have also arguably been impaired by Abdullah's use of the Official Secrets Act (OSA), which gives the government the right to classify as a state secret any document it deems to be sensitive to national security. The government has used the OSA in many instances to avoid scrutiny, including for deals it strikes without tender with politically connected private companies, opposition politicians say.

No-man mission

Abdullah has frequently said that the fight against corruption cannot be a one-man mission. But his actions have hardly inspired cooperation among the ruling elite, let alone at the grassroots. Instead, his government has moved to take down self-fashioned whistleblowers and maintained sharp curbs on the media. The UMNO-backed *New Straits Times* newspaper group, for instance, is currently suing two bloggers for defamation over postings that were sharply critical of the government, and Abdullah has in press interviews supported the legal action.

To be sure, an anti-corruption campaign waged by the leader of a party that arguably institutionalized the practice in Malaysia was bound to be a slippery slope. And after three years in power, should Abdullah try to recommit himself to the fight he would run the risk of dissent within UMNO with new general elections on the horizon. "Abdullah has learned that this is the way to do business in UMNO if you want to stay in power," contended Tian Chua of the opposition People's Justice Party.

If it all sounds familiar, that's because it is. Corruption and patronage within UMNO reached endemic proportions during Mahathir's 22-year rule. He sought through any means possible to catapult the nation rapidly to developed world status by 2020. If someone could get the job done—in business or politics—to Mahathir it often did not matter how as much as when. Those practices continue largely unabated under Abdullah's government, in part because their consequences are not readily visible.

Malaysia still makes a convincing show that economically things are humming along. In the capital city, shiny modern trams dart and slither between glass office towers. Well-groomed highways connect the peninsula's far corners. Unemployment is low. The state-run media gloss over government abuses to paint a picture of economic progress and social harmony. And the unquestioning feudalistic masses digest and echo what they are fed by pontificating politicians.

All the while, however, Malaysia has seen foreign direct investment drop from $3.8 billion in 2003 to $1.4 billion last year. Leaders have struggled to come up with a new vision for the country, with grand pronouncements about becoming an agriculture, biotech and high-tech hub showing few signs of materializing. Meanwhile, corruption is also having long-term adverse social consequences.

Recent opinion polls prioritized the need to tackle graft above rising inflation and unemployment concerns. Political analyst Bakri Musa recently noted on his blog: "We are sending precisely the wrong message to our people. That is, in order to succeed or afford a mansion and other trappings of the 'good life', we do not have to study diligently or work hard but merely ingratiate ourselves to the powerful in order to hog our own little spot at the public trough."

Abdullah's sagging anti-graft campaign promises to become a big issue at the next general elections, which some believe could be called in the coming months. The People's Justice Party has promised to weed out corruption should it come to power, and it has singled out corruption issues as the main plank for building up its meager support base. Yet the party's figurehead, Anwar Ibrahim, has been curiously silent on allegations of corruption linked to Abdullah, UMNO and his family.

Despite his insistence to the contrary, Anwar may be looking to re-enter UMNO, the party he was ignominiously ousted from nearly a decade ago on charges of corruption and sodomy. Rumors abound that he has quietly been cultivating close ties with Abdullah in preparation for just such a move. Despite opposition grumblings and signs of business-as-usual, the general public has hardly shown a level of outrage over recent corruption allegations that would indicate they intend to abandon Abdullah or UMNO's ruling coalition at the next polls.

First published March 21, 2007 (*Asia Times*)

* * *

Malaysia's Blind Path to Progress

In its race to develop, the Malaysian government has always had one eye on Western achievement in terms of science and technology, dynamism, efficiency and pluralism. The other eye has been conscious of Malaysia's Muslim identity and the dangers of falling for the "superficial conclusion that the Islamic system of society and economics is not compatible with the requirements of progress, and should, therefore, be modified on Western lines," in the words of the late Islamist Muhammad Asad.

The speeches of former authoritarian Mahathir Mohamad, who retired in late 2003 after more than 22 years in power, distinguished between Asian and Western values. He devised the "Look East" policy, which cited Japan as a model. Then, in 2001, to pander to Malaysia's 60% Muslim majority, he declared Malaysia an Islamic state. His favorite tune is said to be Frank Sinatra's "My Way."

Of late, the government has been hailing its "balancing act" as a rousing success.

Speaking at a panel titled "Modernization without Westernization" at the World Economic Forum in Davos last month, Deputy Prime Minister Najib Razak said in effect that Malaysia has adroitly combined Islam and modernization to become a beacon of inspiration to the Muslim world. "The Starbucks and McDonald's will still be around, but we still preserve our culture ... We are a fundamentalist Islamic country" that has become a "source of force" for modernization, and is "ahead of the other [thriving Asian economies, such as Singapore, Hong Kong and Taiwan], and they are looking toward us."

But back home a different picture is taking shape, one in which the government has been less mindful of progress than it has claimed; and a worrisome number of people seem to be sinking into a mass consumerist lull of mediocrity, rather than collectively pushing toward brave new heights.

The government has talked a lot about preserving "Islamic" and "Eastern" values. "But many aspects of development haven't really been thought out," said Mohammad Haji Salleh, professor of literature at Universiti Sains Malaysia. "There's been too much emphasis on rapid capitalistic growth."

The price of growth

The Malaysian Institute of Economic Research estimated that the country grew by 7.2% last year. But that growth might have come with a price. A recent United Nations development report found Malaysia to have one of the worst income disparities in Asia, with the richest 10% of Malaysians earning 22 times more than the poorest 10%. Meanwhile, Malaysia suffers from among the highest obesity rates in Asia: 59% of Malaysian go to a fast-food restaurant once a week or more, compared with just 35% of Americans and 11% of Europeans, according to an AC Nielsen's Consumer Confidence and Opinion Survey; it also states that 98% of Malaysians eat at fast food restaurants. Only Filipinos frequent fast-food restaurants more often.

In its bid to join the ranks of the industrialized world, Malaysia finds itself grappling with the challenge of any developing nation: how to incorporate the myriad admirable qualities associated with the West while resisting the seemingly pernicious ones.

From a Muslim perspective, walking this fine line is essential to proper development. Assad, writing in the 1930s, said "there is only one thing which a Muslim can profitably learn from the West, namely, the exact sciences in their pure and applied forms." Wisely, most progressive Muslim scholars today aren't as dismissive of Western achievement as Assad. But blind imitation and consumption remain a concern for most devout Muslims. And in Malaysia, those tendencies have been less tempered than elsewhere in the Muslim world.

They are predictably most pronounced in the capital city. In Kuala Lumpur recently, a European visitor was overheard saying, "Mall culture is more prevalent here than in the States." That might be overstating it, but even Malaysians, from journalists to laymen, often lament that their capital city doesn't offer much beyond shopping. Certainly it does—the much-neglected national library and art museum out along the highway come to mind—but retail shopping, much of it with a global touch, seems to dominate leisure pursuits here.

The Kuala Lumpur retail market was worth RM13.77 billion (US$3.62 billion) in 2004, or 26.7% of Malaysia's total retail industry, according to Retail Group Malaysia, which tabulates the retail data for the Malaysia Retailers Association. The group says an additional 3.23 million square feet (984,504 square meters) of retail space will be built around Kuala Lumpur in 2005, and 4 million more in 2006, much of it in the form of mega- and hypermarket-anchored shopping centers. Knowing this, it seems only fitting that Kuala Lumpur is home to "Southeast Asia's biggest shopping mall."

Word has spread. Arrivals from Saudi Arabia, for instance, many of whom attest that they come for the shopping, were up 53% last year.

And the craze doesn't end in the capital; for the whole of Malaysia, retail sales grew 7.7% last year, and the industry growth rate is soon expected to surpass the country's gross domestic product growth rate.

From a less dollars-and-cents viewpoint, they might be unsettling. But are they cause for panic?

'Courtesy and noble values'

As one travels away from city centers, what distinguishes Malaysia and its healthy mix of cultures becomes more evident; arguably, as Najib suggested, the core remains intact. Even among some urbanites, there is a growing mindfulness of culture and religion. The *tudung*, or Muslim headscarf, for instance, is more visible, even in urban areas.

But some warn against confusing the appearance of spiritual values with actually living them.

"Most Malaysians have not really thought about consumption

and how that is tied to moderation of religion," said Masjaliza Hamzah with the women's right's group Sisters in Islam. "Do they see a link between their religion and work ethics, between their religion and how they should treat others?"

It seems the government is asking the same questions. Premier Abdullah Badawi has talked abstractly a great deal about Islam Hadhari, or Civilizational Islam, which through 10 points sums up his vision for a progressive Muslim society. And last month Abdullah announced a "courtesy and noble values" campaign in which he bemoaned "the erosion of values and the disappearing smile on Malaysian faces." A local newspaper followed up with "The Rude Malaysian Contest," in which readers voted "jumping the queue," "bad driving," "spitting" and "not giving seats to the elderly" into the top offenses.

Some global watchers argue that a breakdown in traditional values is the inevitable consequence of progress and point to fast-developing Asian economies to Malaysia's north as proof. But the concern with Malaysia is the seeming lopsidedness of the government's priorities. "The government has spent the last 20 years to make Malaysia economically viable, but in terms of software, we haven't kept up. We haven't developed critical thinking," said Hamzah. This, she said, is partly due to draconian legislation designed to discourage self-expression and a restrictive, coddling education system that hasn't grown in tandem with the economic sector.

Salleh, the literature professor, worries that these realities, combined with the proliferation of mass consumerism, do not bode well for Malaysia's future.

"I'm afraid if [the tendency] goes unchecked we'll find two divides," he said. "One will be the very rich who own businesses, the other will be a very large number of consumers who tend to forget themselves."

The government has always viewed the majority Muslim Malays

as most susceptible to falling into the latter category; from the 1970s to present the government has upheld an affirmative-action program to improve their work ethic and empower the community. But more than 30 years on, some say Malay "backwardness," as Mahathir called it, remains a nagging problem.

In a speech last week, Abdullah urged the Malays to stop wasting time and develop themselves into "towering" personalities: "The Malays need to change their attitude to one that is more constructive. We need to use our time wisely so that we can better ourselves and become more successful. We should have the objective to better ourselves, our families, our race and country ... spend time to look for good ideas. Look at how you can write that working paper for a business project, or plan how to get your child to succeed in school. Stop wasting time, wasting your energy and wasting your effort."

It's as though the government senses something is slipping away—that if the Malays don't transform themselves soon it might not happen. Perhaps it's no coincidence that last month the religious department here raided a popular nightclub and arrested around 100 patrons, all of them Muslim, for "indecent" behavior. Or why the number of late-night road checks around the capital appear to have increased in recent months.

But then the government ignores or supports efforts that seem to outright emasculate its calls for positive change. "Genting theme park to woo more Malay visitors," read a headline in a local newspaper on January 24. A main attraction at Genting, about a 45-minute drive from the capital, is gambling. Meanwhile, the Education Ministry is said to support co-curriculum programs at the theme park for school children.

The government's task—how to keep the economy humming while meeting the demands and helping preserve the integrity of its various communities—is not an easy one. (Besides Malay Muslims, there are sizeable Chinese and Indian communities on the peninsula, and many indigenous people living in the eastern Borneo states of Sabah and Sarawak.)

But according to Hamzah and others, many of the ruling Muslim elites' gestures, which appear to signify a balanced approach to growth, are self-serving and superficial.

"I don't hear authorities bending over backwards to ensure there's equality, justice, freedom and dignity in their 'Muslim' communities," as stipulated by the Koran, said Hamzah. "We are emphasizing rituals and preserving the 'image' of what the authorities want to define as Islam, rather than internalizing the essence of the principles of the Koran ... in the daily lives of those who believe."

In a word, it's cultural, spiritual and intellectual development some find to be lacking. Others believe that in time Malaysia, which gained independence in 1957, will strike the right balance.

Interest in these and other areas—a greater overall mindfulness—will occur, said Chua Beng Huat, author of *Life Is Not Complete Without Shopping: Consumption Culture in Singapore*. Chua said much of this is already happening in next-door Singapore. "Building of shopping centers has slowed rapidly. Parents are opening up the idea of their students studying film and other arts, whereas 10 years ago they didn't."

The concern is that there is a weak intellectual tradition in Malaysia; and a weaker work ethic, with less overall value placed on education and entrepreneurship than in Singapore.

Also, many of the government's feel-good programs—from Islam Hadhari to Vision 2020, a government initiative that seeks to make Malaysia a fully developed country within the next 15 years—are not being seen through to their fullest. Stability and economic growth have been Malaysia's top priorities and have often been conflated with justice and advancement. Enlightenment is expected to follow—only the cart might be in front of the horse. And with hypercapitalism moving at full-throttle, it may be less a matter of when and more a question of if the trend can be reversed.

First published February 11, 2005 (*Asia Times*)

* * *

Hail, Hail Malaysia's Pak Lah

He gazes down from highway overpasses, building facades, light posts and banners stretched between trees—neck erect, chin dipped a trifle, a glint of humble warmth in his resolute gaze.

The portrayal of Prime Minister Abdullah Badawi as both firm and avuncular helped propel him and his ruling coalition, the Barisan National, to a resounding election victory in 2004. It built trust in his campaign promises to fight corruption without fear or favor, bridge the rural-urban wealth divide and promote moderate Islam. It also raised hopes he would allow for more democratic space after decades of authoritarian rule.

His track record in the four years since has not lived up to the portrait and political marketing. Corruption remains endemic. Islam is more aggressively asserting itself in the public and political spheres. His government has intimidated bloggers and whistleblowers and since November forcefully extinguished rallies calling for electoral reform, racial equality and price controls.

Abdullah's overall approval rating stood at 91% when he became prime minister in 2003. Now, only 38% of Indians and 42% of Chinese, the country's main minority groups, approve of his job performance, according to an opinion poll conducted last month by the independent Merdeka Center. The overall rating has fallen to 61%.

And so the excessive use of his portrait would seem almost counterintuitive, even in the runup to general elections, which are expected to be held in March. "For those who feel deprived it would seem to have the opposite of the desired effect: 'He deprived me and now he's smiling at me'," said the president of Transparency International Malaysia, Ramon Navaratnam.

But there he is flicking by like a shuffling deck of cards on highway lampposts and the road leading to Parliament, in front of the national library and mosque, beside shopping centers, at roundabouts and inside the central train station.

In the historic neighborhood of Kampong Baru, banners welcoming him on February 14 occupied so many lampposts there was little room left for local rock bands to stick bills for their upcoming concerts. One might be excused for concluding that the capital is more awash with portraits of Abdullah than ornaments for Chinese new year.

Political analyst Zaharom Nain says it's a matter of projecting image over substance. "It looks as if his media people are saying, 'Let's maintain that nice-guy image. Yes we've had a tumultuous year, let's try to incorporate those dissenting voices, we're here, we're considering what you're saying and we are doing something about it'."

After the Hindu Rights Action Force held a 20,000-strong march in front of the iconic Petronas Towers in November, protesting what it felt was marginalization of the Indian community, Abdullah's portrait appeared on banners with swirls of Tamil language advertising a meeting with Indian organizations intended to smooth relations.

To be sure, the proliferation of Abdullah's portrait is not just a matter of electoral fervor. It dates to his first days as prime minister, when it was used to cut a sharp contrast with his iron-fisted predecessor, Mahathir Mohamad, said Mustafa K Anuar, associate professor of communications at the Science University of Malaysia. Abdullah's portrait was used to reinforce the sense that a softer, more caring and generous leader had taken over, and it had been "exploited to the hilt," said Mustafa.

Abdullah's face was positioned front-and-center last year on billboards for Malaysia's 50th anniversary, like those found in front of the Ampang Park shopping center in the capital Kuala Lumpur. Those ads depict Malaysia's five prime ministers ascending in size from first to most recent—only Abdullah appears in color, looking decorous and decisive.

Some of those signs, now fading, have been replaced with banners featuring Abdullah for the minor holiday known as Federal Territories Day. Friday's edition of the state-controlled daily newspaper *The Star* featured a photo of Abdullah at a launch for a new model from national car maker Proton with a sticker of his face on the door of the car he stood beside.

Abdullah is not the first prime minister to enlist his self-portrait to cultivate a winning persona. Mahathir's picture was likewise widely plastered in the public domain; the key difference, however, is in the characterization. Mahathir was prickly and authoritarian, "with the courage of his convictions to treat his varied and staunch opposition with contempt," notes Khoo Boo Teik in the book *Beyond Mahathir*.

And rarely did his portrait suggest otherwise: even his smiles tended to look fleeting. His image was nurtured less through the use of his portrait and more through actions and policy—though certainly with the help of his servile groomers in Malaysia's tightly controlled media. In comparison, Abdullah so far has little to claim in terms of policy achievements.

What he does have is a firm but gentle common-man portrait that diverges widely from the actual substance of his tenure. It is a velvet glove for the iron fist; kid-glove treatment for the country's creeping Islamization and unabated corruption; a counterpunch to the growing chorus characterizing him as a draconian leader of inaction and indecision.

On the matter of degree, most people interviewed for this article noted that even Mahathir's face wasn't as omnipresent as Abdullah's. Many of these people hadn't considered how in-your-face Abdullah's mug had become in Malaysia's daily life until this reporter mentioned it, an indication of the sheer relentlessness of the campaign. It has become ubiquitous to the point of being subliminal.

A press secretary for the prime minister said that with the exception of Abdullah's pictures used for the 2004 general election, the Prime Minister's Office had had no involvement in the banners or billboards featuring the prime minister. "We have never been asked about using his image. We never approve anything," she said. She said the use of Abdullah's image was mostly taken up by other ministries and ad agencies such as Big Tree, which is a 100%-owned subsidiary of the country's largest media company, Media Prima. The government-linked Malaysia Resources Corporation Berhad owns a significant portion of Media Prima. "But there is no directive," the press secretary said.

Another employee in the Prime Minister's Office who worked closely on the 50th anniversary advertisements with the Ministry of Arts Culture and Heritage and on other official ad campaigns tells it differently. He said the Prime Minister's Office assists with or at least signs off on most depictions of the prime minister used for official federal campaigns and functions.

"Most [ads featuring Abdullah] need to go through us," he said speaking on the condition of anonymity. "We give the approval to put up certain banners." On ads featuring the prime minister that were not overseen by the Prime Minister's Office, he added, "Sometimes we send letters to take down pictures [of Abdullah] if they're not a good photo."

Which raises the question: is Abdullah seeking to cultivate a personality cult? Professor of sociology at the National University of Malaysia, Abdul Rahman Embong, says not. "He is profiling the leadership of this country," Abdul said, reiterating the point that Abdullah needed to distinguish himself after two-plus decades with the nation's self-proclaimed father of development, Mahathir Mohamad, at the helm.

There's no Little Red Book as there was in China, no songs venerating a Dear Leader as in North Korea, no statues in the square. But there is the use of humble, egalitarian-sounding slogans like, "I am the number one public servant," and "Work with me not for me," to soften the entrenched feudalistic leanings of his party, the long-ruling conservative United Malays National Organization. His nickname, Pak Lah, short for Father Abdullah, feeds the script.

Abdullah may not be in the same league as North Korea's Kim Jong-il, former Iraqi dictator Saddam Hussein or the Soviet Union's Joseph Stalin, all notorious for the personality cults they built around their leadership, but the Malaysian leader has shown a knack for political marketing—similar to the techniques ousted Thai prime minister Thaksin Shinawatra deployed to shore up his administration's grass roots popularity.

With elections around the corner, the question now is whether or not the campaign is working. "No doubt his intention is to camouflage excesses in executive action and abuses perpetuated by his administration," said Ramdas Tikamdas, former president of the National Human Rights Society. "But any reasonably minded Malaysian will have to see this 'uncle' against his stern executive action."

Ramdas may be underestimating the deep feudalistic underpinnings of Malaysia's political culture. Talk to Malaysians about Mahathir's sacking of his former deputy Anwar Ibrahim, who was subsequently jailed on dubious charges of corruption and sodomy, and chances are they will tell you Anwar deserved what he got because he openly challenged number one.

Or ask them about the prime minister's failure to fulfill his previous electoral promises or to even give the impression that he is working toward them and you'll likely hear a call to patience that defies the mounting anxiety about the country's direction under his leadership. What many of these people find more offensive than his poor track record is a foreign reporter questioning the competency of their well-intentioned leader.

That may be changing, though, as Abdullah appears to have ruled with a feudalistic streak of his own, found in his assumption that Malaysians will back him even if he doesn't deliver on his campaign promises. Their loyalty has further been tested by escalating crime rates, business scandals involving Abdullah's own family members, a fast-rising cost of living and concerns about Malaysia's long-term economic outlook.

Abdullah himself seems to recognize that the feel-good factor that he and his spin doctors have devised may be wearing off. "Some of you can say that I'm not good, you can say whatever. But don't say that I don't work. I work very hard. I really mean it and you know it," he was quoted as saying by *The Star* on Saturday (in the article accompanying the photo of the car with his face on it).

Amid the crowded blocks in the mostly Indian historic neighborhood known as Brickfields, Abdullah's image is hard to find, which may be another way of residents there saying they are looking for a little something more than a paternalistic portrait to meet their expectations of what a modern political leader should represent.

First published February 14, 2007 (*Asia Times*)

REVIEWS AND PROFILES

Holding Malaysian Politicos to their Words

Over the years the Malaysian politician has displayed an almost preternatural gift for delivering ear-catching quotes. What his or her words may lack in vision and profundity they often make up for in what they unwittingly reveal about the speaker, if not the broader state of the country's political leadership.

Within the past month alone, Malaysians have been treated to the information minister saying the prime minister's desire to "hear the truth" does not apply to the media; a member of Parliament telling another that the latter's use of a wheelchair is a punishment from God; the country's de facto law minister dismissing the march of around 1,000 lawyers to the country's administrative capital seeking judicial reform as no "big deal" because "1,000 of 13,000 [registered members of the bar]—is that a majority?"

Politicians often deal flippantly in subjects Malaysians are warned not to discuss openly—race, privilege, abuse of power, corruption, religion, even sex. In other nations claiming (as Malaysia often does) to be progressive, such utterances might well curtail the speaker's political ambitions. In Malaysia's race-based and religion-divided political landscape, they have a tendency to announce politicians as party stalwarts and have even been known to advance political careers.

When the education minister waved the traditional Malay dagger in a clear warning to Malaysia's minority communities last year, he was roundly applauded by party delegates. His name continues to be thrown around as a future candidate for prime minister. Any public outrage the speaker may evoke is usually drowned out by a state-run press that spins the comments in the politician's favor—assuming he or she is in favor with the ruling elite. In particularly egregious instances the mainstream media simply omit the quotes.

The lack of accountability may partly explain the frequency with which Malaysian politicians say the things they say and why the jacket of a new book titled, *Malaysian Politicians Say the Darndest Things* is stamped "Vol 1." The book's compiler, filmmaker and writer Amir Muhammad, was motivated in part by the home affairs minister's justification for banning one of Amir's documentaries last year on the grounds that it wasn't violent enough.

The 100 quotes included in the volume span nearly three decades and run the gamut, from obtuse and malevolent to witty and endearing. Some are to be taken with a grain of salt, such as this one from former culture, arts and tourism minister Abdul Kadir Sheikh Fadzir: "[Taxi drivers who cheat tourists] should be lined up against the wall and shot. They are the new enemies, the same as communists. I am not joking, this is a serious matter. If they can be shot, all the better."

Others provide a worrying window into certain senior politicians' worldview, including this 2003 passage from current Information Minister Zainuddin Maidin: "The Indonesians and Filipinos don't even have enough to fill their stomachs. Who are they to lecture us on press freedom? We are more qualified because we have full stomachs."

Collectively the book serves as a light-hearted yet indispensable history marker in a society where the words and deeds of political masters are all too often forgiven, if not forgotten. The sanctimonious are cut down to size—using their own words mots justes in a place where the political elite are infamously averse to criticism and wield a host of draconian laws to protect their fragile egos.

Many of the book's more recent quotations are reminders of how entrenched Malaysia's system of patronage is. It is telling that many of the featured quotes were spoken in an era in which Prime Minister Abdullah Badawi had promised greater transparency and to weed out corruption without fear or favor. Here, for instance, is de facto Law Minister Nazri Aziz last year defending the United Malays National Organization ruling party that Abdullah heads:

"UMNO members only have to answer to the disciplinary committee and are punished according to party regulations for party dealings. They have immunity to laws outside the jurisdiction of the party. This is because their actions in the party have nothing to do with the public business ..." On the previous page a senator laments not having given his son, who was implicated in a scandal, better tips on how to become a fraudster. He is still a serving senator.

Mixed messages

Malaysia is hardly the only country with politicians making egregious remarks. The malapropisms of US President George W Bush alone have already filled books. There's no Mahmud Ahmadinejad threatening to wipe Israel off the map; no Idi Amin saying, "I want your heart. I want to eat your children." (Although Education Minister Hishammuddin Hussein did come close when he said he wanted a "pound of flesh" from an undergraduate who made a rap video clip posted on YouTube which addressed Malaysia's police corruption and discriminatory affirmative action policies.)

What perhaps distinguishes the habit among Malaysian politicians is that as a unit they are exceptionally preoccupied with the country's image abroad. They have invested heaps of time and money toward presenting Malaysia as a world-class country. But what they say often undermines those public relations efforts.

The long-ruling former prime minister Mahathir Mohamad supported bank-busting mega-projects like the Petronas Towers specifically to put Malaysia on the global map of shiny economic success stories. Arguably, however, Malaysia is more associated internationally with Mahathir's famous anti-Western rants, such as the time he said Jews rule the world by proxy, than its first-world infrastructure.

The same country now promoting itself as a progressive role model for the Muslim world has a foreign minister who last year said Muslim nations should consider arming Hezbollah. Its tourism minister in March, during "Visit Malaysia Year," stereotyped Malaysia's growing blogger community as jobless, depraved women.

The comments reflect a larger disconnect here between notions of progress and the business of actually getting there. Comedian and playwright Jit Murad brilliantly captured the gap during a standup performance in May in which he played a Malaysian politician at a press conference espousing Abdullah's "feel good" campaign. "Some people say they are concerned about the increase in reports of violent crimes," the politician says. "We are also concerned—that every day we get reports. Do not worry. We will cut down on the reports that make us feel bad."

Indeed, leadership in the Abdullah era has placed ever more emphasis on appearance over substance. The administration's anti-corruption drive finds cops wearing "I am against corruption" pins, but by many accounts corruption is as rampant as it has ever been. Key institutions like the judiciary, police force and print media are all still badly in need of reform.

Abdullah speaks abroad about Islam Hadhari, or Civilizational Islam, the country's "model approach for development and progress," as atavistic religiosity gains influence in the educational and judicial systems. The rise of blogs and web portals has put the words and deeds of politicians under greater scrutiny, a fact that politicians are all too aware of but have yet to come to grips with. The information minister, for instance, has made a habit of lashing out at bloggers, only to set up himself and the administration for another round of online thrashing.

To be sure, one should not walk away from *Darndest* Vol 1 thinking all Malaysian politicians are buffoons. Malaysia has fared better economically than some of its neighbors since independence and Malaysian leaders no doubt deserve some of the credit. Indeed judging a person by his words alone, particularly his most unflattering, can be a deceptive business. Mahathir, for one, was known to perorate eloquently on a wide range of issues.

Then again, it's hard to overplay the significance of a prime minister who came to office four years ago promising greater accountability and transparency and seeing few tangible efforts toward that end. Curiously the prime minister is not represented in *Darndest* Vol 1. It's a reminder, perhaps, that the printed word can sometimes hide as much as it reveals.

First published November 7, 2007 (*Asia Times*)

* * *

Malaysia Under Mahathir's Shadow

A year has passed since former Malaysian premier Mahathir Mohamad stepped down from ruling this racially estranged oil-rich nation. But unlike retired leaders before him, as varied in disposition as Indonesia's Suharto and former US president Bill Clinton, the sententious provocateur refuses to go quietly. Within the last month alone he has called his former deputy Anwar Ibrahim a homosexual, Americans "very ignorant" and compared the unrest in neighboring Thailand's troubled south to the Israeli-Palestinian conflict.

Mahathir's latest vitriolic remark came last week when he said Muslims would be "tortured" for the next four years after US President George W Bush won a second term. "We are sad that this man who has caused the mass killings in Iraq has been re-elected to lead his country," Mahathir told some 300 people at a gathering to break fast during the holy month of Ramadan. "For the next four years the world's Muslim community will be tortured by this heartless and merciless man."

On top of those comments came the release by Pelanduk Publications of *Achieving True Globalization*, a book compiled from 10 hours of interviews with Kohei Hashimoto in 2003, in which the former premier addresses China, Japan, the war in Iraq, East and West, and whether Islam has a violent streak.

Yet, despite what often appear as nothing more than acid remarks, Mahathir's views do deserve attention. Mixed as it was, the message he sent during his 22-year iron-fisted rule shaped the outlook of everyday Malaysians, and compels one to examine the impact the former premier has had on the country.

For those familiar with Mahathir's worldview, delivered with incessant zeal over his 22-year rule, his latest comments are nothing less than ordinary. In slightly varied form, he's already told us, "The US wishes to convert the whole world to the American way of life"; "[Muslim] violence is not at all related to their religion"; "We [in Malaysia] have our own democracy ... we think [liberal democracy] is immoral and undemocratic"; and "They say I like Japan, and it is true."

The repetition alludes to a man who feels slighted as he looks around a nation trying desperately to move out of his shadow. Malaysia, it could be reasoned, has had little choice: beyond economic considerations, The nation continues to lag behind many of its neighbors in terms of national unity, innovation, human rights, and fighting corruption. (Even in economic terms cracks have begun to appear. Foreign direct investment here shrank nearly one-third from 2002 to 2003. Neighboring Singapore's, however, has doubled over the same period.)

Two sides to Mahathir

At home, and throughout much of the Muslim world, Mahathir was known as a scrappy champion of the Third World; a man who single-handedly put Malaysia on the map with his fiery rhetoric and undertaking of bank-breaking mega-projects such as the Petronas Towers and national car company Proton. In the West, he was seen as little more than a churlish bigot—this was after all the man who blamed the 1997 Asian economic crisis on a "cabal of Jews."

The real Mahathir, of course, is a little bit of both. His resentment toward the West has been well-documented, and is on full display in Achieving True Globalization, in which he spares not a kind word for the West throughout the 146 pages of text. (Curiously neither the United States nor its variant phrasings are listed in the index, despite repeated references to the superpower.)

But with shrewd insight, Mahathir also calls the West to task for its hypocrisy. He singles in on the emotions driving the world's most divisive conflicts and suggests how to allay them; beneath his scorn is an impassioned plea for a more equal and just world.

Both sides are trademark Mahathir. But which Mahathir has left the greater mark on Malaysia?

When, for instance, Mahathir incited international outrage by saying days before his retirement, "Jews rule the world by proxy [by getting] others to die for them," Malaysians insisted they didn't take the comments seriously, that they had long since learned to tune out the autocrat's invective. Around the same time, however, letters of gratitude were published in newspapers, hung in art museums, schools, libraries and office tower lobbies. Many, in one form or another, thanked Mahathir for his "message."

Can this be, that Malaysians have scrupulously discerned the good from the bad from the ugly of Mahathir's rhetoric—and absorbed only the good?

"It must be remembered that for 22 years people saw him on the front page and the first three minutes of electronic media," said Ramdas Tikamdas, immediate past president of the National Human Rights Society in Malaysia. The mainstream media is tightly controlled by the government. "His statements were policy. He was the CEO of a nation. Apart from him there were no voices."

Deputy secretary general of the opposition People's Justice Party, Xavier Jayakumar, added: "We have to start thinking what he was against and in what way this has shaped our attitudes toward the outside world." Until his retirement in October 2003 he was Asia's longest-ruling leader.

An autocrat's anti-Western bent

Mahathir's anti-Western bent is deep-seated; in his collected speeches he painfully recalls a childhood in which he addressed the British colonialists with *tuan*, or master. And the passing of time has not cooled his resentment.

He has been a vocal critic of the Bush Administration's war on terror, but has failed to draw the line between governments and their people; increasingly, he lashed out at the whole of Western civilization. Last year he labeled Westerners greedy and warlike, then challenged "anyone who says my speech about the Europeans is not true," before boasting that Malaysia had "reached a level that we are able to thumb our nose at them."

The trend continued in his interviews with Hashimoto last year, when Mahathir talked of "Eastern magnanimity and Western intolerance," claiming that "in Eastern civilization, we hold the belief that one should not go around killing people to achieve one's objectives." He said "Asia is a collection of continents and different ethnic groups," while the West suffers from a "standardization of every value." As he's wont to do—employing his preferred tactic of fear—he warned oppressed nations that, given half a chance, the US will attack and occupy their lands.

Concerned with the impact Mahathir's markedly cruder venom might have on a nation still struggling to overcome the scars, trauma and xenophobia of a centuries-long history of colonization, the autocrat's former deputy Anwar Ibrahim wrote last year, "We must carefully deal with the confusion between racist or ethnic attitude against European nations or the struggle to oppose injustice. As we question the arrogance of powerful countries, especially the United States, we also have to be consistent in our demand for the freedom of the people and fight against injustice in developing countries."

People's Justice Party secretary Jayakumar said these warnings have not been heeded. He said Mahathir, in more than two decades of iron-fisted rule, virtually legitimized intolerance and even encouraged it among younger Malay leaders. During Mahathir's final speech as the United Malays National Organization (UMNO) president, members of the party's youth wing reportedly handed out free copies of Henry Ford's anti-Semitic book *The International Jew*. Then last month, at the party's annual assembly, youth-wing members warned of trouble for anyone who questioned Malay rights under the affirmative-action program.

"It's not going to be easy to remove the ideas and thoughts that this man has put into the younger generation of Malays," Jayakumar said.

A message for all Malaysians
Not only ethnic Malays have been affected. Most Malaysians,

irrespective of race, echo Mahathir when they opine that a freer press will lead to chaos. And they admit a fear of speaking their minds due to Mahathir's liberal application of the Internal Security Act (ISA), which has seen numerous dissidents locked up indefinitely without trial or charge.

But Mahathir also imbued in many of those same Malaysians a sense of pride and confidence. Some of his most inspiring speeches centered on a simple message: education and perseverance can take you places. He gave them the Petronas Towers and landscaped interstates to cruise on in Malaysian-made cars. The national slogan "Malaysia *boleh*," or Malaysia can, seemed only fitting.

Ultimately, though, Mahathir sent a mixed message. He urged Malaysians to modernize but to reject the West. He then said to learn from Japan, advice that found its way officially as the "Look East Policy." But try as he might he couldn't escape the West. As Mahathir told Hashimoto, "Unfortunately, Japan wants to become Europe or America."

He all but barred the various races in his country from talking through their differences for fear of unrest. Meanwhile, he played the races off each other for his own political advantage. In a word, he truncated discussion but exacerbated resentment. It's no wonder foreigners now and again hear from their taxi drivers about the other races; who else, besides their own, do they dare share their grievances with?

Mahathir told Malaysians theirs was a democratic nation; on the other hand, he deprived them of democracy's fundamentals. In his series of interviews with Hashimoto, he defends Malaysia's state-muzzled press: "Governments, at least, are elected by the people, and thus have a responsibility to them." He goes on to stretch the definition of democracy by calling China a "one-party democracy ... the process of choosing is still there."

In the past, he deemed those who disagree with his government "troublemakers" and vowed to stop them in their tracks. "Listening to the people we don't like is very important," he said.

Despite the contradictions, Mahathir's rhetoric had a remarkable ability to register as a unified whole, mainly because Malaysians trusted where Mahathir was taking them. Under Mahathir, development was the operative term and Malaysia appeared to be zooming there.

But as Malaysians learn that building a nation requires more than steady economic growth—Mahathir's main justification for oppression—they are beginning to question the path they've been led down for the past 22 years. Under Mahathir's eye, corruption got worse; the courts lost their credibility. Mahathir failed to achieve his main objective: to turn the Malays into a viable, competitive, non-government-dependent race.

Moreover, Mahathir's cavalier logic didn't exactly warm Malaysians to the larger world, the same world he told them to go thrive in. Rather, it insisted that the world is primitively divided between East and West, white and brown, small and big, us and them.

This might still find some eager takers in parts of the Muslim world—Mahathir's target audience since retiring. But here the "wisdom" is wearing off. Malaysians want to make good in the larger world. They want to grow up gracefully. Mahathir, meanwhile, a shrinking shadow of his former self, is fighting just to be heard.

First published November 12, 2004 (*Asia Times*)

* * *

Addressing Muslim Rage

Myth of Islamic Tolerance by Robert Spencer (editor),
a book review by Ioannis Gatsiounis

As the forces of fundamentalism and terrorism continue to ravage Islam from within, Muslims have understandably sought to convey to non-Muslims that Islam is a tolerant religion. Since September 11, there has been no shortage of reminders that the root word of Islam means "peace" or that those advocating *jihad* against the West are deviant "hijackers."

Historians wax lyrical about Islam's "golden age" when non-Muslims and Muslims putatively lived side-by-side in harmony and they reassure us that Islam's current crisis is a growing pain, akin to phases other religions have undergone in their early histories. And while a worrying level of ignorance remains—a recent Pew Research Center poll found that only half of Americans were able to identify the Koran as Islam's equivalent of the Bible—education efforts have be so effectively that many non-Muslims have come to believe that unflattering manifestations of Islam are aberrant. Of course these perceptions are rarely based on direct contact with the religion, for, as any outsider who has taken a closer look at Islam can attest, further inquiry produces as many unsettling questions as it does tidy answers.

Why, for instance, are many of the world's most pious and knowledgeable Muslims also the most hostile toward non-believers? Why do non-Muslims face significant discrimination, even in the Islamic world's most moderate nations? (Just last month in Malaysia, 35 masked assailants dressed in robes attacked and partially scorched a commune led by a Muslim apostate.) This is to say nothing of the rights of women in most Muslim countries. Is it all simply a matter of interpretation (ie abuse for personal or political gain), or does the sustained prevalence of such patterns reveal something inherent about the faith?

Few people want to address this last question openly, lest they be labeled anti-Muslim. But as clear answers to the question of what is ailing Islam in the 21st century remain elusive, the writers of *The Myth of Islamic Tolerance*, including Bat Ye'or, Mark Durie, Muhammad Younus Shaikh, Daniel Pipes and David Littman, among others, are within bounds to tackle the issue head on.

Their premise is that contemporary Muslim rage and intolerance is not historically isolated; and moreover, that it is rooted in the religion itself. This is not an easy idea to swallow, if for no reason other than it contradicts what one wants to believe about the world's second largest and fastest growing religion—that at its core it is sane and rational. And there is ample reason to be leery; several of the book's authors are affiliated with Christian and Zionist movements, while some passages come across as hostile and misleading.

Consider the first sentence of the forward written by Ibn Warraq, "Islam is a totalitarian ideology that aims to control the religious, social and political life of mankind in all its aspects; the life of its followers without qualification; and the life of those who follow the so-called tolerated religions [Christians and Jews, which the Koran refers to as People of the Book], to a degree that prevents their activities from getting in the way of Islam in any way."

And yet *The Myth of Islamic Tolerance* warrants our attention. Any study of contemporary Islam would be incomplete without it. Collectively, the essays expose an unsettling fact: that Islam's famed tolerance of non-Muslims has over the centuries fallen well short of an embrace. It is true that Islam calls for no coercion in matters of faith and that it encourages Muslims to respect the People of the Book (Christians and Jews). But it is also true that the Koran incessantly distinguishes between believer and non-believer and calls for unequal treatment of the two. An most obvious example of this is found in the *jizya*, or poll tax, which requires dhimmis (protected subjects) to pay for military protection.

But the authors reveal many other instances of inequality, as stipulated by the Koran and administered at various times throughout history. Non-Muslims living in Muslim societies have not been able to build new churches or temples. They have been required to dress distinctively from Muslims. They have been prohibited from printing their religious texts and selling them in public places or giving them to Muslims and from testifying against a Muslim in *sharia* court.

That some form of these laws still exist, even in ostensibly moderate Muslim countries such as Malaysia, is not the main point, argues editor Robert Spencer. Rather it's that "centuries of enforcement of these laws have produced lingering cultural attitudes," attitudes that can be found not just in extremists and fundamentalists but in some of Islam's most esteemed moderates.

The deeper question is what inspired the centuries of enforcement in the first place? Spencer argues that it was the Koran itself. "A fundamental component of the Koran's view of non-Muslims is the often-repeated and implacable belief in its own superiority." Anyone who's read extensively from the Koran can attest to its mercurial obsession with the non-believer. And indeed a sense of elitism and acuity to otherness are prevalent in many parts of the Muslim world today. *The Myth of Islamic Tolerance* argues there is a strong connection.

However, the book does include flagrant distortions and glaring omissions. In its determination to show that Islam is not as peaceful as "apologists" would have one believe, it refuses to disclose that Islam also has a tolerant side, which also can be traced to the Koran and which has inspired fiqh (Islamic jurisprudence). It also fails to draw parallels between Islam's history and that of other religions—

which would reveal that part of Islam's crisis is linkable to the nature of religion itself.

The book's selective quoting of the Koran would be dangerous reading for anyone who is not familiar with it. That being said, it would be unfair to allege that most of the writers here are quoting out of context—a charge commonly leveled by Muslims at those who cite some of the Koran's more unflattering verses. It would be unfair because such allegations are usually predicated on the notion that the Koran must be understood in its historical context: that it was revealed during a time of great unrest. This line of reasoning contradicts the elemental Muslim belief that the Koran is the unerring and timeless word of God. Muslims also believe that the Koran should be interpreted literally.

And so the significance of these verses cannot be discounted; they have helped shape Muslim attitudes over the centuries. The question is, are they gaining acceptance at a time when many Muslims perceive US President George W Bush's "war on terror" to be a conspiratorial degradation of Islam? The authors' implicit answer is, yes. They lament Edward Said, author of *Orientalism*, which famously critiqued Western study of the Islamic world, for teaching "an entire generation of Arabs the art of self pity ... and bludgeoning into silence any criticism of Islam."

The authors point out how *jihad*, which in its most basic form means struggle, has historically meant mainly one thing: "the legal, compulsory, communal effort to expand territories ruled by Muslims ... at the expense of territories ruled by non-Muslims." And they take aim at American Muslim groups for ambitiously manufacturing a "positive image of Islam ... instead of dealing forthrightly and constructively with the concerns and questions that non-Muslims have had since the [September 11] attacks."

Indeed *The Myth of Islamic Tolerance* sometimes comes across as an indictment that overlooks Islam's complexities; implicit in its message is that if Islam is to make peace with the rest of the world it will have to shy away from itself.

At turns, however, the book proves to be a timely antidote to a prevailing trend in many media and academic circles, which is to reduce Islam's crisis to social rather than religious factors and to heap the blame on the West. It simply struggles to find an enlightened balance.

[*Myth of Islamic Tolerance*, edited by Robert Spencer, Prometheus Books 2005. ISBN 978-1-59102-249-7]

First published August 27, 2005 (*Asia Times*)

* * *

Faith: Part of the Problem

God is Not Great by Christopher Hitchens,
a book review by Ioannis Gatsiounis

What you are about to read is a review that almost wasn't. I mention this at the outset because the incident in question was informed by the book's subject, religion. This was in a bookstore in majority-Muslim Malaysia's glittering symbol of modernity, the Petronas Towers. I had just been told by the sales clerk the store would not be carrying the title, (which as I write this is number three on the *New York Times*' nonfiction bestseller list).

Her face, framed by a powder blue headscarf, turned florid as her eyes clung to the computer screen. I requested to speak with a manager. The clerk ignored me. I asked again. The manager would inform me that members of Malaysia's Internal Security Ministry had swept through the store the day before and "requested" that the title be removed from the shelves.

"So there is no official ban?" I queried.

"No."

"So ... self-censorship?"

The manager glanced over her shoulder, "Religion is a sensitive issue in Malaysia."

"I understand that but should protecting religious sensitivities happen at the expense of free and open inquiry?" In other words, should the rest of us be stunted intellectually because some people of faith are thought to be susceptible to intolerance?

She murmured, "It's not that we don't have the book, it's just we're not displaying it."

It was a subtle concession, Malaysian style, and soon she was retrieving a copy from the back of the store. Book and receipt in hand, I hung a little longer than I might have on its sweeping subtitle, How religion poisons everything.

Hitchens, whom Foreign Policy magazine ranked number five in its list of "Top 100 Intellectuals," is the latest to speak up on behalf of what may prove to be the most momentous movement to grow out of the polarizing events of September 11, 2001.

Most attention has focused on the bloodthirsty call to *jihad* hobbling the Muslim world and its reactionary correlative: Bush's "war on terror." But out of the media glare is a swelling resistance to that mutually reinforcing faith-based nefariousness.

These scrappy humanists include writers such as Sam Harris, Richard Dawkins and Michel Onfray. It is transcontinental. It is traversing the traditional left-right political divide. It looks deeper than the Israeli-Palestinian conflict and colonialism-cum-imperialism in search of a cause for religious extremism, to reveal faith itself as an integral part of the problem.

Like the Enlightenment before it, the movement's guiding principle is reason. Reason of course is at odds with many of religions' most basic assumptions (Jesus was born to a virgin; the Koran is the irrefutable word of God and so on). The difference is two centuries have passed since the end of the Enlightenment. Reason now has more weight in its corner—more science, more philosophy, more knowledge, more humane and sophisticated systems of ethics and justice (ditch the cross burnings and stoning for adulterers, says reason).

"One must state it plainly," writes Hitchens. "Religion comes from the period of human prehistory where nobody—not even the mighty Democritus who concluded that all matter was made from atoms—had the smallest idea what was going on. It comes from the bawling and fearful infancy of our species, and is a babyish attempt to meet our inescapable demand for knowledge (as well as for comfort, reassurance, and other infantile needs)... All attempts to reconcile faith with science and reason are consigned to failure and ridicule for precisely this reason."

At a time when not all Muslims are terrorists but almost all terrorists are Muslims, to paraphrase Abdel Rahman al-Rashed, many reason-based writers, intellectuals and activists taking up the crusade against faith have focused unduly on Islam. Hitchens is less divisive. Without glossing over particulars, he exposes the shared absurdities of faith. "... religion does not, and in the long run cannot, be content with its own marvelous claims and sublime assurances. It must seek to interfere with the lives of nonbelievers [see bookstore example, above], or heretics, or adherents of other faiths. It may speak about the bliss of the next world, but it wants power in this one."

This is Hitchens on sex: "... all religions claim the right to legislate in matters of sex," even though, "Clearly, the human species is designed to experiment with sex ... Orthodox Jews conduct congress by means of a hole in the sheet ... Muslims subject adulterers to public lashings with a whip. Christians used to lick their lips while examining women for signs of witchcraft ... Throughout all religious texts, there is a primitive fear that half the human race is simultaneously defiled and unclean, and yet is also a temptation to sin that is impossible to resist."

Here he is on September 11: "The nineteen suicide murderers of New York and Washington and Pennsylvania were beyond any doubt the most sincere believers on those planes ... Within hours, the 'reverends' Pat Robertson and Jerry Falwell had announced that the immolation of their fellow creatures was a divine judgment on a secular society that tolerated homosexuality and abortion."

Meanwhile, the evangelist preacher Billy Graham claimed to have detailed knowledge of the current whereabouts of the victims, while Osama bin Laden was making similar claims on behalf of the assassins.

Hitchens takes aim at "the tawdriness of the miraculous," commonplace in all religions, from Mohammed's "night flight" from Mecca to Jerusalem to Jesus' resurrection. He says that "if you only hear a report of the miracle from a second or third party the odds [that it happened] must be adjusted accordingly ... and if you are separated from the 'sighting' by many generations, and have no independent corroboration, the odds must be adjusted still more drastically."

This might seem to provide enough logic to humble believers—or at least get them to relinquish fundamentalist convictions. But what religion has on its side is that these miracles—not to mention the sayings and doings of their prophets and saviors and the supposed authenticity of their texts—are "entirely unverifiable, and unfalsifiable."

The men who organized religion do seem to have understood that man's instinctive thirst for logic meant their outlandish claims would eventually be called into question, hence why "all religions take care to silence or to execute those who question them." This,

Hitchens rightly points out, is a sign of their weakness, not their strength. Man is also drawn to wonder and mystery and no doubt this is what makes religion's fairy tales of parted seas and winged horses so alluring. But the mysteries of consciousness and the universe and the magic of music and art and literature meet that need—without insulting our intelligence with tidy explanations.

Hitchens says believers tend to use the argument that religion improves people once they have exhausted the rest of their case. This reminds me of a taxi ride I took last week. The driver said that Malaysia was a "free country." "When I gently pointed out the number of ways in which it is very far from that, he said, "But our government is good and not corrupt, because it has Islam."

Malaysia, of course, is famously corrupt and the Islamic component party he was referring to, UMNO (United Malays National Organization), is no exception; the leader of UMNO, Abdullah Badawi, suggested as much when he won the nation's premiership in 2003 on an anti-corruption platform. By most accounts, corruption has gotten worse under the pious Abdullah.

I was tempted to mention this to my driver and to add that the nation's most devout state, Kelantan, where alcohol is hard to find and there are separate check-out lanes for men and women, is also among the country's most impoverished, with the highest or near-highest drug addiction and HIV and divorce rates. But I intuited that these were things he knew already—just as many Muslims know that the September 11 attacks were not a Jewish conspiracy but committed by fellow Muslims—but that he, like they, were too ashamed to admit it to an unbeliever.

It is undeniable that faith does work in some people's lives. I have met people of all the major faiths whose belief does seem to be playing a positive role—they are considerate, affable, compassionate, clear-eyed and moral in judgment. Hitchens offers this example. His wife had left a large sum of cash on the back seat of a taxi.

The Sudanese driver returned the full amount to the couple's home. Hitchens then offered the driver 10% of the money, to which the driver said he expected no compensation for doing what was his duty to Allah.

On the other hand, history up to the present is laden with examples in which faith produces some real nasty results. In Malaysia, for instance, which is struggling in vain to project itself as a model of Islamic tolerance, several states have made apostasy from Islam a punishable offense. Recently, it was reported that a film is under fire from religious authorities because the local actress shaved her head for the role, which the clerics say violates Islamic doctrine by making a woman look like a man.

To be sure, the most devout among us are often the most uncompromising, hostile, irrational, out-of-touch people with modern realities one will meet. What generally allows a religious person to become a constructive member of society is that he chooses to adhere to some tenets of his faith and discard others—so that he might decide to love thy neighbor regardless of whether he is a homosexual; or provide for the poor while rejecting the contempt some scriptures hold for unbelievers.

But even then one does not need to adhere to the primordial "truths" of religion to be a good person. The "serious ethical dilemmas are better handled by Shakespeare and Tolstoy and Schiller and Dostoyevsky and George Eliot than in the mythical morality tales of the holy books," explains Hitchens.

A major liability of religions is that they seek to canonize truth. They are "fossilized philosophies," as Simon Blackburn in his study of Plato's Republic—"or philosophy with the questions left out," says Hitchens.

By contrast philosophy, science and to a large extent literature are inherently more humble. In abiding by the laws of reason they do not fix permanently to truths but must remain open to new evidence, and adjust their convictions accordingly, or risk being jettisoned en masse, as has been the case with Marx and Trotsky (of course these mere mortals did not promise hellfire for anyone disagreeing with their theories and hence crumbled under the scrutiny of reason).

Hitchens tackles the faith-based argument that atheist and secularist rulers have committed crimes more heinous than the the Crusades and Islamic imperial conquests and the witch trials etc, etc. He calls this claim the "last-ditch 'case' against secularism" and shows how these leaders—notably of fascism, Nazism, and Stalinism—often worked in complicity with religious bodies. Even in instances where there is no such collusion, as in North Korea, people adulate their leaders like gods; the rule and abuse is religious in nature.

The author makes a persuasive case that religion often hinders development, the Islamic Republic of Iran being but one tragic example. He says societies that do not learn "to tame and sequester the religious impulse will consistently be outdone by those that do ... Where once [religion] used to be able, by its total command of a worldview, to prevent the emergence of rivals, it can now only impede and retard—or try to turn back—the measurable advances that we have made."

Hitchens treatise does at times come across as indiscriminately contemptuous, for instance, saying that religion can only impede, or in branding organized religion "violent, irrational, intolerant, allied to racism and tribalism and bigotry." And the faithful will likely use this to discredit the book outright while clinging to their deep aversion to contemplating the decisive role faith itself is playing in our divided world. And yet implicit in Hitchens' recognition that religion is man-made is that it is schismatic; and his encyclopedic grasp of history, on full display here, compels one not to reject his claims out of hand.

Also suggestive in Hitchens' unyielding irreverence is that the faithful are a lost cause anyway; that he is not looking to win over minds whose basic convictions sidestep reason but rather to inspire the rest of us to take a tougher stand against injustices committed in the name of God and to puncture religion's elaborately irrational fortresses ensconcing the gullible impulse.

First published July 7, 2007 (*Asia Times*)

* * *

Malaysia's Leader-in-Waiting

While reporting for this story sources kept telling me that Najib's close friend and political advisor Abdul Razak Baginda was the man to talk to for insight into Najib. After filing the story I headed for vacation in Ethiopia, where I mindfully avoided news about Malaysia. Returning through KLIA airport I passed a TV showing Razak pushing through a barrage of camera flashes. While I had been away he had been charged for abetting two of Najib's bodyguards in the murder of a Mongolian model. The trial is still running nearly two years after it began, which some observers say is a delay tactic to reduce public scrutiny and outrage. The media are barely covering the trial and Najib has not been summoned for questioning.

In the weeks following news of the murder, the mainstream press did not mention Razak's close ties with Najib, referring to Razak simply as a well-connected political analyst; and everyday Malaysians I spoke with during this period said they weren't aware of the connection. The press eventually started disclosing the fact and public awareness seemed to shift accordingly. This is testament to the deep influence the state-run mainstream media maintains, despite the growing influence of independent online sources.

Najib continues to be counted as a front-runner to replace Prime Minister Abdullah Badawi in spite of the murder scandal, and military purchases allegedly involving huge kickbacks that were made under his supervision during his time as defense minister. During our forty-minute interview he displayed a firm understanding of the kind of world Malaysia is entering and the attributes it would need to take on to be competitive. But he has also been a staunch defender of UMNO's status quo, which has in key respects hindered Malaysia's competitiveness and social harmony.

Deputy Prime Minister Najib Razak is widely seen as Malaysia's prime-minister-in-waiting. Being the number two in Malaysia, of course, hardly makes one a shoo-in for the premiership. Over the past two decades three deputies have been unceremoniously dumped, thwarting their political ambitions.

The most infamous axing involved former prime minister Mahathir Mohamad's charismatic deputy Anwar Ibrahim, who at the peak of his popularity was imprisoned on charges of sodomy and corruption in what was widely viewed as a political witchhunt orchestrated by Mahathir.

Najib, 53, is the eldest son of Malaysia's popular second prime minister, Abdul Razak, and nephew of the third prime minister, Hussein Onn. He became the nation's youngest member of parliament ever at the age of 22 and is currently both deputy prime minister and defense minister. But his chances are not being gauged by pedigree or political standing alone.

Unlike some of his deputy premier predecessors, Najib has been careful not to outshine his boss, in this case Prime Minister Abdullah Badawi. On a number of occasions he has publicly declared his loyalty to Abdullah, while insisting that the premier has support at every level of the conservative ruling UMNO.

At the same time, Najib has built strong bonds with the party's old guard, making a contrast with the understated Abdullah. Abdullah's early attempts to curb graft and restore government integrity irked some senior UMNO members, but more recently his high-profile campaign has lost steam. Najib comes off as authoritative and eloquent, if not a bit guarded and calculated, when commenting on issues of national interest.

And should he eventually take the reins of power of this fast-developing though anxious nation, it remains unclear how exactly he would proceed.

That political moment of truth could be around the corner. In June, Mahathir started to level accusations against Abdullah, his hand-picked successor, for being weak, indecisive and allowing his family to benefit from government contracts. Mahathir, 80, hasn't let up since, and the criticism is exacting a toll on Abdullah's credibility inside and outside the party.

This has raised new speculation that UMNO could eventually split into opposing Najib and Abdullah camps. Najib has sought to quell the speculation by declaring his unwavering support for Abdullah and UMNO, which he appears to genuinely view as a source of national strength and unity.

Yet while Abdullah and Najib are cordial in public, there is, according to party insiders, no love lost between the two long-time cabinet colleagues. One account has it that Mahathir preferred to make Najib his successor, but, made wary by former deputies trying to outshine him on his political departure, chose the soft-spoken Abdullah to protect his own interests. In return, it's believed that Mahathir demanded that Abdullah choose Najib as his deputy and groom him for eventual succession.

Indications so far are that Najib is patiently waiting his turn and that Abdullah plans to ride out his term, which expires in 2009. Some analysts predict that Abdullah will call a snap national election some time after March to consolidate his power before party problems further unravel.

But as more Mahathir loyalists line up behind Najib, arguably UMNO's most powerful and respected member, there is a risk of an UMNO-splintering power struggle. Some political analysts contend this could tempt Abdullah to bring former deputy prime minister Anwar back into the UMNO fold. Anwar, widely viewed as a strong reform advocate, is officially barred from politics until 2008, the year before Abdullah's term ends.

Najib, in an exclusive interview last week with *Asia Times Online* at his sprawling office at Putrajaya, the administrative capital outside Kuala Lumpur, said: "Anwar cited that he's siding with [the People's Justice Party]. He has made many, many statements that he ... has no intention of joining UMNO. So I guess we will see Anwar as part of the opposition in the landscape of Malaysian politics." Judging by his body language, though, Najib clearly preferred to change the interview topic.

Economic challenges

Najib readily acknowledges the challenge of transforming Malaysia from a manufacturing-based economy into an innovative, knowledge-based one. "We have to realize that the world is more and more competitive, and I don't think that's quite sunk in across the board in Malaysia," says Najib during the interview. "Unless you go out there, in New York, say, then you realize, looking at Malaysia, through that prism, that you really must put your act together."

In multi-racial Malaysia, that has historically meant preserving tolerance and harmony between the majority Muslim Malays and the sizeable Chinese and Indian minorities. "It is delicate. Once you upset the balance, you unleash forces which you may not be able to control," said Najib. "So we are very wary of doing something that might upset the apple cart."

Striking that balance has involved a controversial affirmative action program, known as the New Economic Policy, introduced by Najib's father in 1971 to help the Malays catch up with the more economic-minded Chinese and imposing curbs to freedom of expression and thought, such as the broadly worded Sedition Act, which criminalizes speech that may "excite disaffection against" the government, or promote "feelings of ill-will and hostility between different races."

The social contract has produced mixed results. It was implemented in response to the 1969 race riots between the ethnic Malays and Chinese, which at the time threatened to tear the young country apart. The program was originally designed to last 20 years but has since been extended indefinitely by the Malay-led government, leading to growing resentment among the Chinese and Indians and a stigma of welfare dependency among the Malays.

Meanwhile, Malaysia's restricted political and social environments for the sake of racial unity has simultaneously stifled creativity and the development of the dynamic workforce necessary to see through Malaysia's dream of becoming a developed nation by 2020. The government's long-term racial balancing act is failing to adequately address modern economic and social challenges, say critics. However, Najib takes issue with such criticisms.

"Policy-wise. UMNO is a very pragmatic party," he told *AToI*. "We don't have any fixed ideology ... because of that we're able to adjust UMNO's policies according to different circumstances." As an example, he cited how UMNO recognized early on that the nation's private sector was weak and through its policies turned it into a viable engine of economic growth.

Last month Najib called for a reexamination of UMNO's race-based policies. "UMNO will not succeed if we just continue to defend the [racial] status quo," he said, according to news reports. "Yes, we can build this and that using the [political] powers that we have, but can we change the attitude of the Malays? That is what we should ask ourselves, as this is the factor which will determine whether Malays can progress further."

At other turns Najib has reaffirmed his commitment to race-based policies, feeding perceptions that the party is far more rigid than its leadership recognizes. Najib is of the belief that UMNO's race-based policies are administered with all of Malaysia's races in mind. "UMNO will continue to be a party that protects the interests of the Malays and Muslims and brings prosperity to all the people in the country," he said in August. To do this, he told *AToI*, the emphasis must be on growth and distribution—but growth first. "Only with growth can we have equal distribution."

But there's an increasing sense around Malaysia that the changes UMNO has made haven't gone far enough. It's become axiomatic—even Malaysia's leaders make the point—that Malaysia has a first-world infrastructure but a Third World mentality. Najib openly admires other countries where social and economic development have synergized, citing America as a prime example. "We do admire a lot of things about America—the fact that they allow creativity to flourish in America. In other societies you don't get that."

Worldly power broker

British-educated, Najib cuts a worldly profile. "I am equally comfortable sitting in a surau in my constituency or having dinner at Simpson's on the Strand," Najib was once quoted as saying, referring to an upscale London restaurant. Najib does not seem to share Mahathir's inferiority complex toward the West, nor does he share the former premier's impulse to scapegoat the West for Malaysia's problems.

Many feel that Malaysia needs a more worldly leader to reach out to the West and maintain the country's competitive edge. The question is whether Najib will take on that crucial role should he become prime minister.

With its myriad races and simmering tensions, Malaysia is not an easy place to govern, and this has over the years informed UMNO's cautious, conservative approach—even though the party's strong majority has given it the power to implement policies almost at will. Previous governments have arguably erred toward abuse and complacency rather than reform. Increasingly that is the on-the-ground perception surrounding Abdullah's stalled reform drive.

It's unclear how much that would change under a Najib-led administration. Najib has in his long political career established a vast network of loyalists, comprised of political and bureaucratic veterans and powerful business brokers, both domestically and overseas. "He is the most well connected politician in Malaysia," notes Shamsul Amri Baharuddin, director of the Institute of Malay World and Civilization, Universiti Kebangsaan Malaysia.

"He's been in six different ministries, and this has helped him build relationships among many different people. And he's shown an ability to dish out the goodies, country-wide, from Kedah to Johor," he added, referring to two states at opposite ends of Malaysia's peninsula.

Najib's power sources begin close to home. His brother Nazir is the chief executive of CIMB, Malaysia's biggest investment bank which maintains a global presence. Nazir and two other brothers, Nizam and Johari, are also involved in GP Ocean Food, the country's biggest integrated fisheries group. Najib's cousin is Hishammuddin Hussein, education minister and son of Malaysia's third prime minister Hussein Onn. Najib's wife, Rosmah Mansor, is also said to wield significant political influence. Najib reportedly maintains close ties with the state oil giant Petronas and with many prominent businessmen, including tycoon Vincent Tan. Najib also "holds the dollar bags of the Defense Ministry," as one Kuala Lumpur-based analyst, requesting anonymity, puts it.

Transparency is scant in Malaysia. The Official Secrets Act, for instance, restricts access to information of public interest, making it difficult to accurately gauge the extent of Najib's influence and connections. Economically, Najib may prove to be a cross between Abdullah and Mahathir. In his public speeches he has called for streamlining approval procedures for potential foreign investors. He has applauded a number of Abdullah's economic policies, including the targeting of value-added large-scale agriculture and hi-tech as future sources of domestic growth. And like Abdullah he has emphasized the need to return to fiscal balance.

Toward that end, Abdullah has scrapped a number of mega-projects that Mahathir initiated. Najib, however, has left the door open to restarting some of those projects, including a deferred double-tracking rail project. As with Abdullah, Najib would also likely pursue a more Western-friendly foreign policy than the sometimes combative Mahathir did. "[The US] respects our sovereignty ... if, for example, they want aircraft carriers to cross our territory they ask for our permission. It's a healthy relationship," said Najib in the interview.

At the same time, it doesn't appear Najib would stray much from Malaysia's draconian tradition toward civil liberties and human rights. He has been known to support restrictions on the media and has defended the use of civil liberty-curbing laws, such as the Internal Security Act, which allows for indefinite detention without trial. Significantly, Najib's office oversees Suhakam, the government's human-rights commission.

"His role has been to dampen Suhakam's role in dealing with rights issues," contends Tian Chua, information chief of the opposition People'sJustice Party. "He has helped Suhakam avoid tackling controversial human-rights cases." Najib has said Malaysia will introduce democratic reforms, but "it must be an evolution not a revolution, not through street demonstrations because this will create anarchy and chaos."

Likewise, Najib has done less than some would have hoped in tackling endemic government corruption. After UMNO's 2004 elections there were numerous allegations of money politics. Rather than calling for an independent investigation, Najib's response was to urge those making the allegations to come forward. If only whistleblowers were protected in Malaysia they might have. Last year, amid criticism that the Abdullah administration's corruption drive had netted only one high-level politician, Najib said, "This is the start of UMNO's fight against money politics. We will continue to pursue it." But no high-level politicians have been formally charged since, and by most accounts Najib hasn't exactly been championing the cause.

Elsewhere, Najib has said that allegations of vote-buying within UMNO should be an internal affair and not probed by the Anti-Corruption Agency. When a code of ethics was introduced by Abdullah in 2004, Najib publicly applauded the move, saying it would deter government officials from abusing power. Critics, however, say the new code is in the main toothless, falling well short of requiring politicians and officials to declare their assets before taking office.

Najib said during the *AToI* interview that he favors new measures to strengthen investigative procedures in corruption cases and to empower the now weak disciplinary commission. And he sounded genuinely concerned about how corruption and corruption allegations could damage UMNO and the nation. Said Najib: "Once the party's corrupted you elect the wrong leaders."

In the preface to his latest book, *Globalizing Malaysia*, Najib stresses the need to turn Malaysia into a "balanced society," one that is caring, knowledgeable and economically vibrant, saying Malaysians must be prepared to "make adjustments and sacrifices as we tread our way forward." Najib's 31-year political career may well lead him to the premiership. But taking the country forward socially, economically and intellectually will likely require breaking with that same past.

First published October 17, 2006 (*Asia Times*)

* * *

Malaysian PM's Competing Instincts Collide

Talk about Premier Abdullah Badawi in the year and a half since he became prime minister has generally been about what he hasn't done. As promises from wiping out corruption to professionalizing the police force to making the government more efficient and democratic have gone unfulfilled, Abdullah has become linked with words like inaction and indecision. Now, however, it's no longer so much inaction that is hampering the administration—he has become more assertive in how it handles everything from religious affairs to migrant workers to press freedom—but the course of the action itself, which in some significant ways eerily echoes that of his predecessor, strongman Mahathir Mohamad.

Mahathir was often criticized for neglecting corruption, provoking other nations, and squelching personal freedoms. When Abdullah took over it was widely assumed Malaysia's standing in these areas would improve. Arguably, to some degree they have. Domestically and abroad, for instance, those who have worked with Abdullah describe him as more accessible and team-oriented than Mahathir. He has okayed dialogues on everything from religious rights to the dreaded Internal Security Act, which allows for detention without trial, and has radically shaped the willingness of most Malaysians to express themselves.

But as political analyst Abdul Razak Baginda noted, "We're seeing a lot of two steps forward and one backward." And the steps backward are increasingly being characterized by the terse officiousness that was a hallmark of the Mahathir era. On April 20, for instance, the Malaysian government banned 11 books, mainly dealing with religion. Abdullah said the books—including Karen Armstrong's acclaimed *A History of God*—"could be detrimental to public order." He didn't elaborate.

In response to an April Fool's joke by a web portal here that chastised the government for not living up to its pledge to curb corruption, Minister in the Prime Minister's Department Mohamed Nazri Aziz said the government would take legal action against the web portal for "telling lies." A few days later Abdullah's deputy, Najib Razak, announced that the government would sue one of neighboring Indonesia's most respected dailies, *Kompas*, for the same offense. A member of Malaysia's ruling coalition then said the "Indonesian media is jealous of Malaysia's wealth and prosperity." Obviously such gestures haven't helped patch relations between the two neighbors, relations that began to sour in February over a maritime border dispute.

Tense dealings were par for the course under Mahathir but unexpected under mild-mannered Abdullah. Yet under the current administration, Indonesia is not the only neighbor with which Malaysia finds itself spatting.

In January Thai Prime Minister Thaksin Shinawatra accused Malaysia of harboring Islamic terrorists responsible for killing hundreds of innocent civilians in Thailand's restive south. Abdullah and his cohorts were outraged by the charge and beat back at Thaksin with some off-the-cuff remarks of their own. A few weeks later the alleged mastermind behind the violence in southern Thailand, Abdul Rahman Ahmad, was arrested by Malaysian authorities. Thaksin wanted him extradited, but Abdullah said the two countries did not have an extradition treaty and that because Ahmad was a Malaysian, he would remain in Malaysia.

Then last month the Malaysian government's decision to send packing one million-plus undocumented workers, mostly Filipinos and Indonesians, sparked off strings of anti-Malaysia protests in Jakarta and caused tension with the Philippines.

It is yet unclear how Malaysia's relations with its neighbors are affecting its standing internationally. During Mahathir's reign, however, Malaysia had a hard time developing credibility outside the Muslim world. Former deputy premier Anwar Ibrahim rallied a wide range of voices, including internationally respected non-governmental organizations, US vice president Al Gore and former Indonesian President B J Habibie to challenge Malaysia on its political and human-rights record and Mahathir's penchant for making anti-Semitic remarks. Meanwhile, Malaysia incessantly peddled itself as a "model Islamic democracy," which finally caught on with Washington in the months following September 11, 2001. But a report last week by the *Washington Post* calls into question the authenticity of Washington's praises. The article alleges that Mahathir spent millions of dollars through US lobbying groups to secure a White House visit and improve relations the US, which hit the skids after Mahathir orchestrated the jailing of Anwar on what many believe were trumped up charges of sodomy and corruption.

In a bitter twist for Abdullah, Anwar is now serving as a visiting fellow at John's Hopkins School of Advanced International Studies in Washington, where he has been using speaking engagements to set the record straight as he sees it on Malaysia. "If you want to be a moderate Muslim country, you cannot condone corruption," he was quoted as saying. He also said Malaysia should not be endorsed as either moderate or democratic. "How do you have free and fair elections when the views of the opposition are not heard? The entire media is controlled by the ruling party and you have free and fair elections?"

Some observers have been quick to blame UMNO intransigence on those who surround Abdullah; the old guard that he putatively opposes. But to some extent Abdullah must be held accountable for their lack of decorum. After all, these officials work under him, and as leader it is Abdullah's responsibility to establish a collective demeanor conducive to achieving his objectives, whether they are to reform the system or improve relations with Malaysia's neighbors. Certainly those who worked closely with Mahathir rarely strayed. Mahathir made sure of this. And in his two-plus decades at the helm he accomplished many of his goals, the result of which caused Malaysia to evolve into the prosperous nation it is today.

To be fair, Abdullah finds himself in a much-overlooked Catch-22. He is rightfully credited for being more tolerant of those around him than Mahathir was, for encouraging them to take initiative and work with, as opposed to for, him. But assuming it's the system Abdullah wants to fix, then giving greater freedom to essentially the same cast of characters who gained their political mileage bootlicking to Mahathir will not help the cause.

That Abdullah is committed to changing the system is at best an assumption, as the last few months have made clear, judging not only by the administration's actions and rhetoric but its outlook as well.

As Abdullah said in an Asia-Pacific radio broadcast earlier this month: "I think if we are talking about reform in Malaysia it is very, very dramatic in the most successful way. What were we before? I believe people should know what were we before when we were under the British ... We were all agriculture ... So everything now has been transformed."

This seems to contrast with the ambitious talk of reform Abdullah adopted before last year's parliamentary elections. More frighteningly perhaps, it represents a complacency typical of Malaysia's ruling elite, in which Malaysia's past achievements are talked up to divert attention from the nation's shortcomings.

Despite the red flags, Abdullah has advanced Malaysia in some key respects, said Chandra Muzaffar, president of the International Movement for a Just World. Last year, for instance, the corruption board arrested 497 people in connection with corruption, the highest number in a given year since the agency's inception in 1967. This hasn't broken the culture of corruption, but it is a start.

Muzaffar also said, "The judiciary is much freer, and in parliament you have much livelier debate. The backbenchers are taking front benchers to task on certain things."

And, as has been noted, in any course Abdullah decides on there will be various factions to contend with—from the business sector weaned on cronyism promoted by Mahathir to the government's myopic old guard to a creeping tide of Islamic fundamentalism. This of course doesn't exempt Abdullah from pursuing institutional change, which according to Muzaffar is "the only real way to change the system."

Malaysians are still waiting for a host of laws to be written up (laws that protect whistle-blowers for instance), and for others, such as the Printing Presses and Publications Act (PPPA), to be abolished. That act requires publications to renew their licenses annually and has ensured that Malaysia's press remains among the most obsequious in Asia.

Some observers say the mere existence of the PPPA does not reflect Abdullah's views on press freedom; reporters are said to have greater access to ministers than they did under Mahathir. But what, if anything, can be inferred from Abdullah's comments during the Asia-

Pacific interview? "The practice of democracy here ... has been most effective, in the sense that there is freedom of expression, and at the same time they [the citizens] have a right to vote and we have never failed to hold an election. Every time within five years there must be one election; we have never failed to do that."

Abdullah has of late, and at times unwittingly, exposed two sides of himself: one set on serving the status quo, the other on helping Malaysia flourish. Time will likely reveal a greater inclination for one or the other. For now they have emerged as the strongest opposing forces within the ruling elite. The irony is, they rest largely within one man.

First published April 29, 2005 (*Asia Times*)

RACE AND RELIGION

The Racial Divide Widens in Malaysia

Malaysia's government regularly cautions its constituents that open and honest dialogue of the "sensitive" subject of race is strictly off limits.

Then comes along the week-long United Malays National Organization (UMNO) annual assembly, at which Muslim Malay party leaders warn the country's minority Chinese and Indians that questioning the special status of Islam and Malays in society will be met with violent doom.

Fists tremble. Daggers are brandished. Party delegates thunder, "Long live the Malays." The very predictability of the chest-thumping is what UMNO members use to rationalize it: "Although some sides were a bit extreme [this year]," said UMNO vice president Muhyiddin Yassin, "it is quite normal to voice feelings during the assembly."

Yet it would be a mistake to confuse this year's assembly with previous party congresses. The Islamic and racist zeal was unmistakably more incessant and explicit, and the proceedings were considerably less tempered with calls for national unity. Remarks by Hasnoor Hussein, an UMNO delegate from Malacca, were typical: "UMNO is willing to risk lives and bathe in blood to defend the race and religion. Don't play with fire. If the [other races] mess with our rights, we will mess with theirs."

What troubles many Malaysians about UMNO's lack of restraint is that it comes at a time when the country appears more racially polarized than it's been in decades. Malaysia's mix of ethnic

Malays, Indians and Chinese has long been resentful of each other and willfully segregate themselves. Those resentments exploded into full-blown race riots in 1969, when ethnic Malays attacked and killed scores of ethnic Chinese.

These days, some 90% of Chinese students attend private Mandarin-language schools. Meanwhile, most Malays attend public schools and most Indians Tamil-language institutions of learning. Two years ago the government initiated a public service program to improve race relations by choosing 18-year-olds to participate in a military style camp. That scheme has been dogged by reports of race-related infighting, however.

Unequal rights

In the face of a creeping Islamization, non-Malays and social activists have recently pressured Malaysia's UMNO leadership to grant equal rights to all of the country's citizens regardless of race or religion—as is guaranteed under the federal constitution.

In particular, they have also become more vocal in questioning a controversial affirmative action program intended to help Muslim Malays catch up economically with the ethnic Chinese, who comprise 55% and 25% of the population respectively.

Started in 1971, the so-called New Economic Policy (NEP) was originally intended to last 20 years but has since been extended indefinitely. That's because, according to the government, its target of 30% Malay ownership of the country's total corporate equity still has not been achieved. According to official statistics, that percentage now hovers around 18%. Yet a study conducted by an independent academic last month contested that figure by claiming that ethnic Malay total equity ownership could already be as high as 45%.

The push for more democracy in authoritarian Malaysia leaves its ethnic Chinese and Indian minority groups particularly vulnerable—a fact reflected in the racial bashing at this year's UMNO assembly.

At the same time, UMNO's preoccupation with racial politics raises growing doubts about its ability to lead the country forward faced with the challenge of China's economic emergence. The party leadership has openly acknowledged the need for Malaysia to change course if it is to remain competitive with its fast-rising neighbors.

Economic growth slowed from 7.2% in 2004 to 5.2% last year, while foreign investment dropped 15% to $3.9 billion. Prime Minister Abdullah Badawi has promoted his concept of Islam Hadhari, or Civilizational Islam, a modernist interpretation of the faith that stresses moderation and technological and economic competitiveness. In that direction, his party has also introduced plans to transform Malaysia into a regional information technology, agricultural and biotech hub.

"We need an economic transformation," Abdullah said in his opening address at the UMNO assembly. Yet tight curbs on personal freedoms, implemented to curb racial tensions, have hindered the open inquiry and innovative spirit necessary to achieve Abdullah's vision. The next phase of economic development will require coincident social transformation, reforms the current race-obsessed political leadership is reluctant to implement.

Past tense progressive

Oddly, UMNO was once a progressive party, championing what seemed a viable vision to improve equity among the races. Even into the 1990s, under the iron-fisted leadership of Mahathir Mohamad, UMNO looked primed to lead Malaysia toward developed country status. The shimmering steel and glass that spangle Kuala Lumpur's skyline are remnants of that now fading vision.

But the plan went awry as UMNO became politically entrenched in power. Meanwhile, Malaysia's social development and technical know-how has not kept pace with its infrastructural achievements. A common concession in Malaysia, even among its own leadership, is that the country has First World infrastructure but a Third World mentality. Now, that dubious distinction is becoming increasingly obvious to outsiders.

The country's leadership must take much of the blame. UMNO has clung to old solutions, such as the NEP, to fix new problems. Put another way, UMNO, which has ruled Malaysia for four-plus decades through a coalition of other race-based parties, has become bitter, cynical and defensive—a party that is emphasizing preservation at the expense of progress.

Even younger UMNO members, once portrayed as idealistic, urbane and liberal, have quickly adopted the traits of the party's old guard—to the point of becoming the face of the party's increasing racist angst. For instance, Abdullah's Oxford-educated son-in-law, Khairy Jamaluddin, who is coincidentally the deputy chief of UMNO's youth wing, warned in September that Chinese political groups would try to take advantage of any split inside UMNO.

When pressured to apologize, according to media reports, the 31-year-old said, "What is there to apologize for? ... I am only defending my race." At the annual assembly, meanwhile, UMNO Youth Chief Hishammuddin Hussein urged the government to reject proposals for an inter-faith commission intended to foster better understanding among Malaysia's various religious groups.

He brandished a Malay dagger, known locally as a *keris*, when speaking. Some delegates, it seemed, urged him to go further. "Datuk Hisham has unsheathed his *keris*, waved his *keris*, kissed his *keris*. We want to ask Datuk Hisham, when is he going to use it?" said UMNO Perlis delegate Hashim Suboh.

Non-Malays are seeking to exploit the fiery tone of the UMNO assembly to their own political advantage. Liow Tiong Lai, youth chief of the Barisan Nasional component of the Malaysian Chinese Association, said the day that the assembly wrapped up, "All of us are Malaysians in this multiracial country and hatred must not exist.

Instead, we must find strength in diversity. We must inculcate love and unity among the races in order to overcome obstacles together."

Malays and UMNO party members will question the sincerity of such remarks, and not without reason. Following UMNO's example, all of Malaysia's major political parties are explicitly race-based, and all have been known to play the race card to shore up their support bases. But only UMNO has the weight of an assembly that has incited anger, mistrust and ridicule of other races.

This year's assembly could mark a dangerous turning point for a country that not long ago was often applauded internationally as a model moderate Islamic nation for its seeming religious tolerance and clear economic achievements. Nowadays, it's altogether unclear if a racially charged UMNO can even manage to maintain short-term social and political stability.

First published November 23, 2006 (*Asia Times*)

* * *

In Malaysia, "Too Sensitive" for Debate

Abdullah's appeasement of conservative Muslims would breed distrust among non-Muslims and contribute to the ruling coalition's poor election showing.

At a time when rage and intolerance are eating away at the Islamic world, Malaysia has stood out as a source of hope. Its Muslims have co-existed peacefully with the 40% non-Muslim population. There has been no major incident of violence committed in the name of Islam on Malaysian soil. It's no wonder Muslim and Western leaders hold Malaysia in high esteem.

Next month their hat-tipping is set to continue, when Prime Minister Abdullah Badawi delivers a keynote address at the sixth Asia-Europe Meeting (ASEM) in Finland. The European Union wants Abdullah to share his thoughts on Malaysia's success in the areas of race relations and inter-faith issues.

If the past is any indication, Abdullah will claim tolerance and unity as enduring traits of the Malaysian people. He will swear by Islam Hadhari (Civilizational Islam), a political and ideological interpretation of the faith that stresses moderation and technological and economic competitiveness.

But back in Malaysia a very different reality is unfolding on Abdullah's watch, one that raises questions about his commitment to Islam Hadhari and may have far-reaching implications for this "model Islamic democracy."

Hardline Muslims have grown more vocal in recent months, demonstrating at forums held by a coalition of non-governmental organizations known as Article 11 that wants the government to put its weight behind the Malaysian Constitution, which guarantees equality and freedom of worship, as the supreme law of the land. Article 11 is concerned that *sharia* (Islamic law) courts have recently taken primacy over civil courts in a number of controversial decisions. The hardliners are also opposed to efforts to establish an inter-faith commission to enhance understanding among Malaysia's various faiths.

The latest protest came on July 22 in the state of Johor Bahru. As Article 11 gathered in an upper-floor hotel ballroom, some 300 protestors gathered from behind a police line at the hotel entrance, brandishing signs that read, "Don't touch Muslim sensitivities," "Destroy anti-Muslims," and "We are ready to sacrifice ourselves for

Islam." In May protestors threatening to storm an Article 11 venue succeeded in bringing the forum to an abrupt end.

And now Abdullah has seen enough. Not from the hardliners, though, as one might expect, but from Article 11. "Do not force the government to take action," he warned the coalition. He accused Article 11 of playing up religious issues and threatening to shatter Malaysia's fragile social balance by highlighting "sensitive" issues. (It is an article of faith in Malaysia that "sensitive" issues should not be discussed openly.)

And yet it is these same issues—race, religion and the affirmative-action program benefiting the majority Malays—that are dearest to most Malaysians' hearts, that are discussed passionately, albeit behind closed doors, within one's own racial community. Abdullah has issued a stern warning to the media to stop reporting on issues related to religious matters. And he has not ruled out using the Internal Security Act, which allows for indefinite detention without trial, against Article 11 members should they continue with their activities.

Abdullah's position is in keeping with a worrying trend of his tenure, and that is to give Islam a peculiar prominence in Malaysia's political and social landscape.

Malaysia's Muslim-dominated leadership has long given Islam priority in Malaysia. The constitution recognizes Islam as Malaysia's official religion. Abdullah's predecessor, Mahathir Mohamad, labeled Malaysia "an Islamic state." And all of Malaysia's five prime ministers have promoted Islamic values in one form or another. The Abdullah era, however, has witnessed a growing number of politicians, religious administrators, authorities and activists making their own rules, pronouncements and judgments on things that are beyond their purview, with some districts even establishing "snoop squads." And *sharia* courts are said to be over-stepping their bounds in making rulings involving non-Muslims.

Abdullah's has been less than resolute in handling Malaysia's creeping fundamentalism, which is not to suggest the former Islamic scholar is promoting an intolerant strain of Islam. To be fair, Malaysia is a tricky place to govern. It requires deftly balancing the needs of the majority Muslim Malays with those of the Indian and Chinese minorities to prevent social unrest.

But by caving in to hardline sensitivities over inter-faith dialogue and the constitution, Abdullah, inadvertently or otherwise, appears to be going beyond merely accommodating the Malay community to the point of empowering its fringes. And the danger in this should not be underestimated, this being an era in which a growing number of Muslims around the world are resorting to intolerance to advance their causes (the publication of cartoons depicting the Prophet Mohammed and the violent assault on free speech in response to it is but one example).

Abdullah's stance against Article 11 could be read as in keeping with Mahathir's belief that greater freedom of expression will stoke inter-ethnic tensions. But Abdullah's position is a recklessly selective application: it is to allow hostile segments of the Muslim community to use free speech to dictate the limits of free speech.

The double standard was on full display two weeks ago, when Abdullah's powerful son-in-law Khairy Jamaluddin rallied members of Abdullah's United Malays National Organization (UMNO) in a protest outside the US Embassy in Kuala Lumpur. Traffic stalled as the mob burned US and Israeli flags and chanted, "Destroy Israel, down with Israel."

Racial and religious sensitivities run deep in Malaysia, and all of Malaysia's communities have inherited legitimate grievances over the years. But those sensitivities may be catching up with the country. Malays, Indians and Chinese have been drifting apart.

A recent survey found that the majority of Malaysians do not trust one another and seek refuge in their own ethnic community—

contradicting Malaysia's elaborately crafted outward display as a paradise of multiculturalism. Abdullah will no doubt tear a page from that book when he travels to Europe for the ASEM meeting, while back home a new chapter is being written.

First published August 4, 2006 (*Asia Times*)

* * *

Malaysia Takes the Rock out of Music

Hours after filing this story I passed a plasma TV in the mall at the base of the iconic Petronas Towers. On the screen was a singer wearing hotpants and gyrating amid a troupe of topless male dancers. Behind them the wall read, "Naughty Girl." Some Arab males stopped to watch, with one mumbling breathlessly, "Beyonce."

So while the government restricted the expression of international pop stars to stave off "moral decay" and tarnished Malaysia's image in the process, Beyonce's cancellation was a hot topic on fan sites and message boards — Beyonce still penetrated into the heart of Malaysia.

This is Visit Malaysia Year and the government is using the opportunity to promote the multi-ethnic country as a regional beacon of diversity and tolerance. But apparently international performing artists are a little less welcome than your average tourist.

In August pop star Gwen Stefani was required to dress "modestly" for her concert here, after the National Union of Malaysia

Muslim Students protested against the scheduled performance on the grounds that she would bring to Malaysia an "American hegemonic background," said the group's president Hilmi Ramli.

Early this month, R&B singer Beyonce Knowles scrapped her debut concert in Malaysia slated for November 1 due to what her agency called "a scheduling conflict," though local record industry sources say it was because the 26-year-old diva thought better of conforming to Malaysia's dress stipulations for international performers. "They have to dress decently ... and behave in a manner appropriate in Malaysia," insisted Culture, Arts and Heritage Minister Rais Yatim, days after Beyonce cancelled her show.

Malaysian authorities have in the past required local rock stars to cut their hair or forfeit the opportunity to appear on television or radio, and frequently remind Malaysians of the consequences for openly addressing "sensitive" issues like race and religion. But it wasn't until 2005 that foreign performers were asked to join the act.

Guidelines require foreign performers to cover themselves from shoulder to knees. They also stipulate no hugging or kissing fellow artists or audience members, no jumping or shouting, no cursing and no exchanging objects between audience and artist. Preventing "moral decay" and preserving Malaysian values are the reasons usually cited for the restrictions.

But what exactly are Malaysian values, and who is defining them? The issue has come to the fore in this multi-ethnic and multi-religious society, as religion asserts itself with renewed vigor in the public and political domain, and Malaysia's sizeable non-Muslim communities feel increasingly marginalized. Deputy Prime Minister Najib Razak recently called Malaysia an "Islamic state," even though Malaysia's governing framework is a secular constitution that gives Islam special importance.

Mohamad Akram Laldin of the International Islamic University in Malaysia says the government curbs on artistic freedom are in the interest of all Malaysians. "When the government takes a decision, they know that ... a big majority of the people will not be happy if such a thing is allowed. That is the reason why they have put [in place] certain restrictions [for performers]."

Razlan Ahmad Razali, chairman of Pineapple Concerts, which was to organize Beyonce's performance here, finds such reasoning specious. He says the dress of performers never becomes an issue until a vocal religious minority makes an issue of it. "Look, compared to 10,000 people who want to watch Gwen Stefani and 100 or 50 or so people doing the protests—you're willing to cave into those people?"

US rock stars Linkin Park and Mariah Carey are notable acts to have complied with Malaysia's dress restrictions. (Carey coincidentally is now appearing in a print ad for a local radio station wearing a short slinky dress with her derriere facing the camera next to the tag line, "Turn me on.")

The government and the Muslim groups it often stands accused of pandering to tend to conflate Islamic values into Malaysian values, and into Asian values more broadly, to rationalize giving Islam primacy in a society where non-Muslims account for 40% of the population. But a look around Malaysia reveals that Malaysian values (like Asian values) are neither static nor homogenous.

Even within Malaysia's Muslim community there is considerable plurality. Indeed, many of those who frequent nightclubs dressed in form-fitting, flesh-baring clothing also happen to be Muslim. A tourism campaign sponsored by the Culture Ministry deems Malaysia "Truly Asia," as in, "With a sparkling and lively melting pot of races and religious [sic] where Malays, Chinese, Indians and the many ethnic groups of Sabah and Sarawak live together in peace and harmony, Malaysia is truly a country that epitomizes Asia."

Solo act of censorship

But then Malaysia finds itself standing alone among Asian neighbors in its handling of international pop stars. On Beyonce's scheduled Malaysian date, she will instead play in neighboring Indonesia, where some 85% of the population is Muslim. She will also perform in Thailand, India, and China. None of those countries have asked Beyonce to censor herself or be anyone other than herself.

Indonesian concert promoter Nia Zulkarnaen was quoted as saying, "I expect Indonesians to see this in a positive light. She is a great singer and her stage act is entertaining. Why should we say no to the way she dresses?"

The Malaysian government is standing firm, however. After Beyonce's cancellation, Rais said his ministry will set up a committee to vet foreign performers and ensure they dress and behave in a way that is respectful to Malaysia as defined by the government. No one can deny Malaysia the right to act on its own terms, a point the government has not been shy to stress.

Former prime minister Mahathir Mohamad was famous for his anti-Western and anti-Semitic diatribes. Ministers relish dismissing international calls for Malaysia to show greater respect for human rights and dignity. International Trade Minister Rafidah Aziz called a speech by then US vice president Al Gore during the peak of the *reformasi* era, which echoed the Malaysian public's cries for greater government accountability and democracy, "The most disgusting speech I have heard in my life." (Rafidah just so happened to be facing numerous accusations of graft at the time, with the head of the prosecution in the attorney-general's chambers saying there was prima facie basis for her arrest and prosecution on five counts of corruption.)

But authorities are now tightening the noose at a time that was predicted to see greater tolerance and integrity among political leaders. Current Prime Minister Abdullah Badawi took over from the long-ruling Mahathir in 2003 preaching Islam Hadhari, or Civilizational Islam, which stresses moderation, creativity and technological mastery. Its 10 main principles include a just and trustworthy government and a free and independent people.

Instead the nation's endemic corruption has gone largely unchecked, while top officials tenaciously defend the status quo and browbeat the public into subservience. After a secretly recorded video clip surfaced last month of V K Lingam, a prominent lawyer, allegedly brokering judicial appointments with Chief Justice Ahmad Fairuz Sheikh Halim, the minister in the prime minister's department, Nazri Aziz, said the identity of the whistleblower must be revealed in order to determine the authenticity of the clip, popularly known as the "Lingam tape."

Nazri's consolation to the whistleblower was that the government could offer him or her plastic surgery. He later said he would push for a Whistleblowers Protection Act to be tabled in parliament. Some are perplexed as to why a prime minister vowing to stamp out corruption without fear or favor didn't make that among his first priorities of business, and why the anti-corruption agency remains under the jurisdiction of the prime minister's office.

Others wonder how the creative revolution the government is looking to kick-start to lead Malaysia into the 21st century can take off with such severe limits to artistic expression. It's perhaps no coincidence that Malaysia's music and arts scene lags behind those in neighboring Indonesia, Thailand and the Philippines. A number of Indonesian bands, for instance, have significant fan bases in Malaysia, while Indonesian media "throw our promotional CDs out," a top Malaysian artist recently told this correspondent.

Image at stake

To be sure, Abdullah's soft, accommodating demeanor cuts a sharp contrast with the surly vicissitudes of his predecessor. And he possesses a handy political tool in Islam Hadhari, which puts a good face on Malaysia's situation when Abdullah convenes with dignitaries abroad. Despite this, the Abdullah era has been riddled with controversies, some involving Abdullah's own family members.

Low points of the last year include a by-election in the small town of Ijok, in which Abdullah's government spent some RM100 million to narrowly defeat the opposition People's Justice Party; a landmark court decision in which a woman was not allowed to renounce Islam and declare herself with a religion of her own choosing; a case where members of Abdullah's United Malays National Organization (UMNO) used the party's annual assembly to threaten Malaysia's minority communities; UMNO officials' intimidation of bloggers for exposing government malpractice; a senior police official and the director general of the anti-corruption agency faced allegations of accepting bribes; a political analyst and security guards with close links to Najib stood trial for murder; and, of course, the damning revelations of the Lingam tape.

These occurrences have begun to curtail confidence in Abdullah and UMNO domestically. Some 1,000 lawyers marched to the prime minister's office in protest after Abdullah said there was no need to set up a commission of inquiry to handle the Lingam scandal. The last time Malaysian lawyers marched was in the late 1990s and the only other time on record was in the 1970s.

Some of these developments are also taking a toll on Malaysia's international reputation. And the government's crackdown on international artists certainly won't stem the tide. "[Beyonce's cancellation] is an opportunity lost for the Malaysian public and for Malaysia's name," said Razlan. "Bringing in these artists is the most direct way to promote Malaysia. They just can't see this is a small issue when it comes to dressing." He added: "They are losing out on the bigger picture ... especially Malaysia's name."

Razlan said international agents "very familiar with the region can't be bothered to offer Malaysia because of the potential problems they foresee." He said Western music acts Cold Play, Christina Aguilera, Eric Clapton and the Red Hot Chili Peppers had all recently bypassed Malaysia in favor of Singapore.

Like Malaysia, Singapore has garnered a reputation for strictness. But authorities there have lightened up in recent years, going as far as to even allow bar top dancing. Officials in the neighboring city-state seem to be coming around to the idea that, at least in entertainment venues, though not the political arena, respect for freedom of expression is good for business.

Mohamad Daud of PUSPAL, a subsidiary under the ministry of culture, arts and heritage responsible for issuing permits and enforcing compliance with the guidelines, said that playing host to international performers was good for Malaysia but that the most important thing is that they comply with government rules and regulations. "We are not worried about the question of what it will do to our reputation."

The Malaysian government certainly cannot be accused of selling out; rather it's chosen to risk negative publicity to prevent the risk of moral decay. And somewhere that's bound to win over some hearts.

First published October 13, 2007 (*Asia Times*)

* * *

No place for Terror in Malaysia

It happens now and then. A suspected terrorist is nabbed in the region, the arresting country claims the paper trail passes through Malaysia, and the Malaysian government goes on the defensive: Our country? No way.

The latest episode came on Sunday, following an eventful week for the region in its battle against Islamic extremism that included the capture of what Indonesian police say is Abu Dujana, the operational commander of the Jemaah Islamiah (JI) terrorist network.

And on Friday, Singapore announced it had arrested five suspected Islamic militants earlier this year. Four were alleged members of JI, with one, Mohamed Yassin, said to have "undergone JI training in Malaysia," according to Singapore's Ministry of Home Affairs website.

On Sunday, the inspector general of Malaysia's Royal Police, Musa Hassan, refuted the ministry's findings.

"There is no JI movement here in Malaysia," he was quoted as saying by the state-controlled daily *Berita Harian*. "The report by Singapore's Home Ministry is not true. I have not heard of and have never received any reports of a JI movement or al-Qaeda in this country."

The cocksureness—about networks that are adroitly covert no less—is illustrative of the government's obsession with preserving Malaysia's reputation as a model of Islamic moderation.

This while neighbors in the region—including the Philippines, Cambodia, Singapore, Thailand and Indonesia—have humbly admitted that terrorists and their sympathizers may be roaming their streets.

Digging beneath Malaysia's shiny veneer of exemplary moderation are reasons to believe that Malaysia is no more immune to being a breeding ground for radicalism.

It is true that Malaysia is economically better off than some of its neighbors, and some analysts draw an inverse correlation between a society's economic prosperity and its fertility for terrorism. But as the recent arrests in economically vibrant Singapore indicate, there are no hard-and-fast rules governing what makes a state vulnerable to terrorist elements taking root.

It is also true that shortly after September 11, 2001, the Malaysian government rounded up dozens of people suspected of having ties to JI. It shut down Islamic schools preaching "deviant" interpretations of Islam. All the while, Malaysia's Muslim Malays who make up 55% of the population have exhibited a great deal of tolerance toward Malaysia's two other main ethnic groups, the Indians and Chinese (and vise versa).

That being said, Malaysian Islam is racialized and highly politicized (compare this with Indonesia where Islam is decentralized and less homogenous). The two main organs of Islam are the long-ruling United Malays National Organization (UMNO) and the opposition Parti Islam SeMalaysia known as PAS. The latter's goal is to turn this multi-ethnic nation into an Islamic state. Both claim to represent the ethnic Malays and employ Islam to stake their claim, knowing that Malays look suspiciously on any concession to other races.

Last week, for instance, PAS's newly re-elected deputy president, Nasharudin Mat Isa, who is said to represent a younger generation of more inclusive PAS leaders, announced, "I am still very much an Islamist." Elsewhere, Prime Minister Abdullah Badawi has shot down the idea of an inter-faith commission, under pressure from Islamic groups. The idea was intended to stem increased tension and misunderstanding between religious groups. In short, narrow-mindedness and self-righteousness on the ground is reinforced by displays of it from the top.

PAS controls only one state in Malaysia, Kelantan, and some analysts are predicting it will lose Kelantan in the next elections, which Abdullah may call as early as this year. It is assumed that if that happens, atavistic, ascetic Islam will be a spent force in

Malaysia. But less support cannot be equated with no support. In fact, the undemocratic tactics which UMNO has used to erode PAS's support—from denying the party media access to withholding state funds—has bred resentment among PAS's core constituency. And there's nothing quite like resentment among the fervently religious to get the balls of radicalism rolling.

Across the border from Kelantan in southern Thailand, Muslim Malay militants have been locked in a bloody separatist battle. Former Thai prime minister Thaksin Shinawatra has alleged that some of the militants were trained in Kelantan, a charge that Malaysian authorities flatly deny. This even though Malaysia's northern border has been notoriously porous; in a trip across the border, my Malay friends accompanying me were allowed to pass into Thailand with merely a wave.

Malaysian authorities say they have since addressed the lax security. But it is naive, not to mention dangerous, to conclude that some Malaysians in a border area where faith runs high and ethnic pull is strong—at a time when a siege mentality is gripping much of the Islamic world—are not susceptible to taking up the Islamic call to *jihad*.

Another factor that may make Malaysians vulnerable to extremist ideology is the fact that Malaysian Islam, resurgent as it is, tends to be ritualistic. Many of my Malay friends recite Arabic of which they don't know the meaning. And I am embarrassed to say I have read more of the Koran (about half) than many of them. This superficial understanding—predicated on the "knowledge" that there is a God, he is the God, it is the gravest of sins to insult Him and His religion (*the* religion)—is vulnerable to manipulation.

Related to that, many of the region's top terror suspects linked to JI, including Abu Bakar Bashir and Hambali, were stationed in Malaysia before settling elsewhere in the region. No investigations that I know of have been carried out to see what impact they had here on local minds. Meanwhile, Saudi Arabian money is helping fund Islamic education in Malaysia, with the puritanical Wahhabi strain of the faith said to have attracted some adherents in the northern state of Perlis.

That being said, the state's mufti, Mohamed Asri Zainul Abidin, has stood apart from staunchly conservative muftis in other states for, among other things, denouncing the practice by Malaysian religious authorities who snoop in search of *khalwat* (close proximity between a man and woman who are not married) on grounds that it violates Islam's respect for privacy; and for advocating a less ritualistic approach to Islam.

Some foreign-policy gestures have not exactly sent an unequivocal message that extremism is unacceptable. Abdullah has said the Western and Muslim worlds should work together to curb intolerance and extremism. He has also appeared frequently in the local media smiling and embracing Iran's President Mahmud Ahmadinejad, whose regime has been linked to terrorist acts in neighboring Iraq. Meanwhile, Malaysia's Foreign Minister Syed Hamid Albar last year suggested sending arms to Hezbollah. It is tempting to brush these overtures aside as meaningless. But they are not, not in an era when many Muslims around the world have adopted a dualistic siege mentality.

The government could also help prevent intolerance from spreading through revising what it allows and prevents Malaysians from reading and watching. The Internal Security Ministry bans books and pressures bookstores not to carry certain titles on the grounds that it will "disrupt peace and harmony."

Last week, it did so in response to Christopher Hitchens' best-selling book, *God is not Great*, which examines the irrational legacy of religious conviction.

Meanwhile, anti-Semitic literature, such as the *Protocols of the Elders of Zion*, is readily available. So are videos glorifying *jihad*.

On a recent visit to the Jamek Mosque area of Kuala Lumpur, I encountered a group of Muslims transfixed in front of a booth selling pirated religious videos. On the screen were bearded mujahideen marching through a forest brandishing machine guns as Koranic verses were recited.

The government has also opted to focus more on symptoms rather than causes when it comes to promoting "peace and harmony," and this may inadvertently be encouraging intolerance. The government has long stressed that religion is a "sensitive" issue and should not be discussed openly. As a result Malaysians find themselves easily offended and ill-equipped to talk through their differences. Resentment festers.

None of this is to suggest that Malaysia is a hotbed for terrorism. The majority of Muslims in the country are moderate and have done their part to preserve Malaysia's social balance. It's just to say the seeds are there, and unequivocal denials by government officials intended to pad Malaysia's image do nothing to change the fact.

First published June 13, 2007 (*Asia Times*)

* * *

The Search for a Malaysian Race

From one vantage point, Malaysia is a shining example of racial and religious harmony in the post-colonial age. It has met the basic needs of its majority Muslim Malays and its Indian, Chinese and native minorities, to the extent that there has been no major racial incident in Malaysia since the May 1969 riots, in which hundreds of Malays and Chinese were killed.

Seen another way, however, the social construct of race pervades the national consciousness at almost every turn. All major political parties are race-based and have been known to use race to advance their own interests. Most Malay students choose to attend national or, increasingly, Islamic schools, while some 90% of Chinese primary and secondary students attend private, Chinese-run schools. Pent-up mistrust, resentment and condescension are a part of Malaysian daily life.

Yet acceptance has prevailed; an acknowledgement by most Malaysians that while the racial situation is far from perfect, there is much to be grateful for. Theirs is a stable, fast-developing country. All Malaysia can take a little pride in that.

Unfortunately, this "success" has not been matched by a collective and concerted effort to improve the "harmony" here—not in the government, not among the *rakyat* (citizens); in large part, the government censures and the public dutifully avoids substantive exploration of the matter.

"There has been a self-satisfaction with the current situation and laziness to deal with certain problems and conflicts," said Sumit Mandal, a historian with Universiti Kebangsaan Malaysia.

The authoritarian government hasn't strayed much from its original post-riot social contract, the New Economic Policy (NEP), an affirmative-action program intended to help the Malays and other *bumiputra* (sons of the soil) catch up economically with the capitalist-oriented Chinese. The NEP and its offshoots have played a crucial role in sustaining harmony in Malaysia. But they have been equally controversial and a source of increased resentment.

This can be better understood by considering what the NEP collectively stood for during its implementation in 1971: a compromise. It was widely thought that Malay economic progress would be matched by political gains for the Chinese and other minorities.

"From a [non-Malay] perspective, there has developed a weary acceptance of the way things are," said Ibrahim Suffian of the Merdeka Center for Opinion Research.

Malay economic advance has been matched not by an increase in power-sharing but by a consolidation of Malay political power. The United Malays National Organization (UMNO) heads a multi-racial coalition known as the National Front (BN), but the leading Chinese party's role has weakened in recent years. Samy Vellu, head of Malaysia's largest Indian party, is widely thought to be a token of UMNO and "more threatened by smart Indians than inclined to help them," as one young Indian businessman put it.

Hopes of gaining equal citizenship have faded for many. And yet potential unrest has been tempered in no small part by the economic prospects available to Malaysians. Gross domestic product looks primed to exceed 7% for 2004. Average household income is $9,000, highest in the region next to Singapore. Unemployment is at 3.5%. Poverty has been slashed from 49% at the NEP's outset to 7% today. Malaysia is the world's largest producer of palm oil, pepper and rubber, and is a destination for migrants.

Thus, despite grumblings of "institutionalized inequality," most Malaysians count themselves lucky, and those who don't are often reminded they should. In *The Chinese Dilemma*, a book that challenges conventional Chinese and other minorities' perceptions of themselves as second-class citizens here, Malaysian businessman Ye Lin-Sheng writes, "If the Malays had come to occupy India and China in a similar manner, how do you imagine the Indians and Chinese would feel? How would they have responded to these intruders? What would they have done? ... I also look at the lot of Chinese and Indian migrants to other countries and that of those who had stayed home. This is enough to make me feel thankful that I am [in

Malaysia] and not there."

Not everyone agrees. Disgruntled Malaysians with the means have been known to relocate overseas. Even the government lately has expressed concern about its "best and brightest" not returning after being educated abroad. It is estimated that 30,000 Malaysian graduates work overseas. Many of them are Chinese.

Khoo Kay Peng of the Sedar Institute, an independent think-tank, links the brain drain to the government's race-based policies. "If you don't create equal opportunity through a meritocracy, in the private sectors, high-quality people will continue to move away."

Which begs the question, how long will the Malays need assistance? The NEP was designed to run 20 years but has been extended indefinitely. Prime Minister Abdullah Badawi warned at last year's UMNO annual assembly that Malays need to abandon their "crutches" or risk ending up in wheelchairs. But Abdullah was met with strong resistance within UMNO, whose members are wont to "protect" the Malays for political expediency at the expense of national unity.

Abdullah has set up a National Unity Council to better unite the races, but few are holding their breath. In his first 15 months in office he has announced a number of grand plans, such as the Royal Police Commission, National Integrity Plan, and Islam Hadhari (Civilizational Islam), but they have not shown substantial results, or necessarily appear determined to do so. The National Unity Advisory Panel, according to a member, has had one meeting since its inception in October and is in the process of trying to schedule a second.

"I don't see any headway in the government's strategy," said social scientist Dr Norani Othman, despite much talk among a band of younger overseas-educated members of UMNO, who have witnessed more egalitarian means of managing multi-racial societies. "There continues to be a lack of critical thinking, of examining how this problem has arisen in the first place."

Some problems can be linked to tactics used by former premier Mahathir Mohamad. He may have coined the term *bangsa* Malaysia (Malaysian race) in 1991, but he arguably did more to emphasize differences than broker unity during his 22-year rule. His finger always seemed near the race trigger. He even took aim at peoples of other nations—Jews and Anglo-Saxons were two favorite targets.

It was under Mahathir that UMNO and the opposition Islamic party, Parti Islam Se-Malaysia (PAS), began trying to out-Islamize each other in a battle for the Malay heartland (fueling both intra- and inter-ethnic tensions). The feud fed an Islamic revival already underway and that has continued to the present.

Abdullah has introduced Islam Hadhari as a vehicle for moderation. But many Malaysians have come to question the motivation and substance of Islam Hadhari. Even if Islam Hadhari proves successful, it alone cannot solve Malaysia's inter-ethnic tensions because Islam is hardly the only force causing ethnic strains.

In *The Chinese Dilemma* Ye suggests that the Chinese could help improve matters by taking a closer look at themselves: "Malay success is always ascribed to the privileges and special support they get under affirmative action, but non-Malay achievement is invariably put down to innate ability and hard work ... have the Chinese forgotten all those licenses, concessions and contracts that they have won through patronage, connections and bribery?" Le encourages them to "try looking at themselves through Malay eyes," but concludes that the possibility of this has been "undercut by more recently acquired feelings of inferiority. Much cultural baggage, then, stands in the way of a change of Malaysian Chinese attitudes toward Malays."

Of course, a less fragmented Malaysia will depend on all communities taking a closer look at themselves and their own legacies of racism, as well as taking greater steps to better understand the grievances of each other's communities. (Indians, for instance, among Malaysia's poorest communities, don't qualify for *bumiputra* perks, yet few outside their own can be found championing their cause.)

But these steps are unlikely to happen if the schooling trend continues and if Malaysians don't learn to talk through their differences. As it stands, race is rarely discussed outside of one's own ethnic community. And the state-regulated media avoids meaningful discussion on the topic.

"The [government and media] should create a sense that people should talk about their differences," said Dr Patricia Martinez, head of Intercultural Studies at the Asia-Europe Institute at the University of Malaya. Instead, there's been a "sheer infantilizing of all of us to the point that we're unable to articulate ourselves on an issue that has become central to defining ourselves as Malaysians."

Martinez, however, cautions against placing all the blame with the government and media. While draconian legislation such as the Internal Security and Sedition acts have been designed to curb freedom of expression, and the mainstream media have with rare exception dutifully toed the line, self-censorship is also a problem. "We self-sensor ourselves more than government sensors us. There's a reluctance [among Malaysians] to be offensive," Martinez said.

That tendency has both helped and hampered community relations. But there's a growing sense that a fully-realized *bangsa* Malaysia will require greater expression between communities.

Movement toward a Malaysian race

Taking the leap, said Mandal, are a handful of film directors, website writers and editors, non-governmental organizations, playwrights and visual artists. One is Yasmin Ahmad, whose film "Sepet," a teenage romance centering on a Chinese boy and Malay girl, will open next month. Without harping on differences, it examines some of the realities and myths about ethnic groups here. And while the conclusions it draws about inter-ethnic relations are far from rosy, Mandal said it also manages to emphasize what many of these artists are highlighting: trans-ethnic solidarities. "There's far more boundary crossing going on [in Malaysia] than some would like to believe," he said, adding that trans-ethnic solidarities are among the least researched features of Malaysian society. [1]

This is unfortunate though not likely to change as long as government policies emphasize race—they keep race at the fore. And yet outright scrapping, as opposed to a gradually repealing, of the ethnocentric policies is unrealistic, and those who have been calling for this tend to think in terms of the aspirations of their own community rather than the whole of Malaysia. Such thinking is potentially as invidious as its advocates claim the current economic arrangement is.

But assuming the government adopts a system of greater equality, one based less on race than actual need, gulfs between communities will remain. This is in no small part because the government has continually manipulated race and consequently it has evolved into a socio-political construct Malaysians centrally identify themselves with (even though, as Mandal points out, identity here extends beyond these boundaries, and even though intra-ethnic divisions may prove to be a greater source of tension than inter-ethnic ones).

Some interest in a multi-racial party has emerged. "What we see is that religious issues divide, even among Muslims themselves," said Syed Husin Ali of the multi-racial, opposition People's Justice Party (PKR). "So we are, though not cutting ourselves off from those issues, slowly disengaging ourselves from them." Ali added: "We don't want to be drawn into issues of religion and race anymore."

The party was founded by Mahathir's former deputy Anwar Ibrahim, who was acquitted in September after spending six years

---

[1] Three years after "Sepet," Yasmin released a sequel called "Mukhsin." In discussing the film with Malaysian friends they referred to it as a Malay movie. This puzzled me: Why not a Malaysian movie? In America, we wouldn't call, say, Spike Lee's "Malcolm X" a black film.

in jail on what was widely thought to be a Mahathir-led witch hunt. And while the party is seen as a Malay party, its platform has been social justice.

The party did poorly in March parliamentary elections, when Abdullah's promise for reform led UMNO to a wide margin of victory. Yet Abdullah has shown few signs of fulfilling his promises, leaving the country without a clear sense of direction and opening the door a crack for Anwar. He hasn't declared his allegiance with a particular party, but his recent comments suggest he may well pursue a multi-ethnic platform.

First published January 15, 2005 (*Asia Times*)

* * *

Mahathir's Mixed Legacy on Race

When Malaysian Prime Minister Mahathir Mohamad told a summit of Muslim leaders on Oct. 16 that "Jews rule the world," he might not have anticipated the international outcry that followed. The following day, Mahathir's spokesmen insisted that the remark had been taken out of context and was not intended to cause offense. But for those who know the record of this mercurial premier, his words might not have come as much of a surprise.

Mahathir, who will step down as prime minister at the end of October after 22 years in power, has long played "the race card" to benefit himself domestically.

To judge by his reception at the International Conference of

Muslim Young Leaders held in Kuala Lumpur in September, his efforts have paid off. The delegation, representing 50 countries, nominated him to succeed Kofi Annan as secretary-general of the United Nations. Every question posed from the ballroom floor seemed to open with lavish praise.

Some credited Mahathir with transforming this once backward nation into an economic success story and preparing Malaysians to thrive in the global marketplace. Others hailed him as an inspiration to the Muslim world, not the least for managing to preserve peace among Malaysia's various ethnic and religious groups—a task perceived as difficult at a time when many nations in the region with substantial Muslim populations are being torn asunder by extremist elements.

In the capital it's easy to see what Mahathir's fans are excited about—from the futuristic frippery of the hub-aspiring airport to the world's tallest buildings. On Bintang Walk, Saudi and Western tourists stroll past upscale boutiques and sip drinks topped with whipped cream at the Coffee Bean Café, as street musicians perform American pop songs.

It all suggests that Mahathir's vision—for Malaysia to be a "fully developed" nation by 2020—is well on track. Even Washington has been enthusiastic. Ever since Malaysia denounced Muslim extremism following the September 11 attacks, Washington has entrusted Mahathir's government with setting up a regional anti-terrorism center. And though the US-led war in Iraq—which Mahathir vehemently opposed—has tested relations, Washington still tends to view Malaysia as a pillar of stability in the region.

But inside Malaysia a different storyline is playing out. There is an undiscussed but palpable skepticism about what will happen after November 2003, when Mahathir's hand-picked successor, Deputy Prime Minister Abdullah Ahmad Badawi, takes over.

One of the keys to Mahathir's success was his ability to appease the Malay Peninsula's three main racial groups: Malays, Chinese, and Indians. He did this despite an affirmative action program that benefits the majority Malays (who make up 55 percent of Malaysia's population of 23 million) and other native groups, known collectively as *bumiputra*.

The issue of race has always been close to Mahathir's heart. He made a name for himself politically with his book *The Malay Dilemma*, which argued that Malays needed to change their "backwardness" or risk being dominated economically by Chinese Malaysians.

But unfortunately, rather than fully addressing the issue, Mahathir essentially made it taboo to talk openly about race. During his tenure as prime minister, he has jailed people indefinitely for questioning the government's race policy. He has heavily censored the press and banned certain films and plays outright. Essentially, in Mahathir's Malaysia only the government can talk about race; and for the most part, it has done so in ways that are both simplistic and inaccurate. In one typical example, an ad that loops on the airport shuttle's plasma screens describes Malaysia as "a land where people of different, races, religions and cultures live in perfect harmony."

A Malay university student told *World Press Review*, "We wouldn't know how to begin talking with the other races about our differences. We talk among ourselves but that doesn't exactly promote tolerance."

By many accounts race relations have gotten worse during the Mahathir years. One high-ranking member of Mahathir's party, the United Malays National Organization (UNMO), said, "There are parallel universes now. We all consider ourselves Malaysian, but we're not exactly Malaysian together. Very different notions of nation have surfaced."

The official, who spoke on condition of anonymity, estimates that 95 percent of Chinese students attend private Chinese schools and 90 percent of Malays attend public schools. Many non-Malays deserted public schools in the 1980s and '90s in the belief that the quality of education was deteriorating as the schools became too Islamic. The result is that some Chinese speak less than fluent Malay, the national language, and that the races often only interact when necessary.

Mahathir tended to put economic considerations first, reasoning that race relations and other social ills would improve as a result of economic gain. When he did talk about race it was to attract political support. Since all Malaysia's major political parties are race-based, political survival often depends on playing the race card. Mahathir, it has been remarked, knows how to play this card better than anyone.

"It's no coincidence that around election time the news channels show footage of the anti-Chinese riots that coincided with Suharto's fall," says Steven Gan, editor of Malaysiakini.com, whose staff computers were recently confiscated when he ran a letter that questioned the Mahathir government's record on race relations.

Many Chinese supported Mahathir, feeling he maintained a conducive political climate for business. But Mahathir's race-based politics—under which Malays are granted a large number of university and government seats—has spurred what one Malaysian Chinese writer termed "a reverse racism of a sort."

Those same policies have found Malays no less resentful of the Chinese; some assert that affirmative action has just made Chinese, the second-largest ethnic group in Malaysia, more nepotistic and determined to succeed. And although Mahathir's economic policy has given rise to a vibrant Malay middle class, many believe that the affirmative action program has made Malays more dependent and less empowered. The prime minister himself has indirectly conceded the point, urging Malays to get rid of their "crutches."

Khoo Kay Kim, professor emeritus of history at the University of Malaya, says Malaysia is home to 50,000 unemployed recent university graduates, the majority of whom are Malay. "A lot of them coasted through school knowing full well that space would be made for them. Sadly, they didn't develop much in the way of employable skills along the way."

Some of the roots of the Malay-Chinese divide can be traced to the decades before Mahathir's reign, and particularly to the Iranian Revolution, which inspired an Islamic revival among many Malays. During those years, nation took a back seat to religion and this increased skepticism about non-Muslims and the "impurities" of the outside world.

But the affirmative action program has seen the emergence of a new divide—among Malays themselves. The Malaysian opposition complains that the program didn't pay enough attention to who needed the assistance most; rich Malays benefited. Resources were wasted. Economic dominance was consolidated.

The Asian economic crisis of the late 1990s led to a political crisis, as Mahathir's deputy prime minister, Anwar Ibrahim, mounted a political challenge. Anwar is now serving a 15-year jail sentence on what many consider trumped-up sodomy and corruption charges.

Feeling betrayed by what they consider Mahathir's dirty politicking, many Malays, particularly those in rural areas, have begun to support the opposition Pan-Malaysian Islamic Party (PAS), which is pushing for an Islamic state governed by *sharia* law. PAS now has political control of two states, and may very well pick up a third in the next election. In its strongholds, there are separate seating areas for men and women. Drinking alcohol and singing karaoke—both popular pursuits here, particularly among the Chinese—are banned. The green-and-white party flag flutters from porches and mosques while children lounge about in knit PAS caps, as though an election is in full swing.

The party's critics charge it with atavism and promoting extremism. PAS officials say the party is merely pushing for a more egalitarian state. Less debatable, says a disenchanted UMNO official, is the effect PAS' emergence and Mahathir's inability to solve race issues is having on the country. "We are experiencing a creeping conservatism. Religious energies are being misdirected. The potential economic and political ramifications are immense." In September, Pakistani officials arrested 15 Malaysian students suspected of being second-generation leaders of the Jemaah Islamiyah terrorist network.

In the meantime, Mahathir has benefited from the US-led invasion of Iraq; he has used Malaysians' sense of indignation to foster unity and distract them from the fissures at home. In July, at his last speech given to the UMNO General Assembly before retirement, he classified people of European descent as greedy, bent on recolonizing the world, sexually immoral, and as "rejecting the institutions of marriage and family...and accepting the practice of free sex, including sodomy, as a right."

Predictably, local media raised no objection to the comments. They have served Mahathir dutifully over the years, to the point that some Malaysians have begun to question how much of Mahathir's reported contributions to the country have been manufactured.

But the episode contains a starker message, one that is practically ingrained here: It is fine to talk disparagingly about other races, so long as the remarks don't target Malaysians.

An assistant of Badawi, who has a reputation for being more open but less charismatic and formidable than Mahathir, says that his boss' challenge as prime minister will be to keep UMNO united. In large part, that will depend on maintaining a sound economy and keeping race relations in check. Many experts say the two are inextricable, and that a faltering economy may well expose the shortcomings of Mahathir's race policy.

In the meantime, there is hope that the transition may help open a new chapter in Malaysian history, in which an honest dialogue about race relations—through universities and the media, and from the lips of the political elite—is encouraged.

In the words of an expatriate black American, who is a basketball coach in Malaysia and says that vacant taxis pass him by when he tries to flag them down in Kuala Lumpur, "We may still have race issues back home, but at least, from time to time, we get together and talk about them."

First published August 30, 2003 (Asi aTimes)

* * *

Malaysia Makes its Case on Conversion

In multi-ethnic Malaysia, where Islam is the official religion but freedom of religion is guaranteed under the constitution, apostasy for Muslims has become a contentious issue.

The majority Malays are born Muslim and changing religions is all but impossible for them. Cases of aspiring apostates are handled by *sharia* rather than civil courts, and according to the tenets of Islam, no Muslim should assist another out of the religion and conversion to another faith is grounds for death.

Authorities are known to monitor Malay converts to prevent them from introducing other Malays to Christian doctrine. Appeals for conversion usually sit unheard, and many would-be apostates don't live to see their conversion officially recognized. As one religious scholar put it, "In Malaysia, there's a way into Islam, but no way out."

A question of religious freedom

According to the US government's International Religious Freedom Report for 2003, "It is official policy to 'infuse Islamic values' into the administration of the country." It is illegal to print the Bible and other Christian materials in the Malay language. Proselytizing of Muslims by non-Muslims is also forbidden, though the reverse is permitted.

Non-Muslims, who make up some 40% of the population, say they face difficulties in obtaining licensing and state funding for their places of worship. The country's new administrative capital is Islamic-themed, and a red-domed mosque is a centerpiece of the planned city but temples of other faiths are hard to come by.

These trends pose challenges for non-Muslims and apostates, said lawyer Lee Min Choon, "but they are not paralyzing." Lee said he believes the government's religious policy is generally conducted with the best of intentions. "The government doesn't have a program to create difficulties for other religions. They want peace for all religions."

Some areas seem to bear this point out, like the mostly Indian neighborhood of Brickfields in Kuala Lumpur, where mosques, Indian and Chinese temples can be found within blocks of each other.

Restricting conversion

Last week Malaysian courts handed down two decisions that centered on freedom, equality, and apostasy. Both were expected to resolve much but may settle little.

The first case involved a married Hindu couple. The husband converted to Islam in 2002—no problem there—but what drew national attention to the case is that according to the wife, her husband also converted their two children to Islam without her consent. The marriage has since ended, but when the wife filed for custodial rights with a civil court, it ruled that only a *sharia* court could decide on her children's custodial rights because they are Muslim. In April, a *sharia* court upheld the children's conversion and awarded custody to the father.

According to Noor Aziah Mohd Awal, a law professor at Universiti Kebangsaan Malaysia, "Any case dealing with Muslims goes to *sharia* court." But the mother could not testify in *sharia* court because she is not Muslim. On July 20, however, a high court granted custodial rights to the mother (and actual custody to both parents). This, said Noor Aziah, sets a precedent that civil courts should decide on custodial cases involving a Muslim and non-Muslim parent. But it doesn't resolve which court should preside over cases involving children who have been converted to Islam without mutual consent of their parents.

"The law needs to be amended," Noor Aziah said, "whereby both parties can go to the same court." She suggested that such a court include one *sharia*-court judge, one civil-court judge and a non-affiliated chairman.

In a separate case last Wednesday, a Malaysian Federal Court ruled that four Muslim apostates did not have the absolute right to renounce their faith of Islam, in effect suspending "one's right to choose his religion," the appellants' lawyer, Haris Mohamed Ibrahim, told *Asia Times Online*.

"We hoped the courts would resolve problems individuals are facing," Haris said, "but the court declined to answer a landmark issue."

According to Shad Salem Faruq, professor of law at the University of Technology MARA, the decision clashes with the international view that freedom of religion should be universally granted. And the question of whether multi-ethnic Malaysia should cater more to Islamic or international standards of law is growing more contentious.

Shad said the main concern of the Malay-led government is

Christian proselytizing. Six and 20 % of Malaysia population is Hindu and Buddhist; 9 % is Christian. "But Hinduism and Buddhism historically have had less of a tradition of proselytizing than Christianity," Shad said.

Besides being illegal for certain Christian materials to be printed in Malay, some states restrict Christians from using the Malay language for certain religious terms, such as "Allah" (the God), lest Muslims be confused.

Despite the obstacles, some Christian proselytizers are busy. Reverend Kumar (not his real name) said he vividly remembers the night Malaysia's Special Branch police, who are in charge of investigating perceived threats to national security, knocked his front gate in the middle of the night. The warning was clear, though it has not stopped Kumar. "I am not afraid," he said. "My work is God's will and I have a worthy cause to fight for. [Malays] have a right to find Jesus."

Kumar says he is partly compelled to "save" Malays because Malays are born Muslim, which he says often makes their allegiance to Islam less a matter of faith than subjugation.

"The Muslims who come to see me to be delivered think the religion treats them as second-class citizens," said Reverend Kumar. "They say they don't know what to believe in, they've just been told to believe in it. They feel empty, and they just follow. They come here because they want something more real."

His evangelical church has 12 branches throughout Malaysia and 30 affiliates. Kumar estimates that 100 Muslims are converting to Christianity every month in Malaysia. He says there has been a marked increase in interest since 9/11, when Muslim terrorists attacked innocent Americans and tarnished Islam's global image. "In the *kampongs* [villages] more people have opened their hearts to our message, and more people are coming to see us," he said.

Some Christian estimates put the number of Malay converts at

30,000. Others say the figure is much lower, but then many converts live in secrecy for fear of harassment from the government and fellow Malays. One Malay convert and former *ustaza* (Muslim religious teacher), now a colleague of Reverend Kumar, said she was disowned by her family for converting to Christianity. Her family has since forgiven her, but she and her children continue to be harried by the authorities. Because she is Malay, her son was officially born Muslim and forced to adopt a Muslim name. In school, despite his protests that he is a Christian, he is forced to sit through Islamic studies, as all Muslims are required to do.

She says she has had her fair share of run-ins with the Special Branch, and her phone was recently tapped. Last year, five religious-police officers visited her home to insist she stop her "activities," which, she said, included assisting drug addicts and battered women. They also apparently involved proselytizing. She admitted to parking herself at a McDonald's wearing a Muslim headscarf to introduce Muslim schoolgirls to the Bible. In Kuala Lumpur, boys who are a part of Reverend Kumar's proselytizing movement frequent mosques.

In the cramped lobby of Kumar's headquarters a magazine headline reads, "Storming the Enemy's Stronghold." The first paragraph explains, "Within the 10/40 window [the area stretching roughly from the Middle East through India, China and into Southeast Asia] lie 62 of the least evangelized nations on this planet." Some Christian proselytizers see this area as all that stands in the way of Christian global dominance.

Shad noted that some Muslim groups proselytize too, though they don't typically face harrassment by the government.

Fear and resentment is growing on both sides, and Dzulkifli Achmad, director of the Research Center of Malaysia's opposition Parti Islam se-Malaysia (PAS), said a greater respect for people of other faiths is necessary.

"I used to seek to convert, but I no longer have the drive," he said. "When you think of the unique fabric of this society, it is in our interest to enhance mutual respect. It is very important for Malaysia's solidarity to appreciate other truths. Proselytizing is a form of disrespect. It is the beginning of the conflict."

Some say mutual respect will require more dialogue between faiths. But the government has recently denied permits for inter-faith dialogues, as it considers race and religion too sensitive to discuss openly.

The government's "protection" of Muslim sensitivities sometimes prevents Malaysians from a collective experience and understanding. Mel Gibson's film "The Passion of the Christ" will show here soon, but Muslims are barred from viewing it.

Nora Murah, a legal officer with Sisters in Islam, said the decision contradicts the Prophet Mohammed's teachings. "The Prophet embraced diversity and inclusiveness," she said.

So, too, did Jesus, Christians would opine. But in the time that's lapsed since those two great men walked the earth, millions have grappled to follow in their footsteps, invariably falling short, usually far short—sometimes shorter than non-believers—and often enough at the expense of their "brothers" and "neighbors," as Malaysia can attest.

First published July 27, 2004 (*Asia Times*)

* * *

Islam Hadhari in Malaysia

In the Muslim world Malaysia is bigger than its physical size would suggest. The Southeast Asian nation of 24 million people is known for its stability, tolerance, and steady economic gains over the last 30 years. Malaysia does not take that reputation for granted; it has strived to live up to it. The latest and most ambitious effort comes by way of Islam Hadhari, or Civilizational Islam, a political and ideological campaign introduced by Abdullah Badawi shortly after he was named prime minister in 2003 that stresses technological and economic competitiveness, moderation, tolerance, and social justice.

In October, US Undersecretary for Public Diplomacy Karen Hughes praised Islam Hadhari as a "powerful example" to all Muslims, and Badawi's deputy Najib Razak assured Mrs Hughes that Malaysia was prepared to share Islam Hadhari with the rest of the world. At home, meanwhile, the government has started promoting ten points of Islam Hadhari, including a just and trustworthy government and protection of the environment. Badawi says Islam Hadhari is not a new concept but an attempt to bring the Muslim community back in touch with the true essence of Islam. And like Islamic movements elsewhere, it envisions a restored and empowered Umma.

Islam Hadhari is to some extent a logical outgrowth of social, political and Islamic realities in Malaysia. The government has long stressed moderation and economic equity in order to keep peace between the Muslim Malays, who make up about 60 percent of the population, and the indigenous tribes and sizeable Chinese and Indian minorities, most of whom are not Muslim. Malay concerns, however, have always been central to government policy. The United Malays National Organization (UMNO), which has ruled the country for forty-plus years, has promoted Malay supremacy since before independence. At its founding, UMNO envisioned a Malaysia ruled by Malays and where Malays would be granted special rights and privileges. [1]

UMNO continues to champion a positive discrimination program that benefits the majority Malays. This commitment first and foremost to the Malays has been a key to its hegemony. But it has also required a conspicuous investment in Islam, for in Malaysia to be Malay is to be Muslim; Malays are born into the faith. And while pulls toward religion and ethnicity have complicated Malay identity, politically these two forces are inextricable: Islam in Malaysia is racialized. Hence, to appear "un-Islamic" is also to be "un-Malay"—a political liability.

Islam Hadhari was created with this politicized terrain in mind and in its short existence has served UMNO well. It was introduced months before parliamentary elections in 2004, giving Badawi's promise to tackle Malaysia's endemic corruption and promote reform a progressive Islamic face. Its emphasis on tolerance appealed to Malaysians of all stripes. The UMNO-led national front went on to post one of its best showings in history, winning 90.4 of Malaysia's 219 national parliamentary seats and 64 percent of the popular vote, and roundly defeating the opposition Pan-Malaysian Islamic Party (PAS). But Islam Hadhari should not be viewed merely as a political instrument. [2] Prime Minister Badawi envisions Islam Hadhari as an antidote to the tide of extremism ravaging the larger Muslim world, at a time when many Muslim nations are struggling to reconcile piety with modern realities. "It is our duty," Badawi said at a conference last year, "to demonstrate, by word and by action, that a Muslim country can be modern, democratic, tolerant and economically competitive."

That fight starts at home, where an undercurrent of Islamic fundamentalism has begun to challenge Malaysia's reputation as a "model" Islamic nation. The influence of conservative religious teachers has grown. Fewer men are shaking women's hands. [3] A growing number of minorities are opting for private education as public schools have become more Islamized. More Malay women are wearing the headscarf. The call to prayer is more ubiquitous, occasionally heard channeled into elevators and over the islands at gas stations. The Muslim moral police, known by the acronym "JAWI" in Kuala Lumpur, have become more brazen and officious, detaining couples for holding hands and threatening to send "deviant" Muslims to rehabilitation centers. [4] In January, JAWI police raided a nightclub and rounded up all Muslim patrons while letting non-Muslims off the hook. Those arrested described JAWI officers as "abusive" and "overzealous." In July, a mob of masked persons in robes attacked a commune run by a Malay apostate. The mob reportedly threw Molotov cocktails, broke windows and slashed car tires. Malaysian police have not arrested anyone involved in the attack, but a day later the state religious department arrested 58 members associated with the sect for practicing a deviant religion. [5] In June, two young Muslim brothers were sentenced to a whipping for sipping Guinness stout.

These developments have been cumulative, and they pose a challenge to the realization of Islam Hadhari. But to what extent? Clues can be found in Malaysian Islam's historical antecedents.

Islam arrived in the Malay peninsula in the 15th century. It was at first mostly comprehended and accepted only by Malay aristocrats, but became more of a general identity marker in the 19th century when large numbers of non-Malays began to migrate to Malaysia. [6] A pronounced recent shift in Islamic identity that reverberates through to the present came with the Islamic revival in the 1970s, known as the "*Dakwah* Movement." Catalysts included the Chinese-Malay racial riots of 1969 and the establishment a few months later of the Muslim Youth Movement of Malaysia (ABIM). ABIM provided young Muslims with an avenue to pursue *dakwah*, or preaching and missionary activity (in Arabic, *dawa*), through universities and in the public sphere. The major consequence of this "rebirth," "reassertion," or "rediscovery" of Islam was that Islam came to be seen as the pillar of Malay identity. The *dakwah* sought to resist the pressures of modernization, reinvent and reconstruct tradition, express anti-imperialist sentiment and promote spiritual renewal. [7] External forces such as the Iranian Revolution and the *dakwah* movement in neighboring Indonesia breathed fresh life into Malaysia's *dakwah*, as did, around the same time, the appointment of Mahathir Mohamad to the post of prime minister in 1981. In the course of his 22-year rule he would oversee Malaysia's dramatic transformation from an agrarian backwater into an industrialized export-driven nation (Malaysia is the US's 10th largest trading partner). The era would also be scarred by a politically charged, sanctimonious battle for the soul of Islam.

Mahathir showed dedication to Islam from the outset of his premiership. In his first year, he established several committees to address law, education, economics, science and technology, as they pertain to "The Concept of Development in Islam." Other clear policy shifts included a declaration to restructure Malaysia's economic system according to Islamic principles, and the establishment of Islamic economic institutions like the Islamic Bank and Islamic Economic Foundation. He also brought ABIM's leader Anwar Ibrahim into UMNO, promised to bring the national legal system more in accord with Islamic law, and boosted Islamic content on radio and television. [8] No less important, he made it official policy not to allow economic development to happen at the expense of spiritual progress—but his failure to achieve this last point, and his increasingly desperate measures to compensate for the shortcoming, fomented the Islamic revival in a way that divided the country and has undermined Malaysia's "progressive" vision for itself.

By the mid-1990s it was becoming abundantly clear that capitalism was Mahathir's top priority and Islam was mostly merely a vehicle by which to sell his vision. Ostentatious mega-projects, including the world's tallest buildings, a hub-aspiring airport and one of the world's most expensive administrative capitals, became symbols of the new Malaysia. A large Malay middle-class had developed. Unemployment and poverty had reached single digits. Mahathir waxed ebulliently of a *bangsa* Malaysia (Malaysian race) and about Malaysia becoming a fully developed country by 2020. But many rural Malays felt they were not sharing in the country's success, and came to doubt how Islamic Mahathir's vision really was. The boom was seen to be disproportionately benefiting the elite. UMNO became synonymous with corruption. An intra-ethnic divide surfaced, in which a growing number of Malays saw Islam as the way to restore justice and accountability. But Mahathir and UMNO did not rise to the Islamic challenge. He dismissed allegations of rampant cronyism and nepotism. In so doing he helped pave the way for "radical" Islamic elements to vie for the heart and soul of Malaysian Islam. [9]

This process was compounded by Mahathir's tendency, particularly during political rough spots, to lambaste the West. He blamed the Asian economic crisis on a "cabal of Jews." He warned Malaysians that given a chance the West would re-colonize Malaysia. Whether it was through championing "Asian values" or his "Look East" policy, which sought to hold Asian countries like Japan up as models of how to progress, Mahathir repeatedly drew distinctions between people and societies during his rule. To confuse matters, his vision for Malaysia, with its skyscrapers, sky trams, hi-tech "cyber" cities and superhighways, had begun to look and feel eerily Western—so that Malaysians were being told to reject Westernization while their prime minister invested heavily in it.

These dual realities shaped the whole of Malaysia but left the deepest mark on the Malay community, for through Islam Malays professed to a system of values that the Islamic revival had taught them was often irreconcilable with Western notions of progress.

In the 1999 elections, a web of social, political and economic factors saw PAS win control of two northern states (or 34 percent of the popular vote, a 14 percent increase from its showing in the 1995 election). [10] The results reemphasized the pivotal role Islam often plays in Malaysian politics, and UMNO subsequently worked more aggressively to prove its credentials. Hence in 2001, shortly after the September 11 attacks, Mahathir declared Malaysia "an

Islamic state," intensifying a long-running battle between UMNO and PAS to out-Islamize each other (at least rhetorically). Meanwhile, Mahathir began to close *madrasahs* and jail "dissidents" suspected of preaching hate. Not a few in Washington deemed him an exemplary ally in its war against Islamic extremism. In response to the invasions of Afghanistan and Iraq, however, Mahathir's anti-Western rhetoric returned to the fore, and has continued with him into retirement.

Badawi and his brand of Islam are widely considered a welcome change from Mahathir's divisive and ostensibly contradictory style of rule. And yet Badawi's more tolerant approach may inadvertently be emboldening conservative government arms, like JAWI and the State Religious Councils. Badawi is not the micromanager that Mahathir was. Mahathir artfully centralized power during his rule. He had the clout to question these conservative authorities and often did, checking their power in the process. [11] Since the nightclub raid mentioned above, Badawi's government has issued new regulations to stem the power of JAWI. It has also pressed Malaysia's 14 states to adopt a uniform Islamic code. (Islam, according to the Malaysian Constitution, is a state as opposed to a federal matter.) But Badawi and his party have been reluctant to condemn the expanding reach of conservative Islam, lest they give PAS an opportunity to denounce UMNO as un-Islamic. UMNO's religious affairs specialists have avoided condemning the idea of an Islamic criminal code, instead maintaining that the time is not right. [12]

Islam Hadhari, it is hoped, will temper these developments. But is it sufficient to stem Malaysia's conservative tide? Most Islam Hadhari promotion efforts thus far have come through seminars, state run press and speeches by the prime minister. [13] The principles have not been put into law or formal practice. And Islam Hadhari may ultimately suffer because of its topdown approach. Grassroots movements, such as the Nahdlatul Ulama and Muhammadiya in Indonesia, each with memberships in the tens of millions, have proven more effective in promoting moderation in the Muslim world. [14] Indeed, most Malaysians would be hard-pressed to name but a couple of Islam Hadhari's 10 points. To the average Malaysian, Islam Hadhari remains a nebulous concept.

Some observers count Islam Hadhari's vagueness among its strengths—to be vague is to be inclusive. As a general concept Islam Hadhari makes for a legitimating canopy against crude efforts to Islamize Malaysia. It provides an accessible terminology to counter Muslims who claim that the only way to be a good Muslim is to support the full implementation of *sharia* law. [15]

Islam Hadhari does not seek to be a doctrinal equivalent to the prescriptive, ritualistic nature of fundamentalism. Rather, says Badawi, it is a practical approach consistent with the tenets of Islam. [16] According to Boston University's Robert Hefner, "Badawi is coming out and showing people in long gowns that you can welcome Americans and investment and still be a good Muslim." [17]

However, it could be argued that UMNO and Badawi's approach to governing has often been in conflict with the principles of Islam Hadhari. Among its ten aims are a just and trustworthy government, a free and independent people and mastery of knowledge. Badawi ran on a platform to stamp out corruption and under his leadership a few high-profile cases have been brought to court. But he has failed to curb the culture that breeds corruption. A veteran UMNO official called the party's 2004 elections the worst case of money politics in the party's history. Certainly undoing a practice that became endemic during the Mahathir era may take years to correct, but so far Badawi's campaign has been less aggressive than many had hoped. The Anti-Corruption Agency remains under the watch of the central government, while cases against several long serving UMNO officials widely suspected of corruption have stalled or been dropped. Press freedoms continue to suffer under Badawi, even on the Internet, which Mahathir said the government would not interfere with. Last year Badawi's government threatened to take action against a blogger after a contributor posted a statement to the blog equating Islam Hadhari and money politics with feces and urine.

Whether these developments embolden PAS and the opposition remains to be seen. At the least they have raised questions about Badawi's commitment to reform and whether Islam Hadhari is the genuine article.

Islamist Radicals

By most accounts Malaysia does not have a problem with Islamic radicalism. Indeed, Malaysia has not undergone a large-scale terrorist incident. But several of the September 11 hijackers met in Malaysia. The radical cleric Abu Bakar Bashir moved to Malaysia and lived there for 13 years beginning in 1985 to avoid more jail time in Indonesia. Hambali, believed to be the leader of the regional militant group Jemaah Islamiah, moved to Malaysia around the same time. He was believed to have lived there for ten years and toured the country, frequently recruiting young Muslims to join his struggle to establish a pan-Asian Islamic state, before being arrested two years ago in Thailand. Earlier this year, the suspected mastermind of separatist violence in southern Thailand, Abdul Rahman Ahmad, was arrested in Malaysia. Azahari Husin, a bomb expert who allegedly helped orchestrate a number of bombings in Indonesia before being killed in a shootout with Indonesian security forces in East Java in November, was Malaysian.

The Malaysian government often advertises that it has adopted a zero-tolerance policy toward extremists. But this does not answer how much influence these covert individuals and their ideologies appreciated before the government took notice of them—what has been their reach? Scant research has been done in this area. What is evident is that foreign Islamic entities have aggressively targeted Malaysia over the last several decades, using tapes, DVDs, pamphlets, the Internet, and formal and informal channels of education to promote forms of Islam that feed extremism. And most *jihadi* websites are stationed in the West or in Malaysia. [18] Malaysia's Islamic Affairs Division has successfully vetted some of this material, but it remains a daunting task. In 1996 the division "identified the existence of forty-seven deviationist groups, 15 of which were described as active and involving some 1,000 followers." [19]

Some government officials have acknowledged that Malaysian Muslims are vulnerable to outside influence because they lack "authentic" knowledge of Islam, and have urged them to follow government guidelines to avoid falling astray. Posing a challenge to this recommended path is the powerful and revered *ulama*, who have shown strong cultural and political affiliation with schools of Islamic thought from the Middle East, particularly Saudi Arabia. [20] Another challenge comes from the covert regional cooperation between militants and their sympathizers. Assistance to the Free Aceh Movement in Indonesia, for instance, has been known to come from conservative Muslim groups in Malaysia. [21]

With the September 11 attacks, Muslim governments were left to contemplate the substance of their own societies and the havoc their zealous elements might inspire. Malaysia was no exception. But outwardly it clung to its clean image, steadfastly reminding skeptics of its reputation as a "model Islamic democracy." "We are a very moderate Islamic country," Badawi frequently tells reporters. This ignores the fact that Islamic identity is not static, and has arguably been less so since September 11, as many Muslims view America's "war on terror" as anti-Muslim. Outrage over America's foreign policy has not spilled into Malaysia's streets as it has elsewhere, but the restraint cannot be equated with a lack of sympathy. A public diplomacy official with the US government said anti-Americanism is more entrenched in Malaysia than in Indonesia. And whereas the US's post-tsunami relief efforts improved America's public approval rating in Indonesia and other Muslim nations, no such change occurred in Malaysia.

Islam Hadhari is then, indirectly at least, a concession that Islam in Malaysia needs fixing. As a senior UMNO official noted, "The growing conservatism that we are seeing is the thin end of the wedge. If left unchallenged, it will germinate into a radical and reactionary force that rejects modernity, generates intolerance and imprisons the minds of Muslims behind the bars of dogma and blind imitation." [22]

Beneath the tip of the iceberg he speaks of is the recent news that 60,000 Malaysian graduates, most of them Malay, are unemployed, due largely to a lack of pertinent experience and poor English and communication skills. This makes Islam Hadhari, with its emphasis on technology, knowledge, skills acquisition and achievement, seem apt indeed. But if it doesn't deliver it is likely to be seen as yet another government program designed to co-opt Islam for political gain—a charge PAS is already making.

Where, however, Islam Hadhari may ultimately alienate Muslim voters looking for a greater commitment to Islam, such "shortcomings" may in fact prove to be a strong selling point with non-Muslims. This could, assuming a large chunk of Muslims aren't abandoned in the process, significantly strengthen UMNO and in turn neutralize the political power of radical elements. In a word, Islam Hadhari will need strong Muslim support to be realized. But realization is not necessary for Islam Hadhari to be politically effective.

Regarding the prospect of substantial numbers of Malays abandoning UMNO, moderation has long been a hallmark of Malaysian Islam. But Malaysia is a racially charged society where politicians have used race and religion for political gain. Moreover, the tug of the borderless brotherhood that Islam calls for is strong here, evinced during the *dakwah* revival and more recently in reaction to developments in Palestine and Iraq. State-run media, Internet sites and Arab media pandering to indignation and victim-consciousness have fueled these concerns. (In June the foreign news editor of a Malaysian TV station told me she tends to select footage of the Iraq war that in effect paints Muslims as victims and Western powers as perpetrators, in part to compensate for perceived bias of Western news giants like CNN.) Anger and self-victimization have not consumed Malaysia as they have other Muslim countries. Obviously, Malaysian authorities want to extend that trend, and they see Islam Hadhari as a vehicle by which to do so. As the UMNO-controlled *New Straits Times* reported in July, "[Islam Hadhari] aims to ... enable Muslims to excel and be a distinctive and glorious group."

Malaysia's Foreign Minister Syed Hamid Albar has said Islam Hadhari will help Muslim and non-Muslim countries communicate better and avert a "clash of civilizations." He said Organization of the Islamic Conference (OIC) countries have acknowledged the role that Islam Hadhari could play to correct the image of Islam around the world. [23] One assumes here that Syed expects Islam's image to improve through the spread of moderate forms of Islam like Islam Hadhari and not just through greater promotion of their mere existence. It is the prospect of the former that draws Western officials like Mrs Hughes and US Deputy Secretary of State Robert Zoellick to Islam Hadhari. As the latter said in May 2005, "I had a chance to talk a little about [Islam Hadhari] with the Prime Minister because we think the Malaysian experience is one that is very important—the tolerance, the moderate Muslim majority country, the development of democracy, the rule of law here...we talked about ways in which, perhaps, the government here could share some of its experience with the Iraqis as well as helping the new Palestinian Authority." The US sees Islam Hadhari as a useful resource in combating Islamic extremism and, correspondingly, may prove willing to help promote it, though no formal arrangements have yet been announced.

How great an impact is Islam Hadhari likely to have on other Muslim countries? Popular websites like Islamonline.net have covered it, and Malaysian officials claim that Islam Hadhari continually receives a warm response from Muslims around the world. [24] There is, though, little evidence to suggest that it is actually attracting support in other Muslim countries—even in neighboring Indonesia and the Philippines, where it seems Islam Hadhari would be most attractive, given the rather flexible interpretations of the faith in those countries. Malaysia is recognized in the Muslim world for its economic growth and social stability. But the influence of Malaysian Islam has been minimal. It is highly political and polarized, and is seen to lack the depth and "authenticity" of strains found elsewhere. If there is a country in the region that could be described as having clout in the larger Muslim world it would be Indonesia, where Islamic schools of thought are more abundant and diverse and there is a rich intellectual tradition. Malaysian Muslims tend to seek inspiration from Indonesia, not vice versa, and Islam Hadhari does not appear to have changed the fact: it has received scant attention in the Indonesian media, chat rooms and mailing lists, and among Indonesian Muslim groups. [25] To take off in Indonesia it will probably need key political support. This is unlikely to come from the ruling government, as the national ideology in Indonesia is secular; Islam does play a political role in Indonesia, and Islamic groups have criticized the government for seemingly non-Islamic behavior, but presidents do their best to appear above sectarian differences. [26] Moving beyond Indonesia, Islam Hadhari's influence may be hindered by the simple fact that different countries have different sets of challenges. Then again, few Muslim governments have formulated let alone articulated a plan to reconcile modernity with the Islamic faith, and fewer still have shown the determination to lead by example, as Malaysia has.

First published February 16, 2006
(ARTICLES, *Current Trends in Islamist Ideology*, Vol. 3)

1 Abdullah, Kamarulnizam (2003) *The Politics of Islam in Contemporary Malaysia*, Bangi, Malaysia: Penerbit, p. 117

2 Interview with Robert. W. Hefner, Associate Director of the Institute on Culture, Religion and World Affairs, Boston University

3 *International Herald Tribune*, May 12, 2005

4 *The American Muslim*, January-March 2005 issue

5 Human Rights Watch Report, July 21, 2005

6 Abdullah, Kamarulnizam (2003) *The Politics of Islam in Contemporary Malaysia*, Bangi, Malaysia: Penerbit, p. 216

7 Hefner, Robert W. and Patricia Horvatich (1997) *Islam in an Era of Nation States*, "Identity Construction, Nation Formation, and Islamic Revivalism in Malaysia" by Shamsul A.B., United States: University of Hawai'i Press, p. 211

8 Mutalib, Hussin (1993) *Islam in Malaysia: From Revivalism to Islamic State?*, Singapore: Singapore University Press, pp. 30-31

9 Abdullah, Kamarulnizam (2003) *The Politics of Islam in Contemporary Malaysia*, Bangi, Malaysia: Penerbit, p. 190

10 Gomez, Terence (2004) *The State of Malaysia: Ethnicity, Equity and Reform*, "Introduction: politics, business and ethnicity in Malaysia: a atate in transition?" London and New York: RoutledgeCurzon

11 Hilley, John (2001) *Malaysia: Mahathirism, Hegemony and the New Opposition*, London and New York: Zed Books, p. 191

12 *Economist*, June 2, 2005

13 Interview with Dr Patricia Martinez, head of the Intercultural Studies Research at the Asia-Europe Institue of the University of Malaya

14 *New Statesman*, September 13, 2004

15 Interview with Robert. W. Hefner, Associate Director of the Institute on Culture, Religion and World Affairs, Boston University

16 IslamOnline.net, March 3, 2005

17 Interview with Robert. W. Hefner, Associate Director of the Institute on Culture, Religion and World Affairs, Boston University

18 Roy, Olivier (2004) *Globalized Islam: The Search for a New Ummah*, New York: Columbia University Press, p. 312

19 Nair, Shanti (1997) *Islam in Malaysian Foreign Policy*, New York: Routledge, p. 152

20 Nair, Shanti (1997) *Islam in Malaysian Foreign Policy*, New York: Routledge, p. 109

21 *Asiaweek*, March 2, 2001

22 *Time*, March 10, 2003

23 *New Straits Times*, July 19, 2005

24 *New Straits Times*, July 10, 2005

25 Interview with R. William Liddle, Professor of Political Science, The Ohio State University

26 Interview with R. William Liddle, Professor of Political Science, The Ohio State University

Malaysia's Islamists Soften the Line

Shortly after Malaysia's hardline opposition Islamic party, Parti Islam SeMalaysia (PAS), lost handily to the long-ruling conservative United Malays National Organization (UMNO) in last March's parliamentary elections, PAS officials conceded that the party's plans to implement an Islamic state in a country where Muslims make up but 55% of the population may have alienated voters, and some sort of revised approach would be paramount to the party's survival.

Last week was the closest the party came to acting on this admittance, when PAS's Youth Chief Salahuddin Ayub announced that PAS will become more flexible in its vision of creating an Islamic state.

The move is a gambit to find common ground with the two other main opposition parties, and leaders of at least one, the People's Justice Party (PKR), welcome the move. "We are in negotiations with PAS and almost at the stage of creating an agreement of various platforms," said PKR vice president Syed Husin Ali.

Ali and PAS leaders told *Asia Times Online* that the parties will re-emphasize the issues that led the opposition to unexpected success in the 1999 elections: namely good governance, human rights, free speech, and fighting corruption and moral decay. More broadly, they plan to uphold the democratic-principled Malaysian constitution, which UMNO has overstepped over the years to introduce various forms of oppressive legislation.

But what PAS and PKR, which together make up the opposition front Barisan Alternatif (BA), are viewing as the path to a bright future strikes others as an unimaginative dead-end reversion to a formula that has, in the six years since the last time BA used it, successfully been absorbed by UMNO. Prime Minister Abdullah Badawi's promise to clean up the corruption, cronyism, and abuse of power that flourished under his long-ruling predecessor Mahathir Mohamad, and his promotion of Islam Hadhari (Civilizational Islam), led UMNO to an overwhelming public mandate in last March's elections.

By trying to restake its claim to progressive reform using the 1999 formula, the BA will have to depend on UMNO to falter. And while Abdullah has been slow to deliver on his promises—Malaysia's ranking in Transparency International's Corruption Perceptions Index actually dropped two spots, to 39, in the year since Abdullah took office—the opposition hardly seems primed to capitalize on this fact.

"A lot of political parties are talking about reinvention," said Khoo Kay Peng of the Sedar Institute, an independent think-tank. "But unfortunately, they come back to the same things" in the same way.

PAS, for one, plans to change the tone of its vision, not the content. "The Islamic state is still our goal in terms of strategy and direction," said PAS central committee member Syed Azman. Rhetoric rather than substance is at the heart of the alteration, and that's unlikely to win the trust of most Malaysians.

Talking with opposition leaders, one senses a touch of despondency setting in and, correspondingly, a creeping fatalism. In authoritarian Malaysia, it's not hard to see why. The opposition is all but denied space in the state-regulated media, which UMNO has milked to brand the opposition as a force of chaos and destruction. The UMNO elite also have routinely altered election regulations to suit their political agendas. And political parties must secure (and are often denied) permits to hold rallies.

Historically, opposition parties have scarcely been able to make inroads in the political landscape in Malaysia. In the few instances in which they have, as in 1999 when PAS won the northern state of Terengganu, UMNO has been known to withhold state funds, making it difficult for the parties to deliver on their promises. Getting battered in March, in elections allegedly fraught with money politics and voter fraud, was hardly reason for optimism in the opposition camp.

But despite these obstacles, said Khoo, "There's too much talk and calculating risk in the opposition, and not enough doing, and building the credibility to change perception."

Added Universiti Kebangsaan Malaysia professor of sociology and development Abdul Rahman Embong, "The situation doesn't seem to be moving into something more forward-looking, into what will rally people."

Last September the opposition got what many thought was the jolt it needed. It was then that former deputy premier and PKR founder Anwar Ibrahim was acquitted after spending six years in prison on what many believe were charges invented by the UMNO elite to thwart his political ambitions. Anwar, barred from formally entering politics until 2008, has signed on as PKR adviser and is thought to be the party's heir apparent (assuming he doesn't rejoin UMNO). He has yet to espouse a concrete political agenda, however.

The slivers he does serve up closely echo his 1999 rhetoric, despite Malaysia's new set of challenges in the time that's lapsed. This is hardly warming the *rakyat* (citizens) to the opposition. Anwar, for instance, according to PAS youth chief Ayub as reported by local media, supports adopting the 1999 formula.

But what are the viable alternatives? Even the most percipient pundits here are short on answers. They don't suggest abandoning the core values of the 1999 manifesto; their point, though, is that if the opposition is to be successful it must be more savvy and aggressive in getting its message across—and that will require adopting more innovative thinking. Turning more to text messaging to circumvent the government's press machine, as the opposition had done prior to the March elections, is unlikely to lead very far. Nor is PKR's reshuffling of several key posts last weekend. "It's the same faces, same mindset," quipped one observer.

PAS's Azman said more substantive changes are likely in the works; PAS's annual meeting is in June. However, he discounted the possibility of a major shakeup in the party leadership. And yet that's what some people think will be necessary for PAS to convince the public that human rights, equality and justice are as integral to the party's goals as an Islamic state. As long as PAS fails to do so, it will most likely hinder the ambitions of other parties that join it in an alliance; they will be guilty by association. The Chinese-based Democratic Action Party (DAP) recognizes this. It broke from the BA in 2001 when PAS started ratcheting up its Islamic-state rhetoric. It is now PAS's hope that by toning down its Islamic-state agenda it can sublate DAP back into the coalition.

But DAP secretary general Lim Guan Eng told *Asia Times Online* that's unlikely, even if PAS revises its stance. "They've said they would tone it down in the past, but that doesn't work," Lim said. "PAS must really leave that past behind."

Lim said DAP will press forward with its democratic-reform agenda without being tempted into another marriage of convenience with PAS. But when asked how, specifically, the party planned to do this, he intimated that no bold strategies are on the near horizon. "We need to continue to stress our own ideals and principles," he said.

First published January 29, 2005 (*Asia Times*)

* * *

The Year of the Rat

If there's one thing the Malaysian government wants visitors to know, it's that a modern, multiethnic harmonious society radiates out from its gleaming capital of Kuala Lumpur. It doesn't take long for guests to get the message. It's unfurled on huge banners in the futuristic, hub-aspiring airport that declare, "One legacy. One destiny" and depict children of the three main races (Malay, Chinese and Indian) holding hands. It comes at comes at you in videos showing ethnic dancers twirling with glee on the air-rail train into town. It's on a wall facing the country's most recognizable symbol of modernity, the twin Petronas Towers: "In celebration of independence, unity, and harmony." And it's in every tourist brochure.

To judge from Malaysia's elections in early March, however, tourist brochures touting racialharmony might not be reaching the audience that most needs to hear the message: Malaysians themselves. Race relations in Malaysia have always been touchy and have occasionally flared into the open. Race riots in 1969 left some 200 people dead when Chinese and Malays clashed in the streets of the capital. The riots scared the wits out of the ruling elite, which moved to tamp down similar displays for these past three decades. But problems have increasingly come back into the open since Mahathir Mohamad, Malaysia's longest-reigning political capo— perhaps best known in the West for his xenophobic and anti-Semitic rants—stepped down in 2002. Malay authorities are aware of the problem, but until recently seemed more concerned about appearances than about the underlying realities that gave rise to them. As Deputy Prime Minister Najib Razak told me in his sprawling office, when I mentioned that some Malaysian friends have confided in me an astonishing degree of contempt for their countrymen of a different race, "That's OK, as long as it is being said within the four walls [of each community]."

Indeed, Malaysians are remarkable in their ability to keep a lid on their resentment. But the pot is simmering, and the lid can't be kept on forever.

Chinese Malaysians worry increasingly about the country's creeping Islamization, and not without reason. According to a 2006 survey, 43 percent of Malays would like to see Malaysia become more Islamic. (All Malays are Muslim according to the constitution, thus Islam here is racialized.) Non-Malay female police officers must now wear the headscarves at official events. Muslim snoop squads, in search of *khalwat* (close proximity between unmarried Muslims of the opposite sex), have invaded the privacy of non-Muslims. Najib last year declared Malaysia an "Islamic State," even though 40 percent of the population is non-Muslim and the country's constitution is secular. The 12-year-old administrative capital of Putrajaya is replete with onion-shaped domes and Moorish bridges. The Persian-inspired Putra Mosque sits next to the Prime Minister's office and is arguably the administrative capital's most iden-tifiable landmark. Indian and Chinese temples are conspicuously absent. The same goes for the area around the Petronas Towers in Kuala Lumpur. A mosque nestled beside an adjoining park broadcasts its Friday prayer via intercom, at volumes loud enough for patrons at the Towers' trendy cafes to hear.

As a result of all this, some 70,000 Malaysians, mostly Chinese, have given up their citizenship in the past twenty years. Still more who have retained their citizenship prefer to live and work abroad. Some 90 percent of Chinese Malaysians now attend Chinese-language schools, finding the public Malay schools too Islamic for comfort. Malays, in turn, see the Chinese pulling inward, and this has accentuated their private accusations that the Chinese are insular, exploitative and greedy—intent on advancing their community's interests above those of the nation. Why, if they are marginalized, do Chinese control most of the economy? (And indeed, the Chinese make up 25 percent of the population and control up to 60 percent of the economy.)

All of these facts served as a preface to Malaysia's latest election season, and the results of the March elections suggest that resentments are not only growing but are also growing more political in expression. Malaysia's Indian community seized the early headlines with some 10,000 Indians rallying in November against the marginalization of the Indian community at the hands of an entrenched Malay leadership.

But it's the Chinese and Malays whose relationship is most strained, as the elections bore out. Chinese and Malays voted in significant numbers for opposition parties, helping to deny the governing National Front coalition (BN) a twothirds parliamentary majority for the first time since 1969 and quadrupling the opposition's foothold in parliament. So goes the Year of the Rat thus far in Malaysia. Malays who defected voted primarily for the Islamist Pan-Malaysian Islamic Party (PAS), and Chinese voted for the Chinesebased Democratic Action Party (DAP). The two parties were once part of an opposition coalition, though DAP has since refused to join hands with PAS until it drops its goal of turning Malaysia into an Islamic state. PAS backed away from the call in the lead-up to the March elections, it having been roundly rejected by non-Muslims and Malays alike in the 2004 elections. Responding to the opposition parties' strong showing in the election, DAP's Secretary General Lim Guan Eng said he hopes that PAS and DAP can work together despite their deep ideological differences.

One might think that tensions between ruling Malays and diaspora Chinese would spill over to affect state-to-state relations between Malaysia and China. Oddly enough, they haven't—at least not yet. The Malay-led government's relations with China are healthy, while the Malay community's opinions of the mainland are positive. Malaysia and China's national oil companies, Petronas and

China National Petroleum Corporation, respectively, are producing oil in Sudan. The two countries are discussing development of the South China Sea, while Prime Minister Abdullah Ahmad Badawi has expressed his intent to deepen cooperation on several fronts, including trade and security.

Nonetheless, Malaysian and Chinese interests do not fully converge. China's rise as a manufacturing hub has attracted foreign direct investment at Malaysia's expense. But Malaysia is managing to tap into rising demand in China for palm oil, rubber and electronics, and Malaysian companies are pursuing constructionand service projects in China, as well. A 2006 survey by Grant Thornton of 7,000 medium and large businesses found that 22 percent of Malaysian companies saw sales increase because of growing demand from China. The future could be even brighter for Malaysia in this regard, since 60 percent of China's exports derive from foreign companies operating in China, and Malaysian Chinese are well placed to do business in China. Malaysian finance graduates and consultants with Chinese language skills are also finding that they can earn up to three times as much in China as they can in Malaysia, and most of their earnings come back to Malaysia in one way or another.

In addition, Malaysia's governmentlinked companies, which are usually run by and employ a large number of Malays, are also making inroads in China. Petronas, for instance, signed a 25-year deal worth $25 billion with China to provide liquefied natural gas starting in 2009—the largest trade deal ever between the two countries. Chinese tourists to Malaysia are also on the rise: Tourist arrivals from China hit 688,209 in 2007, just about double the total of 2006.

The bilateral relationship is not without some tension, however. When a video surfaced in late 2005 showing what appeared to be a Chinese national performing "nude squats" as part of a strip-search by Malaysian police, the Chinese Foreign Ministry filed an official protest. Some local Chinese were incensed as well, interpreting the episode as proof of anti-Chinese bias within Malay-led agencies like the police. It turned out that the woman in the video was not a Chinese national but Malaysian—and an ethnic Malay at that. More consequential, as China lures foreign direct investment away from Southeast Asia, Malaysia is finding it harder to climb the value-added ladder. Its science and engineering talent is under-nurtured, and research and development efforts are not taking off as envisioned. Up to 90 percent of state-led information and communications technology startups have gone under, according to the Technopreneur Association of Malaysia, and many other anticipated startups have chosen to set up shop elsewhere in Asia.

Prime Minister Abdullah has leveraged the state-controlled media here to assure Malaysians that China is not a threat to Malaysia's economy, but concern about Malaysia's longterm economic fitness is growing among the business and political elite. That anxiety has not targeted mainland Chinese despite the fact that Malays generally resent the Chinese disapora in their own country and express no regrets about having expelled majority-Chinese Singapore from Malaysia in 1965, less than two years after independence.

Malay attitudes toward China remain positive for another reason, as well: a lack of security anxiety, thanks to a balance between US and Chinese positions in Southeast Asia. The matter is rather complex, however, and it may not last.

On the one hand, Malaysia enjoys close defense and economic ties with the United States. The US military presence in Southeast Asia helps ensure regional stability and safe travel through the Strait of Malacca, through which a third of the world's oil passes. The United States is Malaysia's number one trading partner, receiving 20 percent of Malaysia's exports in 2005 and accounting for 20 percent of Malaysia's FDI from 2000–05. But as Foreign Minister Syed Hamid explained last year, Malaysia is trying not to align itself too closely with the United States, hence a proposed pipeline that would traverse northern Malaysia, providing an alternative route for Mideast oil headed for East Asia, particularly China. Since such oil currently passes through the Strait of Malacca and around the tip of Singapore, Malaysia is clearly trying to sell the pipeline as an insurance policy to both Tehran and Beijing, who fear the US Navy could disrupt their economies by blockading the Strait at a time of tension or war.

Beyond security and economics, there is a cultural balance of sorts between the United States and China in the eyes of most Malays. American cultural influence in Malaysia is pronounced. On any given night at clubs around the capital, local musicians—Chinese and Indian as well as Malay—can be found aping American pop acts. Clothing trends mirror those in the United States, too. Most Malaysians eagerly seek out Hollywood fare, and Kentucky Fried Chicken is a sort of religion here. At the same time, anti-Americanism among Malays runs deeper here than anywhere in Southeast Asia. Most Malays have been raised on a steady diet of anti-Americanism, whether fed by the rants of Mahathir during his 22-year rule, the state-run media or religious teachers. The Bush era has done little to challenge these crude summations; nor has the country's increasingly conservative brand of Islam. Anti-Semitic literature, notably Henry Ford's *The International Jew*, are prominently displayed by major booksellers. Party officials even handed out free copies of the book at Mahathir's last speech as party President in 2003. This sort of thing makes most Chinese and Indians in Malaysia very uneasy.

Meanwhile, Malaysia's Malay-dominated government resents US diplomats and Western journalists drawing attention to the country's dismal human rights record. The Abdullah Administration has harassed bloggers, crushed street demonstrations with tear gas and water cannons, rejected the notion of an interfaith commission, and placed leaders of the Hindu Rights Action Force under the Internal Security Act, which allows for detention without trial. In late January, dozens of peaceful anti-inflation demonstrators near the Petronas Towers were hauled away in police trucks. Washington's occasional calls for justice are resented because they draw attention to the actual substance of Malaysian "democracy," and because they are seen as a threat to Malay political supremacy.

Some Malays still carp about a speech Al Gore gave here a decade ago in which he applauded Malaysian citizens taking to the street to protest official abuses. All this helps explain the findings of a recent poll in which 70 percent of Malay respondents held favorable views of China while 86 percent held unfavorable views of the United States. After all, China never hectors Malaysia about human rights, and more important, it evinces less concern with militant Islam than the United States. Malaysian Muslims, who tend to view the War on Terror as a war against Islam, appreciate the difference. (Several Chinese Malaysians, on the other hand, have told me that they see Bush's War on Terror as a necessary check against fundamentalist proponents of Muslim domination. One cab driver reminded me that Malaysia's minorities live with the imposition of Muslim values every day of their lives.)

There can be no doubt that, as time passes, the present Malay ruling elite has become more ethnically and religiously chauvinist. Last summer the Prime Minister's son-in-law, Khairy Jamaluddin, sought to discredit opposition leader Anwar Ibrahim, who stands for greater democracy and an end to race-based politics, by calling him "a traitor of the Malay cause." As proof, Khairy claimed that Anwar, Mahathir's estranged the former Deputy Prime Minister, is "a puppet of the United States and the Jews."

Chinese Malaysians are increasingly exasperated with use of the race card at the expense of national unity. That explains to a considerable degree how they voted in March. But the truth is that Chinese Malaysians have not always put their best foot forward over the years. I often encounter Chinese who would rather converse in

English than in Malay, the national language. Many are quick to blame Malays for racial animosity, but when I ask them what the Chinese community could do to improve relations, they are often at a loss for words. As most Malays' chauvinism grows, most Chinese react not by reaching out, but by becoming more insular.

So far, these growing tensions have not affected the larger stakes. The goodwill Malays and Chinese lack for each other within Malaysia is spent instead on the People's Republic of China, for the time being. But it is hard to believe that a wealthier and more assertive China will turn a blind eye to future Malay discrimination, and perhaps violence, against its Chinese diaspora community. The US government will certainly not be available as a balancer in such a circumstance; no US administration will defend blatant anti-Chinese prejudice by Malays, especially if it comes tinged with pogromlike anti-Semitic overtones. Indeed, in such a circumstance the United States and China (as well as Singapore) would share an important interest.

First published May/June 2008 (*American Interest* Vol III No 5)

GEOPOLITICS

Malaysia's Axis Mysteriously Shifting

When Abdullah Badawi became Malaysia's prime minister in 2003, many thought the mild-mannered leader would take a more moderate approach to international relations than his prickly predecessor Mahathir Mohamad, who often locked diplomatic horns with the United States and other Western countries.

But a string of scandals and crimes with international dimensions, some even linked to Abdullah's family members, have put his government's relations with Washington on an uncomfortable footing.

US authorities last month arrested and charged Pakistani national Jilani Humayun for his alleged role in shipping contraband military goods to Malaysia, from where they were re-exported to Iran. He was also charged with conspiracy to commit money-laundering and mail fraud. The sensitive dual-use hardware, which was funneled through an as yet unnamed Malaysian company, included parts for F-5 and F-14 fighter jets and Chinook helicopters.

In April the US imposed sanctions on 14 companies, individuals and government agencies it accused of dealing in advanced weapon technology with Iran or Syria. Two of the companies listed were Malaysian, the Challenger Corp and Target Airfreight.

Moreover, a federal jury in New York last year convicted Singaporean businessman Ernest Koh Chong Tek of smuggling dual-use US military parts to Malaysia for transshipment to Iran's military—a violation of the 1995 embargo the US placed on all exports and re-exports of commodities to Iran without approval by the US Office of Foreign Asset Control. He was also charged with laundering millions of dollars through his Singapore bank accounts in the smuggling scheme.

The US and Iran are currently at diplomatic loggerheads over Tehran's nuclear program, and Washington has frequently accused Iran's military of arming radical Muslim militias in the Middle East, including the Lebanon-based Hezbollah as well as Iraqi insurgents who have targeted US troops. However, at least on the surface, bilateral relations with Malaysia remain cordial.

US officials who spoke with *Asia Times Online* would not comment on the investigations involving Malaysia on the grounds that they involve sensitive intelligence information. And so far there is no evidence to link recent violations of the US embargo directly to Abdullah. Yet security analysts say the recent incidents have put the crucial bilateral relationship on edge.

"I am absolutely sure that the US is watching these developments closely and pressing hard on Malaysia behind the scenes," said Tim Huxley of the Singapore-based International Institute of Strategic Studies.

The US is Malaysia's largest foreign investor, and the two sides are negotiating a wide-ranging free-trade agreement. Kuala Lumpur relies heavily on the United States' military presence to maintain the region's balance of power, particularly vis-a-vis its heavily armed neighbor Singapore. At the same time, Malaysia has been a key ally to the US administration's "global war on terror" in the region.

"Malaysia needs the US and doesn't want to do anything that will tilt the US toward Singapore, Thailand and Indonesia," said Richard Bitzinger, a security specialist at the S Rajaratnam School of International Studies in Singapore. "Both sides will be willing to accept some [security] deficiencies, if they remain at low levels."

Family matters

Yet the recent security lapses have been traced to the highest echelons of Malaysia's business and political elite, raising questions about Abdullah's underlying foreign-policy objectives. There are still huge question marks surrounding the 2004 proliferation case involving Scomi, a company owned by Abdullah's son Kamaluddin, which was allegedly involved in supplying dual-use technology to Libya's clandestine nuclear-weapons program.

Buhary Syed Abu Tahir, a Sri Lankan national with Malaysian permanent residency, sat with Kamaluddin on the board of Scomi-linked company Kaspadu. Buhary negotiated the controversial contract, which had Scomi Precision Engineering build components for centrifuges that were destined for use in Libya's nuclear program. Scomi Group had since acknowledged that its subsidiary Scomi Precision filled a contract negotiated by Buhary to supply machine parts to Libya.

Documents obtained by the Associated Press reveal that Buhary was the chief financial officer of Pakistani nuclear scientist Abdul Qadeer Khan's underground nuclear-proliferation network. How he was able to forge such high-powered alliances with Malaysia's political elite is a question that remains unanswered. When the scandal broke, Abdullah said Buhary would remain free because there was no evidence of wrongdoing.

Months later, in May 2004, Buhary was arrested under Malaysia's Internal Security Act (ISA), which allows indefinite detention without trial. Opposition leaders at the time accused Abdullah of detaining Buhary under the ISA rather than pursuing standard criminal procedures lest Kamaluddin be implicated. Now, Buhary's whereabouts are unclear.

Amir Izyanias, assistant secretary of the government-sanctioned Human Rights Commission, says his staff made contact with Buhary on July 23 at Malaysia's Kemunting Prison, where many ISA detainees are held. However, an official with the Department of

Islamic Development said Buhary is not on his list of detainees.

This all comes on top of the 2005 independent inquiry into the United Nations oil-for-food scandal in Iraq, which cleared Abdullah of involvement but implicated two of his relatives. Abdullah's sister-in-law Noor Asiah Mahmood and her ex-husband Faek Amad Sareef were found to have paid US$10 million through their Mastek company, one of the largest payments among the the more than 2,200 companies implicated in the scandal.

The Iraq Survey Group, which the US set up to investigate weapons in Iraq, listed "Abdullah Badawi" on its names of recipients of the oil-for-food scam though did not clarify whether this was Malaysia's prime minister. Abdullah has admitted to helping Malaysian business people to take part in the UN oil-for-food program, but said at the time the accusations surfaced that he was not personally involved. He has said he merely wrote letters supporting their bid in the program, but thereafter didn't follow up what happened to their bids.

Diversified diplomacy

None of these scandals, of course, were necessarily state-sanctioned. Yet they have notably come at a time when Malaysia's governing elite has shown resistance to democratic reform, clean governance and cultural pluralism, while strengthening ties with non-democratic states like Iran, Sudan and Russia.

It's apparently all part of a larger foreign-policy shift, which Foreign Minister Syed Hamid Albar said in May would help Malaysia "avoid being too dependent on one particular segment" of the global economy—read by some as a reference to the US, which currently receives nearly 16% of Malaysia's exports.

Abdullah's son-in-law Khairy Jamaluddin this month attempted to silence an opposition leader by labeling him "a puppet of the United States and the Jews." Meanwhile, Abdullah's information chief and other ruling United Malays National Organization

(UMNO) elites have recently moved to intimidate bloggers and Web portals for exposing high-level government corruption, while courts have handed down hardline Islamic legal interpretations by denying several Muslims the right to change their religion.

Foreign Minister Syed recently dismissed a US State Department report that cited Malaysia's "failure to show satisfactory progress in combating trafficking in persons." Elsewhere Syed has said that Malaysia and Iran hold "identical views" on a range of global issues, including Iran's right to develop a peaceful nuclear program.

Kuala Lumpur is also playing a key role in integrating Iran into the Asian economy at a time Washington is attempting to isolate that country economically. Last year Syed urged member countries of the Organization of Islamic Conference, in line with Iran's policy, to consider sending weapons to Hezbollah.

To be sure, it could all be politics as usual. Amid Malaysia's ethnic- and religious-tinged political landscape, UMNO politicians are wont to pander to Muslim sentiment, while cooperating with the US and West behind the scenes. Even as former strongman Mahathir blustered on about US-led neo-colonialism and protecting Malaysia's national sovereignty, he simultaneously forged close military ties with the US.

For instance, the two sides in 1994 signed an acquisitions and cross-servicing agreement that allows US Navy ships to visit Malaysian ports for repair and replenishment. The contract was most recently renewed in 2005, during Abdullah's tenure. Each year, US Special Forces train at Malaysia's jungle-warfare school, and bilateral military-to-military cooperation is growing rather than diminishing. And the administration of US President George W Bush has generally applauded Malaysia's security and counter-terrorism efforts.

Muted complaints

Nevertheless, some quarters are growing more wary of Malaysia's geopolitical role.

"The UK has become more circumspect of dealing with Malaysian leadership," said Alexander Neill, head of the Asia Security Program at the London-based Royal United Services Institute for Defense and Security Studies. He said in particular the recent zealously Islamic statements by senior Malaysian leaders "are problematic to a counter-terrorism policy."

There are other geopolitical differences. For instance, while the US and other Western governments fret about the unfolding genocide in Sudan, Malaysia has recently invested heavily in the regime's petroleum resources. Abdullah also cemented military and energy ties with Russia during a visit there in June, according to Foreign Ministry Parliamentary Secretary Ahmad Shabery Cheek. Some have suggested that that overture could be designed to counterbalance the close economic and military ties the US shares with Malaysian neighbor and rival Singapore. Ahmad has denied that Malaysia is in any way becoming a proxy for Russian influence in the Southeast Asian region. While the US aims to build an international consensus in dissuading Iran from pursuing a nuclear-weapons program, Malaysia has recently strengthened ties to the Islamic Republic, including recent negotiations toward a $16 billion oil deal. Malaysia is also constructing a $7 billion oil pipeline that will traverse the north of Malaysia, which industry analysts say will help Tehran deliver more oil to East Asia. The National Iranian Oil Company reportedly has a 30% stake in the joint-venture project, though the Malaysian government has failed to disclose specific details of the deal.

Those opaque dealings have predictably caused a stir in Washington. James Keith, the US ambassador-designate to Malaysia, who is to begin his posting in Kuala Lumpur next month, said at his Senate confirmation hearing in May that he would "emphasize that we are vigorously opposed to business as usual with Iran."

He also said investment ties "offer great promise for further development" and that while he would work to nurture them, as well as military and security cooperation, he stressed, "It will be critical ... for my country team and for me to speak forthrightly about our commitment to fundamental values, including those enunciated in the UN's Universal Declaration of Human Rights."

US security and embassy officials here declined to comment on how the recent string of security lapses involving Malaysia have affected bilateral relations and what steps if any are being taken to prevent future misunderstandings. The two sides last year signed a treaty on mutual legal assistance covering a broad range of criminal matters, including evidence and witness sharing, though it's still unclear whether the pact has actually been ratified by Malaysia.

But that doesn't resolve the fact that US fighter-aircraft parts are, according to Koh during a secretly recorded conversation revealed in a US Justice Department press release, were regularly exported to Malaysia en route to Iran. Security analysts say one reason arms proliferators may gravitate toward Malaysia is that it does not have a comprehensive and specific law on export controls. According to the International Institute for Strategic Studies, "Malaysia lists only 'radioactive and nuclear material, substances and irradiating apparatus' for controls, and not dual-use items."

Malaysia does not have any verification system in place to ensure that exported goods are used for their stated end use or truly sent to their listed end users. Officials with the Malaysian police, Defense Ministry, Internal Security Ministry, Foreign Affairs Ministry and International Trade Ministry did not respond to *Asia Times Online*'s requests to discuss how the government is acting to address these regulatory loopholes. Yet until they are closed, US-Malaysian relations will continue to be tinged with mutual suspicion.

First published August 28, 2007 (Asia Times)

GRAND PLANS

Branding Itself Globally

Social, economic, religious, and political trends since this story ran have undermined Malaysia's attempts to brand itself.

When US-based architect Cesar Pelli was brainstorming his plans for what would become Malaysia's most recognizable landmark, the towering twin Petronas Towers, then Malaysian Prime Minister Mahathir Mohamad required one thing of him: that the building be Malaysian.

"What do you mean by Malaysian?" Pelli reportedly asked.

"We don't know," was the reply.

What resulted, a shimmering polygonal pattern based on Islamic design, hardly captures the essence of multi-ethnic Malaysia.

But then, contrary to Mahathir's request, what really mattered is that the design wowed the world.

Over the past decade, until Mahathir's retirement last year, wowing became Malaysia's raison d'etre, with eye-catching, high-tech-themed megaprojects sprouting almost as fast as banana trees do here.

The logic: that the push would define Malaysia.

But under the more reflective leadership of Prime Minister Abdullah Badawi, there's a growing consensus that those projects didn't so much define Malaysia as momentarily divert attention from the country's less flattering realities.

Now Malaysia is joining a number of countries, from the United Kingdom to South Korea, New Zealand and Canada, seeking to brand themselves to the world in name of foreign direct investment and in an effort to increase their lobbying power.

Branding differs from marketing in that marketing is specific to certain areas, such as tourism.

"Branding a country must emphasize the collective identity of every component of that society," said Michael Kor, creative director of Dentsu advertising in Malaysia.

In a word, it's about selling a personality.

Deputy Prime Minister Najib Razak, whose office is overseeing the drive, has been slipping the issue into his speeches, asking audiences to think about what Malaysia's unique selling point might be.

A national brand council is being organized that will include big names from top local advertising agencies, universities and airlines. Government agents are trekking the globe for insight and inspiration.

"We need to put our house in order," said W T Seah, chief executive officer of Asia Pacific Brands Foundation (APBF), a non-profit organization established in part to assist the government in its pursuit of a clearer, more attractive identity.

"There's no use in having good infrastructures and nice skyscrapers if the human element isn't there to promote it."

Seah elaborated, "We can talk about Malaysia being modern and friendly, but when someone gets a rude immigration officer or must wait a long time to get something simple done, that throws him off balance.

Added David Mitchel, group brand manager of Leo Burnett Advertising, "Successful branding can't be too far from the truth."

People catch on.

Malaysia is a case in point. The government has peddled Malaysia as a "model Islamic democracy," "where different races, cultures and religions live in perfect harmony."

But most visitors who have spent any length of time in Malaysia opine that something closer to the opposite is true.

They complain of inefficiency, corruption, arrogance, indifference, aversion to risk and, increasingly, a creeping fundamentalism among its Muslim majority. Some argue that Malaysia has invested more in appearances than substance.

The new administration under Abdullah is trying to address these points, first and foremost by distancing itself from the truculence that clouded perceptions of Malaysia under Mahathir's 22-year rule, which ended when the iron-fisted leader retiring last year.

But it will take more than just a softer, gentler approach to brand Malaysia.

"It must be channeled through all sectors of society," said Seah.

He cited Malaysia's arch rival, neighboring Singapore, as having achieved this.

"It may be seen as clinical and cold but it's clean, efficient, and business-friendly. These attributes stick in everyone's mind, because it's a concerted effort, from immigration to taxi drivers to government ministries."

The top brand among nations is widely thought to be the United States, having "long been associated with a progressive, dynamic and hip lifestyle ... and quality and excellence," as a local newspaper here recently described the country.

There are other success stories as well. Italy is associated with romance and verve, Germany with engineering excellence, Switzerland with fine craftsmanship, Japan with cutting-edge design and reliability.

Branding is harder for emerging markets, said Charles Cadell, managing director of Leo Burnett Advertising; unlike most European nations, they often lack a widespread pre-conceived notion of personality resulting from history and culture.

Some say Malaysia has the added burden of being a multicultural society—how to define such a nation? But the United States' success contradicts this claim.

The truth is, even monocultural societies find it hard to get everyone to fix on one facet and stand behind it, and that's the key, said Cadell, who recently presented a paper to the Malaysian government on branding.

"It's a huge task. You need a consistent, dedicated group working on a 10-year plan," he said.

Even then, "at the end of the day, communication [and in turn, branding] is driven by individuals, consumerism, and brand contact points, like the back of a can."

More to the point, grand government plans to amend perceptions tend to get overwhelmed by other factors influencing those perceptions.

A few years ago, for instance, British Prime Minister Tony Blair saw the need to brand the United Kingdom, for the same reason that countries such as Malaysia want to brand themselves: to attract foreign direct investment and either maintain or improve their lobbying power.

His plan, channeled through the catchphrase "Cool Britannia," was to shed the UK's stuffy, aristocratic image for a hipper, edgier one. The plan failed.

The lesson suggests that branding must have an organic element, something that the people not only endorse but relate to—and thrive at.

Malaysia knows this all too well. White elephants, pie-in-the-sky, throwing money at something and hoping it will grow—this is how some of Malaysia's megaprojects have come to be described.

Consider Putrajaya, a multibillion-dollar administrative capital set amid the palm tracts between the country's international airport and Kuala Lumpur, which was to be the crown jewel of Mahathir's excess. It might be intriguing from an architectural and planning standpoint (it has started to attract tourists), but Malaysians aren't flocking out there to live as the government had hoped. And the project hasn't achieved one its main aims: to attract foreign investment and spur innovation.

Insiders say in its effort to brand Malaysia, the government is taking on a more patient introspection; it may be months or even years before a concrete strategy materializes.

But in doing so, these insiders caution, Malaysia will need to address the root causes of its negative perceptions abroad, which is tied in no small way to its disrespect for basic demonctratic principles. Not doing so will run the risk of undermining whatever viable brand identity the country adopts.

Will it happen? Najib's comments a few months back suggest the branding push might just be more smoke and mirrors.

In a speech in June, Najib said the positive things about Malaysia need to be played up more. He said he hoped foreigners would spread the news of the country's "racial harmony," while most Malaysians themselves are loath to call their tolerance of each other that.

Then last week Najib excoriated former Malaysian deputy prime minister Anwar Ibrahim for his "single-minded criticism" after Anwar said Indonesia was more democratically advanced than Malaysia.

Anwar has been mounting a reform-minded political comeback since a federal court overruled sodomy charges against him and he was released from prison in September.

"Other countries are saying we are their model ... how much more democratic do you want us to be?" Najib retorted.

More recently, however, Seah told reporters, APBF "wants to point out the inconsistencies that we have in this country."

And it could happen—led by the government's ambitions and the *rakyat*'s (citizens') indubitable optimism and talent—if together they are determined to turn the propensity here for talk into walk.

First published December 16, 2004 (*Asia Times*)

Malaysia's Distant 2020 Vision

A year after this story ran the government announced four new initiatives to boost the nation's ICT industry.

They include the Malaysia Animation Creative Content Centre, eContent Fund Awards, CyberSecurity Malaysia, and KnowledgeGRID. The latter is intended to "provide a national infrastructure that maximizes high performance computing resources to accelerate research and industrial development." The CyberSecurity initiative involves rebranding of the National ICT Security and Emergency Response Centre.

The bell tolls in Malaysia in 2020, the deadline the United Malays National Organization-led government has given itself to deliver the Southeast Asian country from developing- to developed-world status.

Former authoritarian leader Mahathir Mohamad launched the ambitious campaign in 1991, which aimed broadly to create a progressive scientific society and position Malaysia as a regional hub for leading innovative technology companies. The stepping stone of that plan was the establishment of the Multimedia Super Corridor (MSC), unveiled in 1996 as Malaysia's answer to Silicon Valley, which includes a 728-hectare futuristic "intelligent garden" city known as Cyberjaya. The government project is expected eventually to cost US$5.3 billion and usher Malaysia into the information age.

Malaysia was arguably in a better position to take the leap than most developing countries. After years of rapid manufacturing-led growth, its infrastructure was nearly world-class. Regionally, the levels of the country's gross domestic product and education were high. Oil and gas production was providing handsome revenues that could be used to spark technology-oriented spending.

To Mahathir, the MSC and Cyberjaya, which in Malay translates to "cyber success," seemed a visionary, win-win proposition.

Nowadays, nothing informs Malaysia's sense of success or failure more than the fate of its high-tech sector. Yet the so-called 2020 vision is fast falling out of focus. Malaysia's political leaders have at times lamented the country's "first-class infrastructure, but third-class mentality." Private-sector innovation taken off to the degree first envisaged by policymakers. To the contrary, the glaring lack of home-grown technology firms means that holders of information and technology degrees currently make up about 20% of Malaysia's unemployed university graduates, who are said to lack the requisite knowledge and skills.

When the government has tried to fill the private-sector gap, it has often missed the mark. The government's pet Information Communication Technology projects, including the Smart School Project, the Worldwide Manufacturing Web and Borderless Marketing Flagships, have flopped because of mismanagement, overspending and poor execution, critics say. There are recent reports claiming that as many as 90% of state-led ICT startups have gone belly-up, according to Technopreneur Association of Malaysia president Farith Rithaudeen.

That poor record has soured private-sector sentiment and dried up the venture-capital funding for other technopreneurial pursuits, including the startup ICT ventures that should be leading the country up the value-added ladder.

Consider, for instance, the case of Sentinel Technology, a small Malaysia-based research-and-development-oriented ICT firm. Mohamad Asendy, the startup's chief executive officer, said his company recently developed new anti-piracy software that he contends has the capacity to become a global market leader. The company even held discussions with Microsoft's Malaysia division, which according to Asendy was duly impressed with the innovation and encouraged Sentinel to divulge how the technology works so that Microsoft technicians could test its effectiveness. Asendy said he preferred first to formalize legal protection for his firm's innovation, but he lacked the RM300,000 (US$81,500) he needed to apply for a US patent. The Malaysian government offered him a RM50,000 grant, Asendy said, but in efforts to land the additional funding needed to apply for the patent, he was asked in exchange to give up a majority stake in the intellectual property. When he tried to obtain further government funding to patent his innovation, he was first directed to the Internal Affairs Ministry, which after a long wait redirected him to the Science, Technology and Innovation Ministry, he said. From there, he was told he would first have to get MSC status before he could apply for funding. Months later the technology is still not legally protected.

Government hindrances

The government is often at the root of Malaysia's innovation problems, scientific surveys say. A Global Entrepreneurship Monitor, a worldwide research project to be released soon, recently surveyed 45 local ICT experts and 2,000 Malaysian nationals about the country's entrepreneurial environment.

The study's results suggest that government policies disfavor new firms. It singled out the lack of financial support, quality of education and training, and overall market openness as main factors holding back Malaysian entrepreneurs. Bureaucracy, regulation and licensing requirements were said to play a role.

For all these discouragements, however, Prime Minister Abdullah Badawi's government is not abandoning Mahathir's high-tech dream. In part, that's because it's impossible to brush the ambitious scheme under the rug; wired with high-speed fiber optics, the MSC spans a whopping 777 square kilometers. Moreover, the government has poured billions of dollars into the MSC's infrastructure and provided large tax breaks to companies that have agreed to locate there. Meanwhile, Abdullah, who on the whole has not been keen to pursue the profligate megaprojects favored by Mahathir, has nonetheless reaffirmed his government's commitment, some say blindly, to all matters high-tech.

For instance, the Ninth Malaysia Plan, the latest five-year economic-policy blueprint, allocates RM1.5 billion to technology-oriented schemes, a 40% increase from the previous plan. One of the plan's main thrusts is "to raise the capacity for knowledge and innovation and nurture first-class mentality." The document is spangled with terms such as "knowledge-based," "science," "innovation" and "research and development."

To be sure, there have been some bright spots on Malaysia's ICT horizon. In May, US technology giant Dell announced it would set up a technology and development center in Cyberjaya. The center will focus on various value-added projects, including software design, and employ up to 1,000 workers.

Narayanan Kanan, senior vice president of the development division of the Multimedia Development Corp (MDeC), the agency tasked with overseeing and directing the MSC, said the Dell deal was a positive development, though he played down any suggestion that such major foreign investments were out of the ordinary. About 1,500 companies currently have MSC status and as many as 10 new ICT-innovating companies are being added to the corridor's roster each week, he said.

Critics, however, contend that Kanan's assessment is rosy and glosses over some of the hard-market realities looming over the MSC's long-term viability, which if not quickly addressed could spell doom for the enterprise. Many of the foreign MSC-registered companies have established centers here for basic distribution purposes rather than innovative pursuits. The country's ICT sector is suffering from various "market failures," including a severe shortage of seed-funding and angel investors, said Nazrin Hassan, an adviser to the Technopreneurs Association of Malaysia.

Hassan contends there are about seven times as many venture capitalists providing startup funding for technopreneurial ventures in neighboring Singapore. "In order to see growth in technopreneurs you have to take chances [with funding]. Many [Malaysian] technopreneurs have died off waiting for seed funding."

Meanwhile, Malaysia's education system may require an overhaul to spur the sort of innovation needed to move Malaysia up the ICT value-added ladder. As in many Asian countries, the Malaysian school system emphasizes rote learning and quantitative rather than qualitative education, critics say.

"We have not developed a capacity for lateral thinking," said Kuala Lumpur-based educationalist F R Bhupalan. "We have straitjacketed our students and not allowed them to engage in meaningful analysis."

The situation is exacerbated by draconian legislation, such as the Universities and University Colleges Act, which requires incoming university students to take a pledge to the government and bars them from joining political parties. Fear and feudalistic deference have long infected Malaysia's education system and in turn the classroom often punishes rather than rewards creative thinking and risk-taking.

Nor has education funding always been well targeted. The government recently invested RM300 million on a Smart School program for 80 schools, which broadly aimed to center education on ICT. About 60% of the project's funding went toward hardware, and procurements were frequently smeared with allegations of mismanagement and misappropriation.

"Many ICT contracts were awarded to the wrong people, some

with no experience or reputation, but with the right connections," said Chris Chan, chief executive officer of TMS, a Cyberjaya-based Internet company. "We have high tech visualized nicely—the implementation's been flawed."

That raises hard questions about the viability of about 500 new education-oriented projects detailed in the Ninth Malaysian Plan.

Changing tech tack

The Abdullah administration is reacting to the criticism. For instance, this year the government replaced MDeC's chief executive officer with industry insider Badlisham Ghazali, the previous director and general manager of Hewlett-Packard in Malaysia, who has more than 18 years of ICT-related work experience. Rumors abound that more key MDeC posts will be filled with industry players rather than crusty bureaucrats.

If true, such moves could make a big difference, said Chan, who for one doesn't buy the notion that Malaysia's small talent crop—its total population is 25 million—poses a major problem to becoming a global ICT leader.

"You don't need that many people to produce positive change," Chan said. "Appointing qualified, successful enterprisers rather than government appointees is a positive first step."

Kanan acknowledged that the government is trying to change tack. Government policymakers have recently narrowed their focus down to six strategic ICT areas, including software and hardware design, creative multimedia contents, shared solutions and outsourcing, he said.

The government intends to roll out the MSC to other areas of the country and offer new, juicier incentives to attract more multinational corporations, Chan said.

MDeC communicates regularly with the Education Ministry concerning what kind of graduates the industry requires, Kanan said.

The ministry declined to comment on what specific policy steps it has recently taken to encourage more creativity and innovation among ICT students.

Efforts to improve funding for startups, including three funds of undisclosed amounts, have recently been established by the government, but are hardly enough to create the critical mass of technology-oriented ventures needed to realize the government's 2020 vision, Kanan said.

But critics say most of the government's plans lack concrete details, suggesting that it is paying lip service to changing the venture's focus. They recommend providing detailed plans for creating better linkages between local universities and the ICT industry, which would ensure that the curriculum is meeting industry standards and requirements. The linkages would also provide foreign investors with easier access to strategic tie-ups with local firms and encourage the government to invest in more locally produced ICT software and hardware.

Currently the government accounts for about 80% of Malaysia's total annual ICT consumption. And, they argue, Malaysia has in the past performed admirably with its back against the economic wall, particularly during the 1997-98 Asian financial crisis, which Malaysia handled its own way and arguably weathered better than its neighbors.

Until now, a certain mix of talent, pragmatism and will power has enabled Malaysia to develop beyond expectations. Excelling in the ultra-competitive ICT industry, though, will likely require something extra, a formula Malaysia is still grasping for. But it's becoming increasingly clear that excelling in ICT will require something more.

First published August 16, 2006 (*Asia Times*)

* * *

Malaysia Changes Gear

In 2007, Deputy Prime Minister Najib Razak said of Malaysia's biotech plan, "We have to do more than what we have been doing in the past. Just having special incentive packages and promoting investment is not good enough." In Malaysia's 2008 budget, RM236 million was set aside for infrastructure and technological facilities for biotechnology. In March 2008 Minister of Science, Technology, and Innovation Jamaluddin Jarjis, whose ministry was spearheading the biotech plan, was replaced by Maximus Ongkili.

In the early 1980s, Prime Minister Mahathir Mohamad sought to transform this country's agrarian economy into a manufacturing one. Before he stepped down in 2003, manufacturing accounted for 30 percent of Malaysia's gross domestic product, double the sector's share of GDP in 1970.

With a population of 23 million—similar to that of Texas—Malaysia ranks as the 12th largest US trading partner.

But with India and China and, closer to home, Thailand and Singapore, luring away Malaysian investors, the government in Kuala Lumpur feels a need to change course again or risk being left behind.

In April, Prime Minister Abdullah Badawi prodded Malaysia toward the crowded biotechnology sector. The government expects this move to account for at least 5 percent of GDP and 280,000 jobs by 2020. It is set to shell out an estimated $1.1 billion in the first five years of the project.

Mr Badawi is calling biotech a natural fit for Malaysia, home to some of the planet's richest biodiversity, with about 15,000 plant species (compared with 5,000 for Europe). But Malaysia will need to make sense of the forests to tap their potential, which will require attracting substantial investment and top international scientists to collaborate with local firms.

As part of the project, the government is offering biotech companies a 10-year tax-exempt status. A fund will be established to train skilled workers and hire researchers. And a nexus of institutions will be nurtured to become the best Malaysia has to offer in specific sub-sectors of biotechnology.

Skeptics point out that there is little to distinguish Malaysia's incentive package from other nations moving into biotech. They also warn that Malaysia has in the past scared off investors with grand plans that have turned into white elephants. National carmaker Proton, protected by high import tariffs, comes to mind; as does the Multimedia Super Corridor, which stretches from the capital, Kuala Lumpur, to the hub-aspiring airport envisioned as the Silicon Valley of the East. Through tax breaks and other incentives, the $4 billion project was expected to attract the world's top high-tech companies. But a cornerstone of the MSC, the planned city of Cyberjaya, is now home to vacant fields and empty rental spaces.

Government officials say this go-round will be different and that they've learned from past mistakes, namely that success in the world of advanced industry is as contingent upon brain power as infrastructure. (Malaysia is home to some of Southeast Asia's best infrastructure.)

"We are aware of what we need," said Ahmad Zaharuddin Idrus, head of the Malaysian Biotechnology Corp., established in late April to oversee what is being tagged the BioMalaysia plan. "We need to radically move away from our normal way of thinking. We need a transformation in mind-set."

Mr Idrus was referring to the need to establish a culture of innovation, innovation serving as the primary catalyst to growth in biotech. In that regard, Malaysia is not alone. For most Asian countries venturing into biotech, scientific breakthroughs have been slow to materialize; the bulk of biotech innovation continues to emanate from the US and Europe, with 90 percent of Asian innovations coming from one country, Japan.

India's biotech industry has shown promise, offering low costs, a large dynamic talent pool and an abundance of research facilities and universities. So has the nation-state of Singapore, which has poured $200 billion into research since 2000. It boasts 4,000 PhDs, 30 percent of whom are foreigners.

And therein lies half the battle for Malaysia, said Sharon Low, managing director of StemLife, a Malaysian-based biomedical company. "The biggest challenge I think is trying to attract some of the world's best to collaborate with our companies," Ms. Low said.

But how the Malaysian government intends to do so is not clear. It has outlined nine points of focus, which include adding value to the agricultural sector and securing international recognition for Malaysian biotechnology.

But when asked about the how-to of the thrusts, the government has been mostly mum; Minister of Science, Technology and Innovation Jamaludin Jarjis declined to comment on what specifically is being done to attract and develop talent, to ensure close collaboration between industry and universities, and to spur innovative thinking and risk-taking—all points outlined in the nine thrusts.

"There's still so much we're trying to figure out," said a ministry insider.

Which some see as akin to opening a restaurant before the silverware is delivered.

"The nine thrusts sound great, but the telling is in the details, and so far what we're seeing is a very broad-based approach," said David Ho, managing director of Hovid, a Malaysian pharmaceutical company. Mr Ho said the government's exploring of agriculture, vaccine, health care and industrial ventures is cause for concern.

There also is talk of using biotech to upgrade cottage industries and set up industries in remote villages. "Where is all the expertise going to come from?" asked Mr Ho rhetorically.

Ms. Low said the government is wise not to be too specific in its approach initially. "I think the government is doing the right thing by not getting itself too involved in the details, but rather creating the type of environment where private enterprise can feel comfortable making investments."

First published July 1, 2005 (*The Washington Times*)

* * *

Malaysia's MSC: Super Corridor or Dead End?

Nothing in Malaysia so embodies former prime minister Mahathir Mohamad's vision for the nation than the 50-kilometer stretch of palm and rubber-patched plains between the airport and the capital. Known as the Multimedia Super Corridor and ballyhooing world-class infrastructure, it was intended to attract foreign capital, trigger a technological revolution and lead the nation to fully developed status by 2020.

To Mahathir it was the next logical leap. The economy under his feisty 22-year rule had transformed from agrarian-based to export-manufacturing-driven. Why stop there? The MSC is the superhighway Mahathir has paved for Malaysia.

A visit to the corridor's capital, Cyberjaya, though, suggests the dream hasn't entirely lived up to expectations. Five years after ground was broken, it appears as if the 21st century has come and gone. Or hasn't come at all. Weedy, barren fields await the arrival of construction crews. "Smart" condominiums boasting "broadband access" and "online shopping" are running at low occupancy. The main shopping complex is often eerily quiet, as are the wide, flat roadways beneath which lie kilometers of fiber optics.

Some heavy hitters of the information-technology (IT) world such as Fujitsu, Ericsson, and most recently Motorola, have come, lured by tax breaks, grants and other incentives. A creative college plans soon to relocate to Cyberjaya. And around the end of this month the government is expected to make a vote of confidence when it unveils Phase 2 of the MSC, which will link the corridor to other cities around Malaysia and the globe.

But with the Mahathir era fast fading, Malaysians and the world seem less impressed by the grandiosity of the MSC than they did a few short years ago, when Malaysia looked primed to become one of the few countries to make the elusive leap from developing to developed status. Indeed terms that sprinkle Cyberjaya's marketing brochures and landscape, such as "connected," "wireless," "borderless," and "E-ready" verge on passe. ("Dot.com," the boom from which the dream spawned, has wisely gone missing.)

"Malaysia has fiber optics ... so?" quipped one investor.

So do rivals India, Thailand and China, which while not exactly centers of innovation offer similar incentives, and in some cases much lower costs.

MSC officials point out that the corridor is home to 500 companies and since its inception seven years ago has employed 15,000 people, 87 percent home grown, and this surpasses targets. Sliding targets, perhaps; in 2000, officials said they expected the population of just Cyberjaya to surpass 20,000 by mid-2001. Regardless, numbers are rising, say MSC officials.

Mahathir, too, hasn't wavered much from the hard sell. "You

are seeing beautiful buildings which are not empty but full of people working in there. That was what we expected," he said before retirement last year.

Others are less optimistic.

"Somewhere it lost a lot of steam along the way," opined Singapore-based economist Song Seng Wun, adding that too much emphasis has been placed on high tech and innovation, a call Malaysians haven't wholeheartedly stepped up to.

Responding to the concern last week, Science, Technology and Innovation Minister Jamaludin Jarjis urged MSC companies not to overlap and duplicate research, calling this "wasteful."

The government has been loath, publicly at least, to acknowledge that the plan might need an overhaul—that would be to admit a US$17 billion blunder in the case of Cyberjaya alone. But it's becoming harder to ignore.

There's a growing sense around Malaysia that Mahathir's megaprojects may have hindered as much as hampered growth, and dealt as much in appearances as substance. By Mahathir's own admission, they were designed in part to woo potential investors. Two other Mahathir megaprojects make up the bookends to the MSC, the vitreous, streamlined airport to the south and the dazzling Petronas office towers in downtown Kuala Lumpur, until last year the world's tallest buildings; a high-speed express train shuttles passengers to and fro.

As a whole, the stretch pumped the spirit of Malaysia *boleh*, or "Malaysia can." Now when Malaysians utter the phrase it's more often than not with irony. In the case of the airport and twin towers they're starting to look a bit like eyesores, reminders of what once seemed possible; not much has come along to compliment their grandeur. And Malaysia is finding that it takes much more than a high-tech pipe dream to distinguish yourself, raising the unspoken: Is Malaysia plateauing? Must this stable, talented, functional, resource-rich nation rethink itself if it is to live up to its potential?

When Mahathir's deputy Abdullah Badawi took over as premier last October, a sense of optimism swept the country—in no small part because he appeared set to diverge from his predecessor. He tabled a grand railway project and vowed to concentrate more on rural development. That and other promises catapulted his coalition to a huge if underhanded parliamentary election win last month. His vision, however, remains a puzzle.

"There's been talk about shifting priorities, but [the government] has not been clear what direction it's going to take," said economist Jomo K S, adding that rethinking a national strategy is overdue, but "it must be informed carefully."

Perhaps a hint lies in Biovalley, a 200-hectare site set to open near Cyberjaya in 2006, with the aim of attracting 150 biotech companies and $10 billion in investment by 2015. It might prove the equipoise Malaysia needs: a simultaneous investment in the MSC and a deviation from its original focus. Biotech, it almost sounds like a natural fit for Malaysia's fertile equatorial soil.

The verdict on the MSC's fate is still out. And who knows, Phase 2 might capitalize on lessons learned and prove so brilliant as to silence skeptics.

Rob Cayzer, senior manager with the Multimedia Development Corp, the MSC's overseeing body, sees no reason not to be optimistic. "The talent in Malaysia is as good as it is in any other developing country: infrastructure's as good, and so is cost."

He may have a point, but as Malaysia is finding out the hard way, that's no guarantee investors will come.

First published by *Asia Times*

* * *

A Megaproject Bears Witness to Malaysia's Faith in Economic Planning

The Iskandar Development Region is a special economic zone twice the size of Hong Kong, named for the sultan of Johor state and set on the Johor Straits that separate Malaysia from Singapore. A promotional video for its planned facilities describes a place that will offer "shopping as splendid as the grand bazaar in Istanbul" and "a beehive of activity at night where stars won't just be in the sky, but on the stage."

The camera darts and reels between digital renderings of university and medical "cities," an amusement park and a waterfront teeming with life.

Welcome to Malaysia, where utopian megaprojects, meant to wow the world, have become a cornerstone of nation building.

According to the Iskandar Regional Development Authority, the government plans to allocate more than 4 billion ringgit, or $1.2 billion, for the region's physical infrastructure over the five years to 2010. Government media say the target is to attract 50 billion ringgit in investment within five years, and 370 billion by 2025.

Several ambitious earlier developments, such as the aviation hub facilities of Kuala Lumpur International Airport and the sprawling, ecologically friendly administrative capital, Putrajaya, are operating well below capacity around a decade into their existence, but Iskandar, intended to be the nation's next major growth driver, will be different, its planners say. The development rubs shoulders with Singapore and is designed in part to feed off the thriving city-state, as Shenzhen has fed off Hong Kong, offering cheaper land and alternative labor.

Strategic transportation infrastructure in South Johor and Singapore includes two road bridges, two airports, and four seaports clustered at the mouth of the Strait of Malacca, through which a third of all the world's trade passes.

Some Singaporeans are already investing. HG Metal Manufacturing, based in Singapore, has purchased 10.6 hectares, or 26.2 acres, of land for $7.3 million, for a steel manufacturing plant, and may well buy more. Wee Piew, the company's chief executive, said the site was "considerably" cheaper than its equivalent in Singapore. Besides the price, and easy port access, Wee said that he was impressed by "Malaysian officials' willingness to liberalize in the zone."

In an unprecedented move, the government has said it will scrap longstanding national affirmative action policies—which provide preferential advancement for ethnic Malays—in certain service sectors of the development region, including health care, creative industries, consulting and education.

The move is politically risky. The former prime minister, Mahathir bin Mohamad, and several divisional leaders of the governing United Malays National Organization, or UMNO, have criticized it, saying that Malays would not be able to compete with foreigners. But the government has argued that maintaining the restrictions on hiring and investment would hinder the region's ability to achieve its huge investment target—the equivalent of $105 billion over 20 years.

"We are trying to get people to understand that for this to be an international development and to remain competitive we have to make sacrifices," said Iskandar Ismail, director of special projects, strategy and investment research at Khazanah Nasional, the government's investment arm assigned to lead the development.

The gamble is piquing investor interest.

"From an external perspective, the reaction has been extremely positive," said Joseph Tan, an economist at Standard Chartered Bank in Singapore. "Foreign investors I have spoken with are very high on the change."

Easing the restrictions is part of a broader strategy adopted by Abdullah Badawi, Malaysia's prime minister, to stimulate private sector investment by, among other things, allowing foreign investors greater access to Malaysian markets—this at a time when neighboring Thailand, a major competitor with Malaysia in manufacturing and foreign direct investment, is carrying out protectionist policies.

Recent economic trends provide at least anecdotal evidence that liberalization is worth trying. With Malay preference restrictions in place, foreign direct investment in Malaysia has been slipping, to 7.3 percent of gross domestic product last year from 14.7 percent in 1991, according to research by the Singapore development bank DBS. And, in Thailand, possibly reflecting the impact of protectionist policies, economic growth is forecast by the University of the Thai Chamber of Commerce to drop below 4 percent this year, from 5.1 percent last year.

To attract investment, the government is also aggressively trying to cut red tape. Just getting approval for subdividing land into development plots now takes almost 18 months, for example.

Still, even with a streamlined administration—the Iskandar development is being managed by a one-stop regulatory authority—the challenges will be considerable. One of the biggest will be to achieve synergies with Singapore, which will mean overcoming a legacy of distrust in the city-state, Malaysia's long-time rival.

Relations have begun to thaw since Abdullah took over from Mahathir in 2003, and Malaysian officials insist the development is designed to complement rather than compete with its southern neighbor.

Manufacturing is the most obvious fit between the two, and the

Iskandar region allots plenty of space for it; but the development plan also reflects Malaysia's desire to diversify into innovative sectors and services, where head-to-head competition is inevitable.

"We see it as healthy competition, though," said Wan Abdullah Wan Ibrahim, the managing director of UEM Land, the developer of Nusajaya, the core residential, administrative, logistical and service-sector zone intended to drive growth in the region.

"We don't see why we can't both have top quality medical centers," Wan Abdullah said, referring to Singapore and Nusajaya. "People can spend a few nights at their theme park ... and then visit ours."

Nusajaya has yet to name a contractor for a planned "international brand" theme park and officials would neither confirm nor deny reports that Walt Disney might be in the running. They said only that it would not be Universal Studios, since Universal is set to open a theme park in Singapore.

Planners of the development also envision education and medical tourism hubs, and a research and development center focused on areas like electronics and biotechnology. These are areas in which Singapore already has a lead and where it has been willing to pay top dollars to entice foreign talent.

When pressed, overseers of the Iskandar project could point to no concrete plan to do the same.

Some analysts find this omission puzzling. "Where are you going to find people of the necessary caliber to work in Johor, if you are not going to pay significantly more?" Tan, of Standard Chartered Bank, asked.

Existing education and hi-tech clusters, around the capital of Kuala Lumpur and the northern city of Penang, are already struggling to flourish employing homegrown talent. Tan and other analysts warn that skill shortages could turn Iskandar into a development feeding off the rest of Malaysia.

Johor's officials don't see it that way. They expect Iskandar to achieve a critical mass by 2011, when its sheer scale, and its mix of work and leisure facilities, should pull in a self-sustaining flow of foreign dollars and talent.

Yet that strategy brings with it the risk of overcapacity. Attracting initial capital may prove easier than luring crowds to fill the planned resorts, arts and sports centers, museums, yacht marina and amusement park: and if customers don't come, the development officials may find it hard to keep up the momentum.

"That's our job," said Wan Abdullah. "How do we create the life? We are courageously determined to make it work."

First published May 3, 2007 (*International Herald Tribune*)

THE WORLD BEYOND

Western Media Fade, New Media Rise in Asia

The non-Western world routinely alleges that the global media represented by the likes of CNN and the *Wall Street Journal* are tainted with a Western, often pro-US bias. But the ever-growing reach of new media entities providing non-Western perspectives to breaking global news, ranging from powerful new television networks to itty-bitty weblogs, has in effect reduced the claim to myth.

Several commercial and technological factors are driving the shift. Previously prominent English-language news weeklies, such as Dow Jones-owned *Far Eastern Economic Review* and Time Warner-run *Asiaweek*, have dramatically fallen from the print news scene they dominated in the 1980s and into the 1990s. Media mogul Rupert Murdoch sold much of his controlling stake in Hong Kong-based Phoenix TV last year, marking yet another blow to advance his media empire into China.

Many Western media outlets have seen their circulation figures stagnate, and under growing financial pressure at home have severely cut their reporting staffs across Asia. *Newsweek* recently closed its Asia bureau and *Time* has closed down all but two of its regional bureaus.

Meanwhile, the financial-loss-making *Asian Wall Street Journal*'s regional subscription base has stagnated at around 80,000 for well over a decade, and former Dow Jones employees allege those figures are probably overblown through the dubious use of bulk-rate subscriptions and other promotional activities. Signaling a possible further consolidation in big Western media, Murdoch's News Corp on Wednesday launched a US$5 billion takeover bid for Dow Jones.

On the other side, there is a growing demand for non-Western news perspectives. *Al Jazeera* is the most prominent example to fill the void, with a host of television and Internet-based imitators quickly springing in its wake. In November, *Al Jazeera* launched an English-language channel that is more sanitized than its Arabic version and aims at competing head to head with the likes of Cable News Network (CNN) and the British Broadcasting Corp (BBC). It recently set up a news hub in Kuala Lumpur and currently reaches 80 million households globally by cable and satellite.

Sensing the shift in sentiment, not to mention the commercial opportunities, Western media companies are, somewhat ironically, rushing to peddle their own non-Western perspectives. The BBC World Service plans to start an Arabic television service this fall, and the *International Herald Tribune* recently noted: "If the BBC's Arabic TV programs resemble its radio programs, then they will be just as anti-Western as anything that comes out of the [Persian] Gulf, if not more so."

Meanwhile, many people outside the West are still living under non-democratic conditions where state media have aggressively resisted presenting Western perspectives on everything from political history to civil liberties to the "war on terror." Here in Muslim-majority Malaysia, for instance, there was little if any mention in the state press of the Holocaust on its 60th anniversary two years ago.

Granted, in many of these same countries the Internet has become a powerful tool to voice and obtain alternative views. In Malaysia, a handful of courageous bloggers have become so effective in drawing attention to government abuses that authorities are considering censoring them. And while ideals that officious leaders demonize as Western imports, including transparency, accountability and freedom of expression, are frequently endorsed on independent blogs and websites, this is hardly a Western bias, as the content is formulated by locals.

Another factor challenging the notion of Western media bias is that despite the rise of independent media in restricted societies many people in these countries remain committed to the strictly controlled mouthpiece media outlets. I have noticed among Malaysians, for instance, that when given a choice—say on a flight or at multinational coffee houses—between international newspapers such as the *International Herald Tribune* and *Financial Times* and local government-controlled propaganda, they almost invariably choose the latter.

Further, if the world media are "sullied by Western political bias and colored by Western ideological bias," in the words of Felix Soh, deputy editor of online media for Singapore's state-controlled *Straits Times* newspaper, then how to explain the highly distorted, caricatured summations of Western culture and its governments so prevalent in the non-Western world today?

In an essay in the timely book *Understanding Anti-Americanism: Its Origins and Impact at Home and Abroad*, Patrick Clawson and Barry Rubin point out that local and satellite stations in the Middle East are "competing with one another as to which can be more stridently anti-American."

Media in the US may have their share of voices that misrepresent Muslims, but most mainstream media there can hardly be accused of competing to see which can be the most stridently anti-Muslim. It is not uncommon to find, even in what many in Malaysia and across the Middle East consider the "Zionist" *New York Times*, op-eds sympathetic to Palestinian plight. In Malaysia the government has banned the mere "screening, portrayal or musical presentation of works of Jewish origin," while a top editor at the government-controlled *New Straits Times* was axed for running an article critical of Saudi Arabia.

Under fire from all sides, the US government has funded everything from television commercials to broadcast stations to correct what it perceives as distorted news about the US. But as evinced by Under Secretary of Public Diplomacy Karen Hughes' "listening tours" across the Muslim world, the efforts have usually focused more on justifying the administration's policies than on promoting better understanding of the nuances of the superpower's role in world affairs.

At first glance the growing presence of non-Western viewpoints would appear to be a mere matter of leveling the playing field. But we are witnessing an overshooting of anti-Western views in the adjustment. Writing back in 1986, Ahmad Shafaat of the Molson School of Business of Concordia University, Montreal, urged Muslims to combat the "anti-Islamic and anti-Muslim chorus" in media with "pro-Islamic and pro-Muslim material." This dualistic reasoning is rampant today; the post-September 11, 2001, media landscape has, like the world the media reflect and simultaneously inform, become increasingly ideological. Ideologies advance themselves through selective facts, and this explains why purportedly objective media entities so often provide strikingly different coverage of the same event. The problem is compounded when the gatekeepers of one ideology feel those of another have misrepresented the facts, leading to a tendency to overcompensate in their own reporting and the cycle one-upping to continue indefinitely.

What, then, we are often left with is not a mass movement to correct reality but to further distort it, and this has led to a crucial irony: in the information age we are no closer to bridging seismic gaps in understanding. And that is something Western and non-Western media are equally responsible for.

First published May 3, 2007 (*Asia Times*)

* * *

China and the Media

China's "rise" (to borrow the press's catchphrase) is the biggest media story of the new century. And not without reason. China has created 120 million new jobs and lifted 400 million people out of poverty over the last 20 years. Its economy is expanding at a clip of 10 percent, while Shanghai undergoes a blistering infrastructural transformation.

But what these factors will amount to is far from certain.

This has not stopped the press from reporting on China as if it is destined to be the world's next dominant power. The assumed end was captured in the lead of a recent *Asia Times* article: "With China's economic, social, political and cultural renewal, a five-century period of Western domination of the world has ended. One has to make sense of China's complex dynamics to apprehend a new world with Chinese characteristics."

China coverage moreover often lacks perspective. A recent piece in the *New York Times* titled "China's Trade With Africa Carries a Price Tag" typifies this trend. The article accounted for China's growing penetration of the continent: "This year, China pledged $20 billion to finance trade and infrastructure across the continent over the next three years. In Zambia alone, China plans to invest $800 million in the next few years." But it failed to mention what the West's tallies were in this respect, essentially giving the impression that the West is a nonentity on the continent. In fact, two-way trade between sub-Saharan Africa and the US jumped 17 percent in 2006 over 2005 to almost $71.3 billion, and since 2006 the US government has signed trade and investment framework agreements (TIFAs) with Rwanda, Mauritius, and Liberia, while strengthening cooperation with existing TIFA partners, according to the Office of the US

Trade Representative.

Where coverage does emphasize context, it tends to suggest that the West is fading inversely to the degree that China is soaring. The second graph of another *Times* story titled "Chinese Move to Eclipse US Appeal in Southeast Asia" reported that "studying Chinese was an easy one over perfecting his faltering English" for Thai student Long Seaxiong, because, as he puts it, "For a few years ahead, it will still be the United States as No. 1, but soon it will be China."

The piece then goes out of its way to cite instances that make the 19-year-old sound prescient.

If only the crystal ball were so clear. If only American influence was not itself expanding. If only America was truckling to the thought of a new world order. If only Western businesses weren't aggressively securing new opportunities and improving profit margins across Asia. If only the business establishment, and the West's more broadly, didn't have a long history of shrewdly working global commerce to its advantage. If only English did not remain the most practical, hence preferred, second-language of non-native English speakers in much of the world. (As I write this I am on a bus with regional NGO and media reps, the air is abuzz with English—Thais talking with Cambodians, Sri Lankans with Vietnamese, Filipinos with Chinese Malaysians.)

But that's not the sexy storyline. No, it's not new, it's not dramatic; media and audiences are drawn to news, and the bigger the perceived impact the better. This makes the reporting and consumption seem important. The China story fits the bill. It speaks of a tectonic historical shift—the sleeping dragon awakening from a centuries-long slumber to take on the world.

Editors and journalists thus sniff out stories that fit the theme. The stories run, reinforcing the theme.

Some media have challenged these assumptions by drawing attention to the giant hurdles China faces in becoming a major power. *Foreign Affairs* notes in an essay called "The Myth Behind China's Miracle" that outdated one-party politics have produced a timid business culture that is failing to develop key technologies and is keeping domestic firms dependent on the West. "First, China's high-tech and industrial exports are dominated by foreign, not Chinese, firms. Second, Chinese industrial firms are deeply dependent on designs, critical components, and manufacturing equipment they import from the United States and other advanced industrialized democracies. Third, Chinese firms are taking few effective steps to absorb the technology they import and diffuse it throughout the local economy, making it unlikely that they will rapidly emerge as global industrial competitors." The essay notes that foreign-funded enterprises (FFEs) accounted for 55 percent of China's total exports last year. According to the *China Daily*, "Only three out of 10,000 Chinese enterprises have intellectual property rights for their core technologies. Ninety-nine percent of Chinese firms have no patents and 60 percent do not have their own brands." The Organization for Economic Cooperation and Development notes that "Some 55% of China's total exports are attributed to production and assembly-related activities, and 58% of these are driven by foreign enterprises, of which 38% are entirely foreign-owned. In fact, among the top 10 high-technology companies by revenue, not one of them is Chinese."

China's challenges extend to the most basic kind. As rich as city dwelling Chinese are often portrayed by the press, urban incomes average a mere $1,000 a year (in the countryside its closer to $300), and the nation's per capita GDP is 110th in the world. One hundred and fifty million Chinese live on less than $1 a day, notes the World Bank. And yet relying on the mass media one might never know.

One is made to forget that America's economy remains the world's largest and most dynamic. Corporate profits reached a 40-year high in 2005, with before-tax profits topping $1.35 trillion.

Cultural impact remains strong. The world continues to clamour for Western brands. From a balcony in the shopping mall at the base of Taipei 101, the world's tallest building—which, according to a plaque on the observation deck, symbolizes the new Asia—I could not spot a Chinese character amid a sea of Western brand names shining in English from billboards and storefronts. Even financial losses due to the sale of pirated Hollywood films, handbag knockoffs and other imitation goods across Asia are advancing the West's cultural influence.

The picture is not altogether rosy for America. The sub-prime bank loan crisis, an unwieldy trade deficit, a weakening dollar and the war in Iraq are a few glaring sore points, and China's rise couldn't come at a more opportune time—when the West is stumbling. These factors are feeding the rise-and-fall prophecy, but they hardly substantiates it.

In fact, history offers ample reason to be leery of the claim. Twentieth century powers that vied for global supremacy with the West, from the fascist regimes to the Soviet Union, crashed quickly back to earth. Of course no one saw it coming at the time; there is a long history of underestimating America, even in America itself. I recall as a child in New York, my father's friend telling me the Japanese, who had recently bought Rockefeller Center, were on the verge of taking on the rest of the city.

What distinguishes China's "threat" from previous ones is that it is coinciding with the most radical presidency in recent American history. Many Americans (not to mention non-Americans) no longer feel the country is on the right side of history, a progressive defender of good against evil—they are no longer emboldened by a collective sense of righteousness—and there is, as Joe Klein put it, "a danger that, in reaction to Bush's ill-considered boldness, the nation will curl inward now, away from the world, away from the future." Away from greatness. That is, Americans are vulnerable to internalizing the

China hype while overlooking the myriad tools at their disposal to sustain America's ascendancy. This, along with American adversaries' sudden good will toward China, rooted in hope for an antidote to American supremacy, threatens to turn the "rise" into a self-fulfilling prophecy.

The media owe it to the public to more astutely discern hype from reality in reporting on China. At a minimum this will require resisting the temptation to feed the script; and shedding any preconceptions about where China and the West are headed.

There is reason to believe that a portion of this gap will be resolved naturally. Hype tends to be short-lived. Moreover, a number of developments—including China's cozy ties with some of the world's most notorious rogue states, such as the genocidal regime in Darfur; its human rights record; its treatment of neighboring Tibet and Taiwan; its lax attitude toward copyright violation; spying scandals; product safety issues; and opaque military spending—are raising doubts about China's self-proclaimed "peaceful rise."

New York Senator Charles Schumer last month summed up the feeling of a growing many when he said, "I don't believe the Chinese move out of a sense of comity and magnanimity."

Asked by the Chicago Council on Gobal Affairs whether China can be trusted to act responsibly in world affairs, 76 percent of French, 61 percent of South Koreans and 58 percent of Americans said, no. Other polls show that a favorable view of China is below 50 percent in countries as diverse as Lebanon, India, Turkey, Japan and Russia.

It remains to be seen what all this signifies—though that's a story much of the media hasn't yet caught on to.

* * *

Greece Neglecting Needs of Muslim Immigrants

Greece, like Malaysia, is struggling with the notion of religious equality: in Greece they won't build a house of worship; in Malaysia they won't let them stand. Sensitivities of each country's religious majorities have complicated matters, and yet not showing greater respect to their religious minorities will threaten long-term social stability. Malaysia is already paying a price for government insensitivities. The government's destruction of Hindu temples led to virulent street protests in November 2007 and widespread disaffection among Indian voters in Malaysia's 2008 elections.

Since this article ran, Greek authorities have passed a law with the Greek Orthodox Church's backing to construct a mosque in a downtown Athens neighborhood by 2010. A similar law authorizing the construction of a mosque near the international airport before the 2004 Olympics in Athens was scrapped after angry protests by residents and the Church.

In the Malaysian state of Perak the new opposition-led government is establishing a department to address concerns of religious minorities and will encourage the construction of places of worship on government reserve land.

With almost 99% of the population Greek Orthodox Christians, Greece may seem like an unlikely destination for immigrant Muslims. Moreover, its 11% unemployment rate ranks near the highest among European Union countries and it is one of the less developed member states. Nevertheless, some 200,000 Muslims, representing a quarter of all immigrants in Greece, now live in the capital Athens alone, up from 5000 in the early 1990s. The first wave came mostly from neighbouring countries such as Albania, following the collapse of the Soviet Union and the governments it supported in Eastern European states. The second wave arrived after 1995 and included Muslims from farther abroad—the Middle East, South Asia and sub-Saharan Africa. From a geographic point of view, their arrival in Greece makes sense as the country straddles Asia and the West and represents Europe's eastern gateway. It is the only EU country in the Balkans. And its seas bordering Turkey make for a porous border. Greece is also the cheapest point of entry for many immigrants.

Ali, 21, paid an illegal trafficking network 3000 euros to smuggle him last year from Iraq to Greece—half of what it would have cost him to fulfil his aim of entering Germany. Ali, who declined to give his last name, makes about 30 euros a day in construction jobs, when he can find them. More often than not, he cannot, he says, because supply outstrips demand, making it difficult to send enough money home to support his five siblings and mother. His father was killed in 2004 by an explosion.

However, immigrants in Greece, as elsewhere in Europe, are finding themselves a vital component to the work force, taking low-wage jobs—mostly in construction, agriculture and domestic help—that many Greeks decline. And yet this should not be understood to mean that Greece welcomes their presence, said Nassos Theodoridis, director of Antigone, a human rights group.

"There has been a great deal of resistance to incorporating immigrants into Greek society," Theodoridis told *Aljazeera.net*.

Laws in Greece make it difficult for minorities and even minority children born in Greece to obtain equal status. And work permits remain elusive due to high costs, bureaucracy and ambiguities in the law. A study by the European Monitoring Centre on Racism and Xenophobia found that the presence of people from minority groups created higher insecurity in Greece than in any other European Union country. Political gestures of goodwill towards minorities are often met with resistance. The most recent proof of this came in early May when Socialist party leader George Papandreou's decision to nominate a Greek Muslim lawyer for prefecture in northern Greece sparked an outcry. Political rivals in turn feed on the "traitorous blunders" of their opponents, so that the public and politicians reinforce xenophobic tendencies among each other, Theodoridis says.

Alexandros Zavos, chairman of the government backed Hellenic Migration Policy Institute (IMEPO), pointed out that the government is designing a programme that will bring political parties, unions and the influential Greek Orthodox Church together to advance relations between Greeks and immigrants and produce a harmonious multi-cultural and multi-religious society. He said the government's response to immigration so far was not one of neglect and resistance. Rather, he said, immigration is a new phenomenon in Greece.

Munir Abdelrasoul, an imam from Sudan who has lived in Greece for 30 years and speaks fluent Greek, said relations between mostly immigrant Muslims and mostly Christian natives in Greece are good. And political attitudes seem to enhance that sentiment: Greece has maintained good relations with most Arab countries, while many Greeks are staunch supporters of the Palestinian cause. But Abdelrasoul said those feelings of goodwill are being challenged by the absence of a mosque in Athens, making it the only European capital without one.

The Greek government backed a plan to build an Athens mosque in 2000. But a change in government and opposition from locals and church officials saw to it that the proposal never materialised. While officials continue to make statements that support the building of a mosque, little has been done to actually build it.

The ministry of national education and religious affairs "has the right to give all the necessary permits for religious places of worship," said the ministry's press officer Charidimos Caloudis. But Marietta

Giannakou, the minister involved, declined to comment when asked to provide a time frame as to when the government would formally approve construction and what the cause for delay has been.

Some analysts say it is politically risky to push for the construction of a mosque. Greeks were brutally oppressed during 400 years of Ottoman rule and many have come to associate Islam with that painful period of their history.

"Some Greeks equate Turkish rule with Islam," said Marios Begzos, professor of comparative philosophy of religion at the University of Athens. "But Greeks and the Greek government must learn to distinguish between Turks and Muslims."

To some extent they have. Some 150 mosques exist in Greece, mainly in the northern region of Thrace, where an estimated 150,000 Greek Muslims live, and the Orthodox Church has donated 300,000 square feet worth an estimated $20 million in west Athens for the purpose of a Muslim cemetery. But the symbolic void of a mosque in the capital threatens to overshadow these gestures.

The absence has drawn international attention. Leading up to the 2004 Olympic Games there was talk in the international Muslim community of boycotting the games. And the Saudi government has pushed strongly to fund the construction of a mosque and cultural centre. The construction of the cultural centre raised concern among the Greek community, given the Saudi government's reputation for promoting a strict interpretation of Islam.

The Greek government has since promised to fund and oversee construction of the mosque, sans the cultural centre. Location is said to be the last main sticking point. A spot near the airport was once being considered but few Muslims live there. There was talk of renovating a mosque leftover from Turkish rule in the shadow of the Acropolis that has since been turned into a folk art museum. But it is very small—not suitable for a Friday prayer—and a symbol of oppression to many Greeks. Land adjacent to where the cemetery will be constructed is now said to be the most likely candidate.

In the meantime Muslims in Athens pray at 20 non-official prayer centres around the capital, most of which can hold no more than a few dozen people.

Abdelrasoul said Muslims in Greece are likely to remain patient on the issue. "Good relations between Muslim and Greeks are ancient. But I hope officials will come to understand that when people feel respected and accepted in a society they feel more satisfied and inclined to honour that society."

First Published June 1, 2006 (*Al Jazeera*)

* * *

Promoting US Values in Muslim Lands

Malaysians have long been sensitive to official Western attempts to push for greater democracy in their country. The Bush Administration's unscrupulous adventures abroad heightened that sensitivity; the call lost its moral legitimacy. This is not to suggest that Malaysians don't yearn for a more humane form of governance. Many do, as the 2008 election results attest. And Malaysia is not opposed to learning from Western industrialized democracies. But as long as the West advocates democratic ideals more through dictation than by example the effort will be met with suspicion and resentment.

It has become virtually axiomatic to suggest that a "war on terror" led by force is destined to fail. As the retired US General Wesley

Clark noted recently, "This is not World War II: when we kill people we make matters worse." And so the question in many Washington policy circles has shifted from whether America should change course to how.

Prospective answers are emerging, as evinced by a recent conference here titled "Terrorism, Security and America's Purpose: Towards a More Comprehensive Strategy." Top policy analysts offered practical steps for America to get back on track, such as seeing to it that rule of law governs all of Washington's foreign policy. The conference also tackled important issues, such as the "Strengths and Limitations of Democracy Promotion as a Strategy for Fighting Terrorism."

However, it generally paid scant attention to Muslim sensibilities, as has most dialogue and literature emanating from policy circles urging revision to the country's foreign policy strategy. What "they" want is still assumed to be what we want. That is, these stirrings of dissent have preserved the same basic conviction that inspired the country's current course: That the basis of the solution is (whatever disagreement there is over the means) to promote American values in Muslim lands.

Keeping on in this way runs a serious risk of emasculating Washington's battle for hearts and minds, as we saw the Tuesday before last in Saudi Arabia. It was then that new Under Secretary of State Karen Hughes, who's in charge of spreading America's message abroad, told an audience of the kingdom's educated elite that she hoped to see the ban on women driving lifted.

When an audience member told Hughes that Saudi women were happy as they were, she was applauded. Indeed promoting American-style democracy to enhance national security has figured largely in American foreign policy as far back as when Woodrow Wilson was president. And arguably Washington's efforts on this front have not only made America but the world safer.

But in Islam, America confronts a civilization that, however diverse, is collectively sensitive to attempts by the West to impose its will: the colonial period is largely forgotten in the West but remains an open wound throughout the Muslim world. Heightening this acuity is President George W Bush's "war on terror," which many Muslims view as a war against Islam. In other words, as Muslim ears are still ringing from the destruction in Iraq and Afghanistan America returns to say, "ps: here are some values for you."

Foreign policy experts justify this imposition by not seeing it as an imposition at all; after all, the Muslim world hungers for democracy. But this overlooks the telling findings of a University of Michigan study: that support for many of the values commonly associated with democracy, such as gender equality and freedom of speech, is weak in the Muslim world.

This may be due less to any deep-seated aversion than backlash to the "impurities" of globalization. What's certain, however, is that Muslims have become wary of Washington's intentions. I've often during my recent travels in the Muslim world that America doesn't "get Islam." The opposite is equally true, that many Muslims don't grasp America (hence the $1.2 billion the US allocated to public diplomacy last year, double what it spent in 1980, with more on the way). The difference is, America, not Islam, is doing the peddling. It is fighting the Islamists for no less than the soul of Islam, for the allegiance of the ostensibly undecided moderate middle. Why, then, does so much of the advisory discourse and literature on America's national security and public diplomacy, while acknowledging Islamic lands as the battlefront, make only passing reference to Islam?

The Koran, for instance, the covenant by which Muslims are to live, is seldom cited; concepts central to Muslim existence, such as tawhid (oneness of Allah) and ijmah (consensus), are rarely mentioned, let alone considered. Part of the problem can be traced to the precepts of American politics. Christianity heavily influences discourse and policy on the right. Many left-leaning elites come from a secularist tradition. There is virtually a built-in resistance to getting to know Islam better.

September 11 fed the resistance, when it became all but official policy not to listen. To listen was to be a relativist or worse an apologist. The obduracy eventually proved fatal to America's foreign-policy objectives, and Washington has since stressed the need for more dialogue. "If we don't have long-term relationships with Muslim populations, we cannot have trust. Without trust, public diplomacy is ineffective," 9-11 Commission chairman Thomas Kean said last year.

But only selective listening and dialogue has materialized. The tendency to talk to persists, and it's not likely to change any time soon, for several reasons. Firstly, "Institutional self-reform is rare; the conscience is willing, but the culture is tough," in the words of historian Jacques Barzun. Secondly, America's foreign policy agenda is in essence a campaign of conversion—not from Islam per se but in how Islam defines itself. Conversion attempts, by their nature, don't seek to understand—they look beyond it. They start from the premise that one's own values are superior to those to be converted. Thirdly, Washington is convinced that the Muslim world is the source of a most elusive and potent danger: a threat not only to our borders, as with the Cold War, but to our subways, classrooms, ballparks and suburbs. Containment will no longer suffice; conversion is necessary. And the sooner the better. Fear and a sense of urgency are driving the dialogue on foreign policy.

Unfortunately, this puts Islam "at the center of a fault line dividing the West and the Rest [which] leads us away from an understanding of attitudes in the Muslim world," noted political scientist Mark Tessler.

This is not to suggest that US foreign policy should cease to promote American values; some do bind mankind. But to be effective the strategy, and the dialogue seeking to improve on it, must more substantively engage the Muslim world, as opposed to doing so in so far as it serves American interests.

Until then, a sign seen at a recent anti-Iraq War protest in Washington, DC, will echo the fears of many Muslims. It read, "Be nice to America or we'll bring democracy to you."

First published October 20, 2005 (Asia Times)

* * *

Hollywood Still Seduces the World

President Bush's foreign policy is said to have unleashed an intense and potentially irreversible strain of anti-Americanism around the world, one in which the line between hating American leaders and culture is blurring.

And yet Hollywood, a symbol of US "hegemony" if ever there was one, is appreciating greater success abroad than at home. International ticket sales now account for 60 percent of overall box office receipts, up from 40 percent three years ago. Home-video sales are said to be the fastest-growing revenue sector in Tinseltown, and that doesn't include the millions watching pirated copies. Meanwhile American television shows attract a record number of foreign program buyers, even though licensing fees have increased sharply in most markets.

So what gives?

Part of the answer lies in trade liberalization. Part rests with shrewder, more global-minded marketing. Major studios are beefing up their overseas divisions and signing foreign partnerships. Warner Bros., for instance, recently penned a $2 billion deal with Abu Dhabi's largest real-estate firm, Aldar, to build a studio and produce films and videogames—thus targeting the Arab world, 60 percent of which is under 25 and regarded as entertainment hungry.

Lower labor costs and fewer regulations also inspire moves abroad. Major Hollywood studios set up production houses in China, to better tap growing interest in films. Hollywood's production costs decreased in 2005 by 4 percent while marketing costs jumped 5.2 percent.

The industry has always welcomed international talent, from Marlene Dietrich to Sean Connery, but as Hollywood pushes its product aggressively abroad, executives view international talent as ever more critical in promoting films abroad.

In "The Kingdom" Jamie Foxx stars beside Palestinian actor Ashraf Barhom, who plays a brave Saudi Arabian police officer. "The Last Samurai" stars Tom Cruise and Japanese actor Ken Watanabe, scoring well in Japan. Brazilian actress Alice Braga joins Will Smith in "I Am Legend." Hollywood tackles transnational hot topics like religion ("Kingdom of Heaven"), terrorism ("Munich"), deadly viruses ("I Am Legend") and the oil trade ("Syriana").

In short, Hollywood is thinking bigger and bigger—with no less than the world in mind.

But none of this sufficiently explains why Hollywood enjoys unprecedented success abroad in an era of rampant American-bashing. The common explanation for the contradiction has been that the world makes a distinction between American culture and its foreign policy; that the more sweeping variety of anti-Americanism is confined mostly to intellectuals and religious zealots.

But over the last few years in Europe and Asia I've encountered more ordinary citizens baldly denouncing America. It is not just

America's politics, they carp, but "hypocritical" values, a "hollow" pop culture and disbelief about voters reelecting Bush. A poll from the Pew Global Attitudes Project supports such anecdotal evidence, finding that favorable opinions of American people among Indonesians dropped from 56 percent in 2002 to 46 percent in 2005, and also fell in Great Britain, Poland, Canada, Germany, France, Russia, Jordan, Turkey and Pakistan. To be sure Bush's foreign policy and his successful reelection bid precipitated a broader disdain for America, and that makes Hollywood's growth abroad all the more noteworthy.

Still, typical "all-American" fare plays well in international theaters. "Spider-Man 3" was the biggest worldwide opener in history, raking in $375 million. "The Simpsons Movie," featuring "America's first family," grossed nearly $333 million abroad, double what it did stateside. Hollywood's most successful titles abroad tend to be special effect-heavy ("Titanic," "Harry Potter," "Pirates of the Caribbean" "Jurassic Park") and animation and digital wizardry ("Shrek" "The Lion King" and "The Incredibles"). Ironically perhaps these films tend to do better than those critical of the US, such as "Fahrenheit 9/11," "Syriana" and "American Beauty." Moo Hon Mei, marketing director for Twentieth Century Fox Malaysia, said this trend has remained largely undisturbed in Southeast Asia over the years and "doesn't look set to change anytime soon."

Either way, viewers of Hollywood pictures are hard pressed to ignore that they are invested in an American product—the American flag here, the country's natural splendor there. Hollywood tendentiously celebrates America's unique brand of dynamism, from its confidence and cool to its technological and creative preeminence.

And generally people like what they see, a fact reflected not only in the numbers Hollywood posts, but in official backlash and its impact. In December, China banned the release of US films for at least three months. The success of American films at the expense of local fare is said to have influenced the decision. South Korea relies on a quota that requires local films to play 146 days of the year, a number halved as part of the US-Korea bilateral trade agreement, yet to be ratified.

In March Javad Shangari, a cultural adviser to Iranian President Mahmoud Ahmadinejad, accused Hollywood of being "part of a comprehensive US psychological war aimed at Iranian culture," in response to the film "300," which some critics suggested was anti-Persian. A government spokesperson added "Cultural intrusion is among the tactics always used by the aliens."

In Malaysia, authorities barred moviegoers from Mel Gibson's "The Passion of the Christ," to protect Muslim "sensitivities," but pirated versions were readily available at stalls around Kuala Lumpur. China's street corners are rife with pirated Hollywood movies, and young Iranians adore American films, often edited or banned.

Hollywood even finds itself prevailing in places where people hold unfavorable perceptions of American culture. "Pirates of the Caribbean 3" and "Shrek the Third" were top box office hits in France. The French of course are known to claim they are above America's "shallow" culture. In the Pew poll more than 60 percent of Lebanese said Americans were greedy, violent and immoral, yet Lebanon is one of Hollywood's hottest markets in the Middle East.

Hollywood's portrayals of America as a den of iniquity may feed such misconceptions. But the fact that Hollywood is a hit in such places signals, at the least, a healthy fascination with the "depravity" of America, and more likely, a gap between what people say and what they actually think about the country. A young Malaysian woman accounted for complexity in her relationship with America when she articulated her affinity for Hollywood in broad terms, saying that it enabled her "to imagine doing things not practiced or accepted at home."

Hollywood doesn't specialize in just "sin," though, and it's not just a peak of sin audiences are lining up for. "[Hollywood] allows people abroad to learn about American society and especially affluence, fashions, consumption patterns, etc., that people are interested in, never mind their anti-American attitudes," said Paul Hollander, editor of the essay collection "Understanding Anti-Americanism."

Edward Said lamented US power in this respect, that is, ideological power: "All cultures tend to make representations of foreign cultures... to master or in some way control them. Yet not all cultures make representations of foreign cultures and in fact master or control them." This representation is sometimes expressed dialectically, vis-à-vis depiction of the self.

With anti-Americanism reaching record highs, Hollywood is not only a powerful ideological tool, but arguably a necessary one. The success of Al Gore's "An Inconvenient Truth," for instance, reminded the world that, yes, some US politicians genuinely have the world's interest at heart.

Same goes for "Charlie Wilson's War," in which Tom Hanks plays a former Texas congressman whose empathy for the plight of Afghans during the Soviet invasion compels him to help arm the Mujahideen resistance. Since September 11 that arming has become most synonymous with the rise of the Tailban and Osama bin Laden, and the film does not gloss over the shortcomings of US foreign policy. "This is what we always do, we go in with our ideals and we change the world and then we leave, we always leave," says Wilson. But the film also conveys that US is far from the "Great Satan"; that American ideals count for something and that some in Washington are committed to assisting the weak and oppressed. Perhaps most importantly, in our era, the film challenges the fallacy that America is fighting a war against Islam. The rogue CIA operative played by Philip Seymour Hoffman says, "America doesn't fight religious wars. That's why I like living there." Staunch anti-Americanists may disagree with the claim. But that's not the point. It gets you thinking.

In "The Kindgom" US special forces are sent to Saudi Arabia after a bomb explodes inside a Western housing compound there. The film conveys that American idealism can be naïve and cause friction. But it also depicts America as a country concerned with justice and able to collaborate with unlikely allies to work toward the common good. "America's not perfect, not at all, I'll be the first to say it, but we are good at this. Allow us to help your men go catch this criminal," Foxx's character tells a Saudi prince.

The point here is that Hollywood's "window" complicates the world's relationship with the US. It challenges the malicious simplifications of American politics and culture, inculcated through politically motivated critics, religious institutions, governments, schools and media.

In doing so, Hollywood challenges the impulse to dismiss and demonize, and in our polarizing world it could do much worse.

First Published January 28, 2008 (*YaleGlobal*)

Epilogue

Post-election Malaysia presents the country with an unprecedented opportunity to fulfill its preoccupation of becoming a First World nation. What was essentially a one-party state now involves an opposition advocating greater accountability, democratic space and more progressive economic policies; leaders and their parties feel pressed to either rise above the country's political culture of mediocrity or risk alienation if not extinction. Malaysians are contemplating a more pluralist approach to nation-building. Officials who months ago ruled with an air of impunity are being pressured to apologize for racist remarks and investigated for abuse of power. The greater balance in government means Malaysians will be exposed to alternative views and learn more about the nation's strengths and weaknesses. Malaysia has been blessed with a golden opportunity to tap its unlocked potential.

But many obstacles to realization remain.

A culture of tribalism, feudalism and oppression runs deep; even the newly empowered opposition has struggled to transcend racial squabbling. The ruling government continues to harass advocates of free speech and accountability. The electorate system remains tilted in the ruling coalition's favor. The mainstream media is still controlled by the coalition. Some quarters in UMNO want to replace Abdullah Badawi as party president, not because he is an obstacle to reform but because they seek cosmetic change so the party can get on with the status quo. In fact the whole enterprise of reform is at risk of falling prey to appearances—whereby the foundations of a progressive democratic society are prevented from taking root but the public is left with the impression that democracy was given a chance but didn't work out. This could lead Malaysia to regress down the same path it yearns to leave behind, similar to the way Russia has reverted to dictatorship after Boris Yeltsin gave Russians the impression he had introduced them to democracy, and it was madness, when in fact his coterie was not made up of democrats but criminals who became oligarchs.

A failure by the opposition to deliver on its promises could set such a scenario in motion, with the public falling back into the hands of an unreformed UMNO. Put another way, contrary to popular belief, UMNO will not necessarily have to reform to survive.

The public must resist being manipulated by race and religion. Given half a chance, desperate politicians will work these volatile issues to their advantage. At around the time of this writing it has been reported that a former official who lost his seat in the general election is trying to galvanize Malay support by objecting to non-Muslims wishing to use the Arabic term for God in their sermons and literature. Mahathir in his bid to topple Abdullah Badawi and revitalize UMNO is telling the Malays they have lost their political power.

Ethnic minorities can help minimize the impact of these manipulations by less stridently calling for on an end to the Malay-centered affirmative action program, while reaching out across race lines to find an alternative system that accommodates all the races. Indeed some of the program's critics are as racially motivated as its defenders, and political opportunists on both sides of the divide will twist the tension to their advantage at the expense of national progress.

The public meanwhile must not grow satisfied with its role in the 2008 elections. It cannot afford to sit back and assume leaders will fulfill their aspirations implicit in the vote swing. Political participation is a process; constant pressure and involvement is requisite.

Addressing these issues will help ensure Malaysia doesn't squander an extraordinary opportunity.

Index

A
Abdullah Badawi 9, 15-16, 18- 22, 25-26, 32, 36, 38, 39-53, 56, 59, 61-63, 67-79, 83-84, 86-91, 97-98, 114, 118-120, 123-131, 137-143, 146-148, 151, 153, 157-158, 161-162, 166, 173, 174, 178-181, 185, 187, 193-195, 201-206, 211, 213, 218-219, 221, 223, 229, 232-234, 263
Abdul Kadir Sheikh Fadzir 38, 51, 96
ABIM, see Muslim Youth Movement of Malaysia
abuses 21, 42, 44-47, 50, 56, 78, 90, 196, 240
ACA, see Anti-Corruption Agency
al-Qaeda 150
Al Gore 52, 128, 146, 196, 260
Al Jazeera 240, 252
America 104, 122, 181, 244-247, 253-261
American 81, 100, 106, 109, 144, 162, 167, 170, 179, 185, 195, 197, 241, 244, 246-247, 253-261
Amnesty International 36, 38, 45
Anti-Corruption Agency (ACA) 70-71, 76-77, 125, 179
Anwar Ibrahim 15-18, 20, 23-24, 33, 35-37, 57, 61, 79, 91, 100, 103, 120, 128, 160-161, 165, 176, 188, 196, 215
Asiaweek 185, 239
Asia Times 15, 19, 23, 35, 39, 41, 47, 53, 58, 63, 69, 71-72, 79, 86, 91, 99, 105, 110, 117, 120, 126, 131, 139, 143, 149, 154, 161, 169, 172, 186, 189, 202, 207, 215, 222, 242-243, 256
Australia 56

B
Barisan Nasional (BN) 15-17, 19-25, 31-33, 36, 54-57, 86, 138, 156, 186, 192
BBC 17, 240
Berita Harian 150
BERSIH 60
Bible 106, 168, 171
Biovalley 229
blogger 22, 55-57, 77, 86, 98-99, 148, 180, 195, 205, 240
blogs 22, 40, 55, 57, 98, 180
BN, see Barisan Nasional
British 24, 102, 122, 129, 214, 240
Buddhism 170
bumiputra 155, 158, 163
Bush, George W. 97, 100, 102, 109, 111, 195-196, 205, 246, 254, 256, 258
business 22, 24, 51, 53, 59, 62, 68, 71, 73-75, 78-79, 84, 91, 97-99, 123, 130, 147, 149, 164, 185, 193-194, 203-204, 206, 213, 244-245
by-election 23, 148

C
Canada 211, 258

Chandra Muzaffar 68, 130
China 90, 100, 104, 137, 146, 156, 171, 192-197, 223, 227, 239, 243-247, 257-259
Chinese 16-22, 24-26, 32, 40, 42-43, 45, 49, 54, 55, 58, 61, 70, 85, 87, 120-121, 135-136, 138, 142, 145, 151, 154-159, 163-165, 168, 173, 175, 189-197, 243-247
Christian 107, 113, 167-171, 248, 250
Christianity 44, 170-171, 254
Clinton, Bill 99
CNN 183, 239-240
corrupt 16, 18, 51, 53, 67, 69, 114
corruption 9, 15-18, 20-26, 3-33, 36-37, 42-43, 46, 48-51, 53, 61, 67-71, 73, 76-79, 86, 89, 91, 95, 97-98, 101, 105, 114, 125-130, 146-148, 165, 174, 177, 179, 186-187, 205, 213
crime 21, 26, 43, 91
Cyberjaya 216-217, 219, 221, 224, 226-229

D

DAP, see Democratic Action Party
democracy 19, 23-24, 31, 36, 42, 52, 60, 62, 100, 104, 128, 131, 136, 140, 146, 181, 183, 196, 212, 253-256, 264
Democratic Action Party (DAP) 17, 18, 20-25, 32, 71, 189, 192
demonstrations 33, 37, 38, 43, 48-49, 53, 58-59, 62, 124, 195
divorce 44, 114

E

ECM 51, 75-76
election 9, 10, 15-17, 19, 21, 23-25, 31-32, 34-36, 38, 48, 51, 53-54, 57, 60, 63, 69, 72, 78-79, 86, 87, 89-90, 119, 125, 129-131, 139, 148, 151, 161, 164-165, 174, 177, 179, 186-190, 192, 229, 263-264
Election Commission 32, 72
Europe 34, 104, 140, 143, 159, 185, 223, 225, 249, 257

F

Far Eastern Economic Review 239
Financial Times 241
fundamentalist 31, 80, 113, 196

G

Genting 84
Germany 213, 249, 258
globalization 9, 17, 254
Greece 248-252

H

Habibie 31, 128
Harakah 21
Hezbollah 98, 153, 202, 205
Hindu 44-45, 49, 87, 168, 170, 195
Hindu Rights Action Force (Hindraf) 49, 51, 87, 195
Hishammuddin Hussein 25, 55, 97, 123, 138
Hong Kong 80, 230-231, 239
human rights 33, 35, 37-39, 41-43, 45, 47, 49, 51, 53, 55, 57, 59, 61-63, 101-102, 124, 128,

146, 185-186, 189, 195, 196, 203, 207, 247, 249
Hussein Onn 123

I

Ibrahim Suffian 21, 33, 156
independence 9, 31, 39, 41, 49, 54, 59, 75, 99, 173, 190, 194
Independent Police Complaints and Misconduct Commission 43
India 146, 156, 171, 223, 225, 227, 247
Indian 16, 20-22, 24, 26, 40, 42, 45, 49, 53-55, 58, 61, 70, 85-87, 91, 120-121, 135-136, 142, 145, 151, 154, 156, 158, 163, 168, 173, 190-192, 195
Indonesia 31, 33, 35, 37, 99, 127, 146-147, 150-151, 175, 178, 180-184, 202, 215
Indonesian 31, 35, 38, 127-128, 146-147, 150, 180, 184, 258
inflation 16, 21, 26, 78, 196
injustice 16, 36, 103
Institute of Southeast Asian Studies 46
Institute of Strategic and International Studies 47
Internal Security Act (ISA) 33, 37-38, 46, 49, 52-53, 104, 124, 127, 141, 195, 203
International Herald Tribune 185, 234, 240-241
International Movement for a Just World 68, 130
Internet 15, 18, 33-34, 40, 43, 55-56, 179, 181-182, 221, 240
Iran 38, 116, 153, 201-202, 204-207
Iraq 100, 153, 162, 166, 178, 182-183, 204, 246, 249, 254, 256
ISA, see Internal Security Act
Iskandar Development Region 230
Islam 9, 17, 20, 26, 33, 35, 38, 44-45, 48-49, 54, 56-58, 80, 83, 85-86, 98, 100, 106-115, 135, 137, 140-142, 144-145, 147-148, 151-153, 157-158, 167-187, 191, 195-196, 251, 254-255, 260
Islam Hadhari 44, 48, 83, 85, 98, 137, 140, 147-148, 157-158, 172-175, 178-180, 182-184, 187
Islamic 17, 20, 24, 31, 36, 40, 44, 47, 54, 57, 61, 80, 106-110, 114-116, 127-128, 130, 135, 139-145, 150-153, 155, 158, 164-165, 168-169, 171, 173-178, 180-181, 183-185-187, 189, 191-192, 204-206, 211-212, 242, 254
Islamization 43, 55, 89, 136, 191
Israel 97, 142

J

Jamek Mosque 59, 60, 154
Japan 80, 100, 104, 177, 213, 225, 247, 257
Jelutong 22
Jemaah Islamiah (JI) 150-152, 180
Jewish 46, 114, 241
Jews 98, 101, 107, 112, 158, 161, 177, 196, 204
Johor 123, 140, 230-231, 233-234

K

Kamaluddin 73-75, 203
Kedah 20-22, 59, 123
Kelantan 19-21, 114, 151-152
keris 25, 138
Khairy Jamaluddin 22, 25, 51, 59, 72-73, 75-76, 138, 142, 196, 204
khalwat 153, 191

Koran 85, 106, 107-109, 112, 152, 254
Kuala Lumpur 1, 11, 17, 23, 43-44, 47, 49, 54, 68, 81-82, 88, 120, 123, 137, 142, 154, 162, 168, 171, 190-191, 202, 205-206, 214, 220, 223-224, 228, 230, 233, 240, 259

L

Lee Kuan Yew 68
Lim Guan Eng 23, 25, 189, 192
Lim Kit Siang 71, 74

M

Mahathir Mohamad 17, 21-22, 32-34, 36-38, 40-41, 43-47, 50, 52, 57, 61, 67-69, 71, 74, 76, 78, 80, 84, 88-91, 97-105, 119-120, 122, 124, 126-130, 137, 141-142, 146-147, 158, 160-166, 176-179, 187, 190, 19-196, 201, 205, 211, 213-214, 216-219, 223, 226, 227-229, 23-232
Malacca 47, 51, 135, 194-195, 231
Malay 16, 18, 21, 25, 40, 49, 52, 54-55, 57, 61, 70, 84, 85, 95, 103, 121, 123, 135-136, 138, 142, 152, 155-156, 158-159, 161, 163-165, 167-177, 182, 190-192, 194-197, 217, 232, 264
Malays 17-18, 20-21, 2-26, 36, 40, 42, 45, 49, 51, 54, 58, 67, 7-73, 84, 90, 97, 103, 105, 114, 120-122, 135-136, 138-139, 141-142, 145, 148, 151, 154-158, 163-165, 167, 170-171, 173, 175-177, 182, 186, 190-197, 204, 216, 231
Malaysian Chinese Association (MCA) 55, 138
Malaysian Strategic Research Center 37, 72
Malay supremacy 25, 52, 173
Mandarin 42, 136
Marina Mahathir 44
MCA, see Malaysian Chinese Association
media 1, 15, 18, 20, 22, 31-43, 49-50, 53, 55-57, 60-61, 70-71, 77-78, 87-89, 95-96, 98, 102, 110-111, 117, 124, 127, 129, 138, 141, 147, 152-153, 159, 166-167, 182, 184, 187-188, 194-195, 230, 239-247, 261, 263
Merdeka Center for Opinion Research 16, 21, 33-34, 87, 156
Muhammad Muhammad Taib 55
Multimedia Super Corridor (MSC) 216-219, 221, 224, 226-229
Muslim 17, 20-21, 31, 35-37, 40, 42, 44-46, 70, 80-85, 98, 100-101, 105-111, 120, 128-129, 135-136, 139-142, 144-146, 151-154, 161-162, 167, 169-175, 179, 181-185, 191, 196, 202, 205, 213, 240-242, 248, 250-256, 259
Muslims 17, 45, 54, 58, 81, 85, 100, 106-109, 112, 114, 122, 139-142, 145, 153-154, 160, 165-175, 179-184, 186, 191-192, 196, 205, 241-242, 248-252, 254, 256, 264
Muslim Youth Movement of Malaysia (ABIM) 37, 175-176

N

Najib Razak 20, 22, 54-58, 80, 82, 117-127, 144, 148, 173, 190-191, 212, 215, 223
National Integrity Institute 68
National Integrity Plan 46, 68, 70, 157
Newsweek 26, 239
New Economic Policy (NEP) 20, 49, 121, 136, 155-157
New Straits Times 62, 75, 77, 183, 185, 241
New York Times 38, 110, 241, 243
New Zealand 211
NIP 46, 68, 70-72
North Korea 90, 116

O

Official Secrets Act (OSA) 77, 124
Ooi, Jeff 22
opposition 15-26, 31, 32-34, 38, 46, 52-53, 55-57, 59, 61, 71, 74-79, 88, 102, 120, 124, 129, 148, 151, 158, 160, 165, 171, 174, 180, 186-189, 192, 196, 204, 250, 263-264

P

Pan-Malaysian Islamic Party (PAS) 17-18, 20-21, 24, 33, 61, 151-152, 158, 165-166, 171, 174, 177-178, 180, 182, 186-189, 192
Parti Islam SeMalaysia (PAS), see Pan-Malaysian Islamic Party
PAS, see Pan-Malaysian Islamic Party
Penang 20-21, 23, 25, 45, 60, 233
People's Justice Party (PKR) 17-20, 24, 56, 160, 186, 188-189
Perak 20, 60
Petaling Jaya 17
Petronas Towers 9, 54, 87, 97, 101, 104, 110, 143, 190, 191, 196, 211
PKR, see People's Justice Party
police 9, 37, 42-43, 46-47, 50, 54, 56, 59-62, 68, 71, 75-76, 97, 98, 126, 140, 148, 150, 157, 170-171, 174-175, 191, 193-194, 196, 207, 257
poverty 40, 50, 156
press 34, 38, 77, 89, 96, 98, 104, 117, 126, 130, 163, 178, 189, 207, 240, 243, 245, 250
Printing Presses and Publications Act 42, 130
Proton 39, 88, 101, 224
Putrajaya 120, 191, 214, 230

R

race 9, 10, 15, 17, 24-26, 40, 42, 49-51, 54-55, 61, 67, 79, 84, 95, 104-105, 113, 121-122, 135-141, 143-145, 147, 149, 151, 153-155, 157-161, 163-167, 169, 171-173, 175-177, 179, 181-183, 185, 187, 189-191, 193, 195-197, 264
race card 24-25, 51, 139, 161, 164, 196
racism 22, 68, 116, 158, 164
Rahim Noor 61
Raja Petra Kamarudin 56
rakyat 155, 188, 215
Ramadan 100
Ramon Navaratnam 87
reformasi 49, 52, 61, 146
religion 20, 44, 50, 54-55, 57, 67, 82-83, 95, 100, 106-107, 109-117, 127, 135-137, 139, 141, 143-145, 147-149, 151-155, 157, 159-161, 163, 165, 167, 169-175, 177, 179, 181-183, 185, 187, 189, 191, 193, 195, 197, 205-251, 257, 264

S

Sabah 85, 145
Saddam Hussein 51, 90
Sarawak 85, 145
Saudi Arabia 82, 153, 181, 241, 253, 257, 261
schools 15, 26, 43, 53, 76, 84, 102, 136, 151, 155, 163, 164, 171, 174, 181, 184, 191, 205, 220, 261
Scomi 72, 74-75, 203
Selangor 20

September 11 106, 109, 111, 113-114, 128, 151, 162, 177, 180-181, 242, 255, 260
Singapore 46, 68, 80, 85, 101, 149-151, 156, 185, 194-195, 197, 202, 206, 213, 220, 223, 225, 228, 230-233, 241
Sisters in Islam 38, 83, 172
Socialist Party 52
Southeast Asia 35, 40, 82, 171, 194-195, 224, 244, 258
South Korea 38, 211, 259
Special Branch 170-171
students 26, 38, 53, 57, 85, 136, 155, 163, 166, 220, 222, 244
Suharto 31, 33, 37, 99, 164
Switzerland 213

T

Taiwan 38, 80, 247
Tamil 49, 87, 136
Terengganu 21, 188
terrorism 52, 106, 150, 154, 205-206, 257
terrorist 49, 53, 112, 127, 149-151, 166, 170, 180
Thai 90, 127, 152, 232, 244
Thailand 100, 127-128, 146-147, 150, 152, 180, 202, 223, 227, 232
Thaksin Shinawatra 90, 127-128, 152
The Star 32, 88, 91
Transparency International Malaysia 87
tudung 82

U

UMNO, see United Malays National Organization
UMNO Youth 55
unemployment 40, 50, 78, 156, 176, 248
United Kingdom 211, 214
United Malays National Organization (UMNO) 17, 21, 22, 25, 36, 38, 40, 45-46, 49-58, 67, 69, 73-75, 77-79, 97, 103, 114, 118-125, 129, 135-139, 142, 148, 151-152, 156-158, 161, 166, 173-174, 176-179, 182, 183, 186-188, 205, 231, 263-264
United States (US) 46-47, 52, 75, 97, 99-101, 103, 109, 124, 128, 142, 145-146, 162, 166, 168, 173, 176, 181, 183, 185, 194-197, 201-202, 204-207, 211, 218-219, 223, 225, 239, 241-245, 252, 254-256, 258-261
university 39, 53, 163-165, 167, 175, 212, 217, 220-222, 225, 230
US, see United States

V

Vision 2020 68, 85
Voice of People of Malaysia 33

W

Wall Street Journal 239
Washington Times 226
Women's Aid Organization 45

Z

Zainuddin Maidin 22, 57, 96